Year of Crisis,
Year of Hope

Recent Titles in Contributions in Ethnic Studies
Series Editor: Leonard W. Doob

Nations Remembered: An Oral History of the Five Civilized Tribes, 1865–1907
Theda Perdue

Operation Wetback: The Mass Deportation of Mexican Undocumented Workers in 1954
Juan Ramon Garcia

The Navajo Nation
Peter Iverson

An Unacknowledged Harmony: Philo-Semitism and the Survival of European Jewry
Alan Edelstein

America's Ethnic Politics
Joseph S. Roucek and Bernard Eisenberg, editors

Minorities and the Military: A Cross-National Study in World Perspective
Warren L. Young

The Emergence of Ethnicity: Cultural Groups and Social Conflict in Israel
Eliezer Ben-Rafael

Minority Aging: Sociological and Social Psychological Issues
Ron C. Manuel, editor

From Colonia to Community: The History of Puerto Ricans in New York City, 1917–1948
Virginia E. Sánchez Korrol

Human Rights, Ethnicity, and Discrimination
Vernon Van Dyke

Year of Crisis, Year of Hope

Russian Jewry and the Pogroms of 1881–1882

Stephen M. Berk

Contributions in Ethnic Studies, Number 11

Greenwood Press
WESTPORT, CONNECTICUT • LONDON, ENGLAND

Library of Congress Cataloging in Publication Data

Berk, Stephen M.
  Year of crisis, year of hope.

  (Contributions in ethnic studies ; ISSN 0196–7088 ;
no. 11)
  Bibliography: p.
  Includes index.
  1. Jews—Soviet Union—History—Pogroms, 1881–1882.
2. Soviet Union—Ethnic relations. I. Title.
II. Series.
DS135.R9B47   1985   947'.004924   84–25216
ISBN 0–313–24609–2 (lib. bdg.)

Library of Congress Catalog Card Number: 84–25216
ISBN: 0–313–24609–2
ISSN: 0196–7088

First published in 1985

Greenwood Press
A division of Congressional Information Service, Inc.
88 Post Road West
Westport, Connecticut 06881

Printed in the United States of America

10 9 8 7 6 5 4 3 2 1

Copyright Acknowledgments

For permission to quote from the following sources, grateful acknowledgment is hereby
given:

Simon Dubnow, *History of the Jews in Russia and Poland from the Earliest Times Until the
Present Day* (Philadelphia: Jewish Publications Society of America, 1916).

Paul Mendes-Flohr and Jehuda Reinharz, *The Jew in the Modern World: A Documentary
History*. Copyright © 1980 by Oxford University Press, Inc. Reprinted by permission.

Chapter IV, "The Bridge to Revolution," appeared in slightly different form in *Soviet Jewish
Affairs*, 7, no. 2 (1977) under the title "The Russian Revolutionary Movement and the
Pogroms of 1881–1882," and is reprinted by permission.

To
my parents
BLANCHE AND BERNARD R. BERK (1915–1972)
for their constant love and support.

Contents

Series Foreword

"Contributions in Ethnic Studies" focuses upon the problems that arise when peoples with different cultures and goals come together and interact productively or tragically. The modes of adjustment or conflict are various, but usually one group dominates or attempts to dominate the other. Eventually some accommodation is reached, but the process is likely to be long and, for the weaker group, painful. No one scholarly discipline monopolizes the research necessary to comprehend these intergroup relations. The emerging analysis, consequently, inevitably is of interest to historians, social scientists, psychologists, and psychiatrists.

In our times we have come to associate overt atrocities against Jews with the ghastly horrors of the Nazi Holocaust. This book turns our attention to another tragic event in Jewish history, the "catastrophe for Russian Jewry," that occurred during a fifteen-month period beginning in April 1881. The underlying and precipitating factors responsible for these pogroms are deduced from available published and archival materials and from survivors of that period. The events were quickly publicized in the press and by word of mouth in Russia and also throughout Europe and the United States. Russian intellectuals tended to remain "indifferent, hostile, or only ambiguously supportive of the Jews" as the pogroms' demerits and merits—yes, merits—were discussed.

Jewish communities in Russia did not immediately disintegrate, only gradually did millions of Jews leave the country with which they had been seeking to identify their destinies. The principal migration was to the United States, which turned out not to be the anticipated "Golden Land." Many American Jews from Western Europe had "a feeling of contempt" for these Eastern Jews and were made anxious by their arrival, but others provided significant assistance. Gentile Americans, too, were both hostile or unaccommodating and friendly or helpful. Gradually the immigrants of those days have become another group with

long memories in our pluralistic society. A relatively small number of
the refugees have had profound effects upon Zionism and Israel.

Scholarly historical accounts have an interest in their own right even
when the unique components in what they describe are stressed and
when the combination is never likely to be repeated exactly. The history
of the pogroms, however, transcends its uniqueness and poses, particularly for historians and social scientists bent on generalizations, a host
of challenging problems. Why have Jews been the target so frequently
throughout the centuries? Does mob violence directed toward property
and human bodies always assume a similar form? Under what circumstances does one group literally as well as figuratively attack another
group? What are the immediate and far-flung repercussions not only
upon the victims and the persecutors but also upon interested and dis-
interested outsiders? How long and for what reasons does a tradition
like anti-Semitism linger within a society? How can barbarisms be prevented? And of course: do we—any of us, any society anywhere—wish
to progress beyond the point at which even petty or symbolic pogroms
become intolerable: or can we?

Every reader of this book will have his own answers to such questions.
Inevitably, depending on his personality and his scholarly bent, he will
also pose other challenging and perplexing questions. One prediction
is certain: he will not be left unmoved.

Leonard W. Doob

Preface

In the spring of 1881 a series of anti-Jewish pogroms swept over Russia and changed the course of Jewish history irrevocably. In response to these terrible events, the three million Russian Jews, nearly all of whom originated in that part of Poland which had passed under Russian control in the course of the late eighteenth century, rose from their torpor to become active participants determining their destiny.

The assimilationist tendencies which had been so pronounced among Russian Jewish intellectuals and students during the reign of Alexander II slowed dramatically, as many Jews suddenly despaired of the possibility of rapprochement (*sblizhenie*) with the Russian people, and turned back to the Jewish community. For the masses of Russian Jews who had not engaged in the heady debates on rapprochement the pogroms appeared as an omen confirming the impossibility of remaining in Russia.

The first months of 1882 saw the birth of a vast emigration movement that did not spend itself until 1914. By that time close to two million Jews had left the Russian Empire, the great majority making their way toward the United States. Simultaneously, hundreds and later thousands of Jews left Russia for Palestine, where they laid the basis of the Yishuv, the modern Palestinian Jewish community. Support for Palestine as a solution for the Jewish Question was substantial also among those who remained in Russia; by 1885 organizations advocating the creation of a Jewish polity in Palestine had been formed there. Russian Zionism, which was to have such an enormous impact upon the subsequent history of the Zionist movement, as well as the Yishuv and the State of Israel, was a direct consequence of the pogroms of 1881–1882.

In addition to the call for emigration, there occurred a dramatic revitalization of Jewish self-consciousness. Educated and affluent Russian Jews concerned for the well-being of their coreligionists in Russia but opposed to emigration now boldly rose to defend Russian Jewry, vociferously championing the cause of Jewish civil rights in Russia. Russian Jewry was marching, to America, to Palestine, and toward the goal of a democratic and progressive Russia.

It is the purpose of this book to focus attention upon these very significant developments for Russian Jews by closely examining the period from April 1881 to December 1882. In the course of the study not only are the Russian pogroms and the Jewish response scrutinized but so also are the reactions of various segments of Russian society to the anti-Jewish movement. The work concludes with perhaps the most dramatic consequence of the period, after the pogroms themselves—the arrival of thousands of Russian Jews in America to encounter the New World for the first time. In a very real sense the pogroms that began in the spring of 1881 marked the beginning of the end for one center of Jewish life, that of Eastern Europe, and the birth of two new ones, the large and prosperous American Jewish community, and the renascent Jewish State of Israel.

Throughout this book I have used the words "Russian Jews" and "Russian Jewry" to mean Jews living in Lithuania, Belorussia, and the Ukraine, and the small but influential group living in St. Petersburg. Polish Jewry living in what at one time was called Congress Poland does not, for the most part, enter into this work, although it most certainly deserves a study of its own. All dates for events occurring in the Russian Empire, as well as of publications, laws, and documents originating there, are Old Style, in the Julian calendar, which was in use in Russia up to 1918 and is, for the nineteenth century, twelve days behind the Gregorian calendar of the West. Events taking place outside of Russia as well as non-Russian written material are dated on the Gregorian calendar.

The published materials I have read in preparing this book are almost all in Russian, Yiddish, Hebrew, German, and English. One short but important source, the Romanenko declaration, which appears in Chapter IV, is in Ukrainian. The sections dealing with the pogroms, the Russian and Jewish responses to them, and the Jewish accommodation to America, that is, most of this book, are based on published primary sources. The first chapter, focusing on Russian Jewry before the pogroms, draws on the secondary literature, although some primary material is used. In almost all cases, both primary and secondary sources were used in their original language of publication; the most notable exceptions are the English translations of Simon Dubnow's two-volume history of Russian and East European Jewry, the diary of George Price, Isaac Linetski's novel, *Dos Poylishe Yingel*, the work of the Soviet historian P. A. Zaionchkovskii, and one poem by Y. L. Gordon.

The transliteration of Russian words follows the Library of Congress system. There is no widely accepted transliteration scheme for Hebrew and Yiddish words and, therefore, the lead of the *National Union Catalog* has been followed even when common sense would dictate otherwise. Hence a much-cited authority appears as Tcherikower rather than as the better transliterated Cherikover. Terms that might be unclear to the reader, particularly those in Russian, Hebrew, and Yiddish, are explained in the Glossary.

Acknowledgments

I owe thanks to many people who gave me assistance in a number of ways. Mina Goldberg's inaugural dissertation on the year 1881–1882 in Russia was written in 1933 for the University of Berlin and appears only in a handful of libraries. It is a very short but fine piece of work, which I read after beginning research on this book. It confirmed my belief that the subject was worthy of study. To the best of my knowledge Goldberg, who was from Kovno in Lithuania, was murdered with almost six million other Jews during the Holocaust.

When I began graduate work in history at the University of Chicago, Louis Gottschalk, a distinguished specialist on the French Revolution, spoke emphatically to beginning students on the importance for the scholar of good reference librarians. How right he was. This book could not have been written without the help of David Gerhan, Cheryl La-Guardia, Bruce Connolly, and Zena Shevchik, superb practitioners of their craft at the Union College Schaffer Library. They were indefatigable, as was Fawn Murphy of the Inter-Library Loan section, in the search for needed books, articles and newspapers. I am also indebted to Dina Abramowicz of the YIVO Library, who guided me to many important sources.

Shimon Paktor, Yaffa Lown, Nadja Jernakoff, and George Slusarczuk provided assistance in the difficult task of ensuring precise translation of material from Yiddish, Hebrew, Russian, and Ukrainian, respectively. Shimon Paktor also introduced me to the world of Yiddish scholarship and inspired me to learn Yiddish so as to gain insight not only into the pogrom era, but into the rich and vibrant world of East European Jewry. I will always be grateful to him for this. Yaffa Lown showed me the beauty of Hebrew poetry, and Nadja Jernakoff, a fine Turgenev specialist, drew my attention to his views of the pogroms.

No scholar operates in a vacuum. Authors are always indebted to those who act as sounding boards for ideas and offer criticism, advice, and support. Rabbi Richard Rubenstein, one of this nation's most gifted analysts of modern Jewish history, was kind enough to read the manuscript and make some helpful and positive comments. My colleagues Joseph Finkelstein, Manfred Jonas, and Donald Thurston, former and present chairs of the History Department of Union College, gave needed encouragement and assisted me in obtaining institutional support. That support came from the Union College Humanities Faculty Development Fund and I am grateful for the research grants it provided. Erik Hansen, a prolific and important author of articles on modern Dutch history, and a prodigious reader of historical scholarship, was always available for assistance. Malcolm Willison, a former colleague in the Sociology Department of Union College, helped mightily in the preparation of the manuscript for publication. Charles Gati and Robert Sharlet, my colleagues in Russian and Soviet studies, have always, by virtue of their fine scholarship, served as inspirations and models.

Typing of the draft and final manuscripts was done by student aides, particularly Kathy Gould, and by Rita Michalec, secretary to the History Department. Michalec provided service above and beyond the call of duty. She labored day and night on the manuscript; and without her assistance it most certainly would not have been completed.

Only my family can fully appreciate the labor that went into this project. I thank my children Natalie, Matthew, and Beverly for tolerating a father who was very often short on both temper and time. Above all, I thank my wife Roberta. Her equanimity, patience, good sense, and optimism sustained me through many difficult hours. I have truly been blessed with a woman of valor.

Year of Crisis,
Year of Hope

I

The Great Reforms

FROM NICHOLAS TO ALEXANDER

In 1855, Nicholas I, who had governed Russia for almost thirty years, died. The reign of the *gendarme* of Europe had been a harsh one. Economic developments and some barely perceptible movement in the direction of the emancipation of the serfs notwithstanding, censorship, repression, and execution bore down heavily on the Russian Empire. It was the two million Russian Jews of that empire, however, who experienced the worst. They lived in an area known as the Pale of Settlement which had been clearly demarcated in the Statute of 1835. It embraced the provinces of Grodno, Vilna, Volhynia, Podolia, Minsk, and Ekaterinoslav; the Bessarabian and Belostok *oblasts*; the province of Kiev, but not the city of Kiev itself; Kherson Province except for the city of Nikolaev; the province of Taurida, minus Sebastopol; the provinces of Mogilev and Vitebsk, except for the rural settlements; the Chernigov and Poltava provinces without the crown and Cossack settlements there; and the existing Jewish communities of Kurland, Riga, and Shlok. Within the Pale, Jews were permitted to move from place to place, and to acquire land and property except for estates possessing serfs.[1]

Under Nicholas I, Russian Jews had become the target of government policies designed to facilitate their assimilation into Russian society and, as far as the Tsar was concerned, their ultimate conversion to Russian Orthodoxy. The most odious of these policies was the *rekrutshchina* or the conscription system introduced by Nicholas in 1827. The law ordered the conscription into the Russian army of a certain quota of young Jews, between the ages of twelve and twenty-five. The government hoped that these Jews, by living in a Russian ambiance, would quickly divorce themselves from their Jewish background and begin to experience rapid assimilation. Although the law stipulated that the Jewish recruits should be granted religious freedom, in practice, an extremely brutal process of Russification was initiated. Some Russian officers, upon receiving the Jewish conscripts, had them forcibly baptized or compelled to eat forbidden foods. The conscripted children were often beaten and starved into attending church services. Worst of all, the representatives of the Jewish communities, who were charged by the government with the task of providing recruits, were not reluctant to fill quotas by sending children down to the age of five. If service in the Imperial Army for the mass of Russian soldiers was an almost life-long sentence to hard labor, then for the Jews the experience was even more difficult, since it meant, in many cases, ripping out and destroying their religion and traditions, or at least having them constantly assaulted.

Alexander Herzen, the future founder of Russian socialism, happened to meet a group of young recruits marching north and gives a poignant description of their plight. Herzen talked with the officer guiding the children.

"Whom do you carry and to what place?"

"Well, sir, you see, they got together a bunch of these accursed Jewish youngsters between the age of eight and nine. I suppose they are meant for the fleet, but how should I know? At first the command was to drive them to Perm. Now there is a change. We are told to drive them to Kazan. I have had them on my hands for a hundred *versts* or thereabouts. The officer that turned them over to me told me they were an awful nuisance. A third of them remained on the road [at this the officer pointed with his finger to the ground]. Half of them will not get to their destination," he added.

"Epidemics, I suppose?" I inquired, stirred to the very core.

"No, not exactly epidemics; but they just fall like flies. Well, you know, these Jewish boys are so puny and delicate. They can't stand mixing dirt for ten hours, with dry biscuits to live on. Again everywhere strange folks, no father, no mother, no caresses. Well then, you just hear a cough and the youngster is dead. Hello, corporal, get out the small fry!"

The little ones were assembled and arrayed in military line. It was one of the most terrible spectacles I have ever witnessed. Poor, poor children! The boys of twelve or thirteen managed somehow to stand up, but the little ones of eight and ten.... No brush, however black, could convey the terror of this scene on the canvas.

Pale, worn out, with scared looks, this is the way they stood in their uncomfortable rough soldier uniforms, with their starched, turned-up collars, fixing an inexpressibly helpless and pitiful gaze upon the garrisoned soldiers, who were handling them rudely. White lips, blue lines under the eyes betokened either fever or cold. And these poor children, without care, without a caress, exposed to the wind which blows unhindered from the Arctic Ocean, were marching to their death. I seized the officer's hand, and, with the words: "Take good care of them!", threw myself into my carriage. I felt like sobbing, and I knew I could not master myself....[2]

The impact of the *rekrutshchina* on Jewish communities was traumatic. Yiddish folk songs of the period reflect the fears and tensions felt by parents and children. Everything that could be done to avoid military service was done, including the deliberate maiming of young boys. The fact that the Tsarist government made Jewish community officials responsible for selecting and rounding up the young men divided the communities and created enormous tensions. It was charged with some justification that community leaders, nearly always drawn from the rich and the learned, made sure that their own children did not serve but, instead, yielded up to the government the children of the poor.

The *rekrutshchina* was only one of the policies implemented by the government of Nicholas I for assimilating and ultimately converting the Jews of the empire. Education was also viewed as an effective device to achieve this end. Under Nicholas and his Minister of National Enlightenment, S. S. Uvarov, with the assistance of the "learned Jew" Max Lilienthal, special government schools, the crown schools, were established for Jewish children. New institutions of higher learning designed to train rabbis and teachers were also created by the government. No amount of government persuasion or coercion, however, could convince the Jewish masses, still in the throes of religious enthusiasm and extremely suspicious of a government that had visited the *rekrutshchina* upon them, to send their children to the government schools or accept the graduates of the state-sponsored seminaries. That they were not wrong is proven by documents emanating from Uvarov's ministry and from Uvarov himself. They testify to the government's ultimate goal of the conversion of the Jews to Russian Orthodoxy.[3]

Nonetheless the government or crown schools did have an impact on the subsequent course of Russian Jewish history. The small number of students in the schools, most of whom came from poor families or, conversely, from upwardly mobile middle-class Jewish homes, received an education that was very, very different from that received by the overwhelming majority of their coreligionists. In contrast to the latter, who attended the traditional *heder* and *yeshiva* with their total emphasis on religious studies, particularly the study of the Talmud, the students in the government Jewish schools received a more secular education, in which the teaching of the Russian language was the most distinguishing feature. The several thousand graduates of these schools were among the first Jews to have a familiarity with Russian culture. They would also be the ones to take the first steps into the broader Russian society and to create a new Russian Jewish culture.

In addition to the students at the government schools, the number of Jews who had acquired secular knowledge was increasing by the slow but inexorable spread of the Haskalah to Eastern Europe. The Haskalah, the Hebrew word for enlightenment, with its connotation of secular learning and religious reform, had been carried from its place of origin in Germany to various East European areas, most notably to Galicia in the Hapsburg Empire. There Joseph Perl and Nachman Krochmal in the first half of the nineteenth century fought for the spread of European culture among.the Jewish masses and a breaking of the hold held by Hasidism on these masses.

It was only a matter of time before the ideas of the Haskalah would push into the Russian provinces that bordered upon Galicia. By the end of the 1830s there already existed a small but growing number of disciples of the Haskalah, or *maskilim*, in Russia. Isaac Bar Levinsohn, Simha Pinsker, and Abraham Gottlober fought battles analogous to those that were being waged in Galicia. The creation of new schools for Jewish students where arithmetic and science, the Russian language, and Russian history would be taught became a cardinal point in the program of the Russian Haskalah. The Russian *maskilim* placed great emphasis on the writing of new religious textbooks to teach the fundamentals of Judaism and, at the same time, thwart "the harmful influence" of the Talmud. The teaching of manual trades to young Jews and the wearing of clothes similar to those worn by the rest of the Russian people were also included by the *maskilim* in their program to reform Jewish life in Russia. Levinsohn, in particular, advocated a regeneration of Jewish economic life by resettling one-third of the Jewish population in the countryside.[4]

In Vilna, Minsk, and especially in the new city of Odessa, the Haskalah sunk deep roots. Established at the end of the eighteenth century in an area that had recently been taken from the Ottoman Empire and therefore named New Russia, Odessa was not weighed down by tradition. Since it was a major seaport, it was also exposed to new ideas and diverse peoples, including, by the early 1820s, some Jews from Galicia. As early as 1826 the first Jewish school for secular education in Russia had opened in Odessa. Forty years later Odessa would be in the forefront of Jewish communities advancing the cause of secularization and enlightenment.[5]

The result of this dissemination of the Haskalah was a growing tension within the Russian Jewish community. On the one side there existed a small but influential group of young men and women educated in secular subjects able to converse and read in Russian or Polish and at the same time very much antagonistic to what they considered to be the antiquated, primitive, and even barbaric practices of the Jewish masses. The *bête noir* of the new group was the *hasidim*, the followers of Hasidism, against whom they directed ferocious hostility. The reformers were so zealous in their attempts to bring modernity and enlightenment to the rest of the Jewish community that they even established contact with the government of Nicholas, requesting that the government utilize coercion against their benighted coreligionists for the sake of their enlightenment. Abraham Gottlober went so far as to defend the government's policy of Jewish conscription.

On the other side there remained the overwhelming majority of the Russian Jewish community. Reeling under the *rekrutshchina*, suspicious of Uvarov's educational schemes and caught up in their own religious enthusiasm, Russian Jewry followed its orthodox and traditional leadership and adamantly refused, in the period before 1855, to acquiesce in the efforts of government officials and *maskilim* to change, in one way or another, the fundamental nature of the community. Between the two camps of Jews there existed suspicion, contempt, and outright hostility, a situation that was to be exacerbated with the accession to the throne of a new Tsar and the beginning of a remarkable reign.

The proponents of change in Russia received a major boost from the Crimean War. Russia's ignominious defeat, its first major defeat since the early eighteenth century, set off a wave of introspection and soul-searching on the part of virtually all educated Russians, including those in the highest spheres of government. Gradually, by the second half of the 1850s, the government, including the new Tsar, Alexander II, and the more perceptive elements in the bureaucracy, reached the conclusion that some very drastic changes had to be introduced in Russia to strengthen the state against foreign attacks, as well as to guarantee domestic tranquility. The result was a series of reforms, the most famous of which was the emancipation of the serfs on February 19, 1861. This transformed Russian society; the reign was regarded by contemporaries and succeeding generations as the "Era of the Great Reforms," and Tsar Alexander II became known as the "Tsar Liberator."

The condition of Russian Jewry fell within the purview of the government's reformers. In the late 1850s and early 1860s those government officials concerned with the Jews became convinced that their emancipation and the amelioration of their position were consistent with the contemporary spirit. Moreover, emancipation not only would lead to the end of Jewish isolation and facilitate Jewish assimilation, it would make the Jews an asset to the empire.

Unfortunately, as in the case of nearly all of the reforms promulgated in this period, those involving Jews were only halfway measures. The government drew back, here as elsewhere, from carrying each reform to its logical conclusion. Alexander's underlying conservatism, coupled with so many officials' fear of the unknown, restrained the government. The emancipation of the serfs was not as beneficial as had first been thought; there was no capping of the reforms with a new political departure, a constitution; and there was to be no emancipation or significant amelioration of the position of Russian Jews.

As a matter of fact, Alexander probably did not hold the Jews in very high regard. One Jewish memoirist of the period, Jakob Maze, recalls a visit made by the Tsar to Kerch in 1876. Maze and his fellow students were scheduled to meet their beloved Tsar. When the monarch passed by and reviewed the students, Maze received the shock of his life.

As he was nearing my group ... I was struck speechless by the following conversation between the Tsar and the commandant of the fort. "Who built these breastworks, the Greek Orthodox people or the Jews?" the Tsar asked. When the commandant replied that both had shared in their construction, Alexander observed, "the inferior breastworks must have been built by the Jews."[6]

Whatever his personal feelings were about the Jews, Alexander did heed those of his officials who advocated reform legislation. The first and most dramatic piece of legislation was issued on the day of the Tsar's coronation, August 26, 1856, and must have generated great excitement among the Jewish masses.[7] It abolished juvenile conscription, the worst feature of the *rekrutshchina*. There followed a series of other reforms. On December 2, 1857, the fifty *verst* zones along the Prussian and Austrian frontiers, which had been closed to Jews in April 1843, were opened again. Jews were to be permitted to live in the frontier zones of the border provinces of the west, as well as in those of Bessarabia, after October 27, 1858. In 1859, Jewish merchants of the First Merchants' Guild were granted, subject to certain conditions, the right to trade and reside all over Russia. In 1860, Jewish soldiers who completed their term of service in the Guard regiments were permitted to remain permanently in the capital.

The Tsarist government established the principle that rights and privileges were to be granted to Jews as rewards for Jewish educational achievement. The law of November 27, 1861, granted Jews who finished a university program and received higher academic degrees, such as the Magister, Candidate, or Doctorate, the right to live and work outside of the Jewish Pale, as well as to receive government employment. Additional legislation provided that the same rights were to be given all Jews with a higher education regardless of the nature of the diploma. Together with ordinary university graduates, this group now included pharmacists, dentists, *feldshers*, and midwives. Merchants of the First and Second Merchants' Guild on December 11, 1861, were granted the right of permanent residence in the city of Kiev, the mother of Russian cities, while all Jews were permitted temporary residence in certain quarters of the city.

There was a long list of new laws affecting the Jews. On June 28, 1865, all of Russia was opened to Jewish artisans and their families. In Russian Poland, where Jews had lived under disabilities that had originated centuries before in the old Polish-Lithuanian Republic, the position of

Jews also was improved. An imperial *ukaz* issued in 1862 permitted Polish Jews to acquire land in all Polish cities and removed all residential restrictions in Russian Poland. This same law also made Jews eligible as witnesses for all legal documents, and gave the testimony of Jews in criminal cases the same validity as that of non-Jews. In 1868 the government eliminated the law forbidding Jews to move from Russian Poland to the Pale in Russia, and vice versa. A series of military reforms begun in 1859 made Jewish service in the army less onerous and humiliating. Finally, two of the important reforms that followed the emancipation of the serfs, the 1864 *zemstvo* or rural self-government reform, and the judicial reform law of this same year, did not have, as had been the custom with previous legislation, any restrictions on Jewish participation. In sum, while the many new laws concerning the Jews were hedged about with all sorts of qualifications, and provided substantial advantages for only a very small segment of Russian Jewry, leaving the rest of the community in the same abysmal condition as before, there seemed to be no doubt that government policies and attitudes toward the Jews were moving in a totally new direction.

The government's friendly initial disposition toward the Jews was paralleled by demonstrations in Russian society of sympathy in behalf of Russian Jewry. In 1858, for example, the magazine *Illiustratsiia* (Illustration) in St. Petersburg published an anti-Semitic article, "The Zhids of the Russian West," *zhid* being a pejorative term for Jew, equivalent to the English "yid." The Jews were castigated for being filthy, rapacious exploiters of Christians. I. Chatskin and M. Gorvitz rose to the defense of their fellow Jews in the influential periodicals *Russkii Vestnik* (Russian Messenger) and *Atenei* (Atheneum). In a counterattack, *Illiustratsiia* heaped abuse on Chatskin and Gorvitz, referring to them as "Reb Chatskin" and "Reb Gorvitz," and claiming that their pro-Jewish position was motivated by greed. This action aroused literary circles in St. Petersburg and Moscow; 140 writers, including some of the foremost literary personalities in Russia, signed a statement declaring that "in the persons of Messrs. Gorvitz and Chatskin all society, all Russian literature, are insulted."[8] The fact that the statement did not address itself to the general question of the status of Jews in the empire was deemed irrelevant by Jewish intellectuals, who were enraptured by the spectacle of Russian writers going to the defense of Jews, with the implication that Russian Jewry was a part of the Russian people.

The Russian press, including government organs, reflected the new philo-Jewish mood of the late 1850s. In 1858, an article in the *Russkii Invalid* (Russian Veteran), published by the Ministry of War, spoke of the need to view the Jews in a new light:

Let us be worthy of our age; let us give up the childish habit of presenting the Jews in our literary works as ludicrous and ignominious creatures. On the contrary, remembering the causes which brought them to such a state, let us not forget the innate ability of the Jews for the arts and sciences; and by offering them a place among us, let us utilize their energy, readiness of wit, and skill as new means for satisfying the ever-growing needs of our people.[9]

The long night the Jews had endured under Nicholas seemed to be over.

THE NEW JEWISH INTELLIGENTSIA

The positive attitudes expressed by the Russian government and leaders of opinion in Russian society had a dramatic impact on the mood of the small Jewish intelligentsia. Both its newer Russified and the older Hebraic segments felt a tremendous optimism about the future; they believed that a new dawn had come. Emancipation, they held, would soon be enacted, and with it would come the *sblizhenie* (rapprochement) between Jews and Russians that the Jewish intelligentsia saw as the ultimate solution to the Jewish question in Russia.[10]

In the first half of the reign of Alexander II, the most articulate commentators on "the Jewish question" were the Jewish periodicals in Odessa between 1860 and 1871.[11] These were *Razsvet* (Dawn), *Sion* (Zion), and *Dyen* (Day) in Russian, *Ha-Melits* (The Mediator), in Hebrew, and *Kol mevaser* (The Voice of the Herald) in Yiddish. The very name *Razsvet* (Dawn) was testimony to the faith of that periodical's editors, Osip Rabinovich and Joachim Tarnopol, that a new age indeed had dawned for the Jewish people, one in which the Jews would emerge from darkness to light, from degradation to emancipation. The Jewish people were finally to take their rightful place in the family of nations.

Although differing in nuance and in the emphases given to various themes, the Russian-Jewish periodicals *Razsvet*, *Sion*, and *Dyen* did in fact have a common focus. All three expressed the belief that emancipation was in the offing and that the Jewish community had to prepare itself for the demands of the new age. While some contributors believed that the Jews had to reform themselves in order to receive emancipation from the government, the editors of all three publications did not share this view. They believed that Jewish emancipation was the natural right of the Jews. They were human beings and should be emancipated regardless of the degree of internal reform among Russian Jews. Nonetheless, the reform of Russian Jewry was imperative for its own sake. Internal reform would eliminate the poverty and ignorance that characterized Jewish life and would enable the Jews to deal effectively with the many problems of modern life, including that of equal citizenship in a modern and progressive state. Internal reform meant a modern educational system in which secular subjects were taught. *Dyen*, in particular, was a champion of the crown schools. Linguisitic Russification was also important, since without it *sblizhenie* was virtually impossible. Rabinovich stated this succinctly in *Razsvet*. "Our homeland is Russia; just as its air is ours, so its language must become ours."[12] *Sion* agreed that Russian Jews should learn Russian, but it also maintained that in the modern world there was a place for Hebrew, the language of the Jewish nation.

Yet, all the talk of reform and Russification should not obscure the fact that the editors and the majority of contributors to these three Russian Jewish periodicals did not call for the total assimilation of Russian Jewry. Their goal was not to create Russians of the Mosaic faith. These Russian Jewish intellectuals believed that the Jews were a distinct national-religious group, which should not have to jettison its identity for the sake of attaining civil rights in a modern Russian state. There was still room for Jewish communal life, with at least some institutional trappings, in schools and social welfare organizations, as well as in religious institutions.

The Hebrew periodical *Ha-Melits* dwelt on some of the same themes and added new ones. It advanced the same call for limited Russification, but the editor, Alexander Tsederbaum, also sought to revive Hebrew and make it once again a living language for the Jewish people. He also supported secular schooling along with rather radical ritual and religious reform. Judaism had to reflect the modern spirit, Tsederbaum and his contributors argued. Law codes created hundreds or thousands of years ago could not be expected to be useful in contemporary life. *Ha-Melits* also dwelt on the need for social reform within Russian Jewry. The marriage of young teenage boys and girls, for example, was considered especially destructive, since it led to unhappy marriages and prolonged dependency, and it decreased economic productivity and perpetuated ignorance. In a vision similar to that of the Russian Jewish press, Tsederbaum and the *Ha-Melits* writers sought a modern Jewish community growing from its ancient Hebraic roots to live in rapprochement and amity with the rest of Russian society.

Kol mevaser, a Yiddish weekly which appeared in 1862, was the only one of the Jewish periodicals designed for a mass audience. This was the reason why Tsederbaum, a fervent *maskil* and hebraist who believed that Russian Jews should speak Russian as well as Hebrew, decided to also publish a Yiddish periodical. When other *maskilim* bitterly protested, he responded by saying that Yiddish had to be used in order to communicate with the masses of Russian and Polish Jews. He stated that his publishing a Yiddish paper would even facilitate the disappearance of the "jargon," since implementation of the ideas to be advanced in *Kol mevaser* would lead to its abandonment. In fact, however, Tsederbaum's Yiddish weekly did not contribute to the demise of Yiddish, but played a major role, by standardizing spelling and grammar, in helping it to flourish.

In terms of themes, *Kol mevaser* focused on the question of internal reform of the Jewish community. The editors realized, in view of the periodical's somewhat less educated readership, that a negative antipodal image would be useful to draw the reader's attention and stimulate his ire. Given the *maskil* views of Tsederbaum and his cohorts on the paper, it was perhaps natural that *Kol mevaser* focused on Hasidism as the bane of Jewish life in Russia. The *hasid* was depicted as superstitious and ignorant, at war with the secular world. The relationship beween the *hasid* and his spiritual leader the *tsadik* was strongly condemned as a primitive carry-over from a bygone period.

The languages in which *Kol mevaser* and *Ha-Melits* were written differed from that of *Razsvet*, *Sion*, and *Dyen*, and the themes of the journals varied, but the new Jewish intelligentsia which edited and contributed to them agreed on one basic idea. In addressing themselves to the new conditions of life facing each individual Jew and Russian Jewry as a whole, they maintained a profound commitment to a future Jewish identity and cohesion. The Jewish people as a distinct collective body was not to disappear in the new age.

The greatest influence on the Jewish intelligentsia was not exerted by Tsederbaum, Tarnopol, and Rabinovich. A small but gifted group of writers and poets, whose books and poems appeared in the Jewish periodicals on a serialized basis, reflected and shaped the attitudes of many in that generation of the sixties and seventies. Writing primarily in Russian, but also in Hebrew and Yiddish, these writers were the first in a long and distinguished line of Russian Jewish literary personalities who sought to lead their people to a better life.

Yehudah Leib Gordon's Hebrew poem "Awake My People!" (Hakiza Ammi), which appeared in 1866 in the periodical *Ha-Karmel* (Carmel), was the reveille for Russian Jewish youth. Its call for Russification and secularization, and its optimism concerning the future epitomized the feelings and aspirations held by many young Jews in the 1860s.

> Awake, my people! How long will you slumber?
> The night has passed, the sun shines bright.
> Awake, lift up your eyes, look around you—
> Acknowledge, I pray you, your time and place....
> The land in which now we live and are born—
> Is it not thought to be part of Europe?
> Europe—the smallest of Earth's regions,
> Yet the greatest of all in wisdom and reason.

This land of Eden [Russia] now opens its gates to you,
Her sons now call you "brother"!
How long will you dwell among them as a guest,
And why do you now affront them?

Already they have removed the weight of suffering from your shoulder,
They have lifted off the yoke from your neck,
They have erased from their hearts gratuitous hatred and folly,
They give you their hand, they greet you with peace.

Raise your head high, straighten your back,
And gaze with loving eyes upon them.
Open your heart to wisdom and knowledge.
Become an enlightened people, and speak their language.

Every man of understanding should try to gain knowledge;
Let others learn all manner of arts and crafts;
Those who are brave should serve in the army;
The farmers should buy ploughs and fields.

To the treasury of the state bring your strength,
Take your share of its possessions, its bounty.
Be a man abroad and a Jew in your tent,
A brother to your countrymen and a servant to your king.[13]

Several years later Gordon, in another poem, "For Whom Do I Toil?" (Lemi Ani Amel), bitterly lamented the headlong rush to assimilation which led some young Jews to abandon not only Jewish values and the Hebrew language but Jewry itself. They were going too far. For them *slianie* (confluence or a pervasive assimilation) and not *sblizhenie* was the goal and it broke the poet's heart.

The one man whose literary endeavors best expressed the mood of the new generation and probably had the greatest influence on it as well as upon those Russians interested in Jewish affairs was Lev Levanda. This graduate of a government rabbinical school, who became a teacher in a crown school, and later a "learned Jew" attached to the governor-general's office in Vilna, became a passionate advocate of internal reform, an ardent Russian patriot, and an equally enthusiastic Russifier.

The very first issue of *Razsvet* carried an article by Levanda, "Several Words about the Jews in the Western Borderlands of Russia," which severely criticized Russian Jewry—and not the Russian government—for the sad plight of the Jews. "What poverty, what material and moral squalor," he wrote.[14] The Jews had to change the values and attitudes that they lived by. Moreover, the Jews had to alter the economic bases upon which they constituted their lives. The Jewish male's total absorption in the study of the Talmud, which led him to abdicate his responsibility for the economic well-being of his family, was, according to Levanda, at the root of the problem.

On the issue of Russification, not only in its linguistic sense but in terms of profound attachment to the Russian state, Levanda spoke for many young, educated Jews in Lithuania, Belorussia, and the Ukraine when he defended the crushing of the Polish revolution of 1863. He chastised the Polish nobility for its centuries-long persecution of the Jews, and to his question, "Was Poland a fatherland to the Jews?" he answered with a resounding "No."

His passion for Russification reached its zenith in the novel *Goriachee Vremia* (Turbulent Times). In it he praised Russia for bringing the Jews out from barbarism and, in discussing the Polish revolt of 1863, Levanda has his Russian Jewish protagonists proclaim, "We stand with Moscow." At the end of the novel, after much soul-searching, Levanda's hero, Sorin, expresses the mood of an entire generation when he cries out that "under the flag of Russification, we shall receive a fatherland."[15] The tragic events of 1881 and 1882 would inflict a terrible wound on this fervent preacher of *sblizhenie* between Russians and Jews, who believed that the future of Russian Jewry was so brilliant.

Levanda's rival for the affections of the Russian educated Jewish youth was Ilia Orshanskii, an extremely talented young scholar of the late 1860s and the 1870s, who wrote for *Dyen* and who died at the age of twenty-nine. Orshanskii, too, championed linguistic Russification and internal reform but operated with a different style and used another genre. Whereas Levanda used fiction, Orshanskii wrote insightful, scholarly articles on the economic, social, and legal aspects of Jewish life in Russia. His book *Russkoe Zakondatel'stvo o Evreiakh* (Russian Legislation Concerning the Jews), dealing with the history of the legal disabilities of Russian Jewry, was considered a classic by his contemporaries. He echoed Levanda in supporting Russia's quashing of the 1863 rebellion and by calling upon Russian Jewry to act as a bulwark of Russification in Russian Poland, Lithuania, and Belorussia. Like Levanda and many of the Russifiers he believed that the integration of Russian Jewry into Russian culture was desirable and inevitable; but he differed from the more fervent Russifiers in that he believed in a natural process of assimilation, in the inexorable fusion of the Jews with a dominant Russian culture without coercive government policies acting as a stimulus. Orshanskii stood with those who argued that existing Russian legislation concerning the Jews had a deleterious and counterproductive impact upon Jewish social structure and integration into Russian society. Let the Jews be emancipated first and then all of the needed social, economic, and religious reforms would follow with alacrity.[16]

What distinguished Orshanskii from other writers and what gave him great popularity was his passionate defense of the Russian Jewish community against its many detractors. He maintained that Jews are a creative and productive people, not always middlemen. His studies of contemporary Russian Jewry depicted the roles played by Jews as artisans, in agriculture, and in animal husbandry. Even as middlemen, Orshanskii claimed, the Jews contributed positively to the economic well-being of the peasantry. He totally rejected the idea that Jews were responsible for the great poverty and perpetual inebriation of the Russian peasantry, stating boldly that both social illnesses were caused by the general backwardness of Russian society and that only when this changed would these be cured. A firm believer in Russification, Orshanskii maintained a powerful emotional tie to the Jewish masses and, like most of the Russian Jewish intelligentsia, hoped that Jewish institutions would be preserved after emancipation. His premature death in 1875 deprived Russian Jewry of one of its most brilliant spokesmen, a loss that would be felt deeply in the coming years.

Both Levanda and Orshanskii were speaking to a growing audience. In the 1860s and 1870s Russification spread fairly rapidly among Russian Jewish youth. The apparent liberalism of Alexander II's reign, the heightened attractiveness of Russian literature and culture, the aggressive policies of Russification pursued by the government in the period following the Polish revolt of 1863, and the granting of rewards and privileges by the government to Jews possessing Russian diplomas contributed to this process. Jewish enrollment figures in the gymnasiums of the empire testify to the strength of the movement. In 1859, for example, 159 Jewish students constituted less than 1.5 percent of total enrollment. By 1863, 3.8 percent, or 547 students, were Jewish. In 1870 Jews constituted 5.5 percent of the student body, 2,047 students. The figure reached 11.5 percent in 1880. These zealous participants in Russification experienced emotional and intellectual trauma in the period of the pogroms that was to follow.[17]

Moshe Leib Lilienblum and Isaac Joel Linetski represented that part of the new generation of educated Russian Jews that was not completely wrapped up in the cause of Russification, although they, too, urged familiarity with Russian society and civilization; but they were very much concerned with reforming the basic structure of Russian Jewry. They were partisans of "inner reform." In the Haskalah tradition, Lilienblum began his public career as an outspoken champion of religious reform. His series of articles, "Orhot Ha-Talmud" (The Ways of the Talmud), in the Hebrew newspaper *Ha-Melits*, advanced the proposition that Judaism was not a stagnant religion and that Talmudic authorities had always sought to reconcile Judaism with the spirit and needs of the time. He appealed to prominent Russian Jewish religious leaders to begin the task of interpreting Jewish religious law in a rational and modern way so as to eliminate the traditional obstacles that stood in the way of modernizing Russian Jewry.

Lilienblum was a true child of the times, what the great historian Dubnov called "a martyr of enlightenment." Like many of his contemporaries, he suffered for his liberal views. Orthodox religious leaders in his wife's town of Vilkomir harassed him to the point where, for physical security, he had to flee to Odessa. In this young and dynamic seaport, already a center of the Russification movement, Lilienblum entered a new phase in his intellectual development. He abandoned his program for religious reform and concentrated instead on the need to restructure the economic underpinnings of Jewish life. He preached the need for Jews to learn a manual trade, and by 1880 he had become an advocate for agricultural work among Jews. On a more general level, Lilienblum urged that Jews become students of the natural sciences: "The more we discover about the laws of nature, the greater will be her usefulness to us."[18]

In this second stage of his career, Lilienblum reflected the various currents of thought swirling through the Jewish community of Odessa in the late 1860s and 1870s. Emphasis upon manual labor and agricultural work was emphasized by old Haskalah circles as well as by the most affluent Jewish elements who had become absorbed in the task of regenerating Russian Jewry through economic reform. Lilienblum's stress on natural science as a palliative for the problems of both Russian society and the Jewish community reveal his coming under the influence of prominent Russian thinkers, most notably Dmitri Pisarev. Regardless of the sources of his ideas, in the end, as one Jewish writer put it, Lilienblum remained a *yeshiva bocher* (yeshiva boy). Every program he advanced could be defended by quotes from the Talmud. In the disastrous years of the first Russian pogroms, 1881–1882, this seeker of a cure for the ills of the Jewish people would draw heavily upon one particular aspect of the Jewish tradition and discover the solution to the Jewish problem in Zionism or, as it was then called, Palestinophilism.

Isaac Joel Linetski was different. Although he, like Levanda, made his mark as a writer of fiction, the similarity ends there. Levanda was educated in the spirit of the age, in crown schools, and had quickly entered into the world of the new Russian Jewish intelligentsia. His novels and short stories, written in Russian, are serious attempts to advance the idea of Russification and, to a lesser extent, a program of internal reform. Linetski, on the other hand, was born to a Hasidic family, was educated in the traditional way, and married at the age of fourteen to a young girl of twelve. Moreover, his most important literary contribution, *Dos Poylishe Yingel* (The Polish Lad), was written in Yiddish and is a hilarious, if biting, satire of Hasidic life.

Perhaps because it was written in Yiddish, Linetski's book enjoyed a readership probably greater than that of most other literary publications of the period. It was also one of the few works, outside of some religious tracts, that was read by the Jewish masses of Eastern Europe. The Yiddish poet, Abraham Reisen, recalled that his father read aloud installments of *Dos Poylishe Yingel* to the family every Friday night and that neighbors were also invited in for the occasion.[19] The book appeared in serial form in *Kol mevaser* in February 1867, but the readers became so impatient that the paper published the whole book as a supplement before it was finished in the periodical.

Better than anyone else, Linetski was able to elucidate the internal dynamics of Hasidic life and the harmful impact that Hasidism had upon the Jews of the empire. Linetski portrayed the sad lot of traditional Jewish women, oppressed, held in contempt, and suffering from a terrible inferiority complex, yet at the same time doing herculean labor in the home and in business: "Even during my stay in paradise [the womb] I was in mortal fear of one thing—of coming into the world as the daughter of a Polish Hasid."[20] In another passage he states: "Though a Polish Jew may be a miserable louse, a stammerer, and a booby among his fellows, he is still considered a man, the lord and master over the prettiest, the most erudite and accomplished women."[21]

Superstitious faith in miracle-working Hasidic rabbis, the greed and hypocrisy of these leaders, the slavish devotion of the *hasid* to his rabbi, even at the expense of his own family, all were attacked by Linetski. He also lambasted traditional Jewish education in the *heder* and lamented the dearth of secular knowledge among the Jews. He did not close his eyes to those aspects of life in the Pale that even the most radical critics of traditional Jewish life were reluctant to touch; alcoholism, sexual promiscuity, and cowardly and obsequious behavior on the part of Jews in their dealings with Gentiles. Tendentious and highly polemical, the book had an enormous impact on Russian and East European Jewish life and gave its author a fame and notoriety which would never again be his, although he, too, would be affected by the events of 1881–1882 and would play a role in the great debates of those years.

Levanda, Lilienblum, Orshanskii, and Linetski were striking a three-way balance. They endorsed a certain amount of Russification and a large dosage of internal reform, but they also believed in the necessity of maintaining Jewish communal identity. There were other Jewish writers, however, who, while also believing in internal reform and in linguistic Russification, gave primacy of place to the preservation of Jewish culture and the regeneration of Jewish national consciousness among Russian Jews. They feared that with the coming of a progressive government in Russia and new economic conditions, Russian Jewry would repeat what had happened in Jewish communities in Central and Western Europe—they would assimilate to the point of abandoning all communal and national sentiment and perhaps even their religion itself.

The preservation of the Jewish national idea drew its inspiration from a number of sources. The traditionalism, large numbers, and high concentration of Russian Jews, compared to Jewish communities in Western Europe, guaranteed that assimilation would never have the field to itself in Russia as it did in other parts of Europe. The increasing anti-Semitism of the last part of Alexander II's reign, discussed in the next chapter, and which was manifested not only among lower and déclassé elements in Russian society but also by high-ranking government officials and prominent literary personalities, led at least some educated Jews to reject the possibility of even *sblizhenie* and to seek a solution to the Jewish problem elsewhere. The growth of national movements throughout the European continent, particularly on the Italian peninsula, also stimulated the development of national consciousness among some Jews who had received a secular education and therefore were not oblivious to the nationalist impulse in European civilization. Jewish nationalism, like the drive for rapprochement and assimilation, was a product of the Haskalah.

Abraham Mapu, the father of the modern Hebrew novel, was a champion of the Russian Haskalah. His novels espoused the cause of knowledge, manual labor, and cultivation of the soil. But his major contribution was to elevate the sense of national consciousness found among Russian Jews, which included a yearning for Palestine. His two romantic novels, *Ahabat Sion* (The Love of Zion) and *Ashrat Shamron* (Guilt of Samaria) took his readers out of their squalid towns and villages and brought them to the pastoral beauties of Bethlehem and the Carmel. They were able to smell the lilies of Sharon. *Ahabat Sion* paved the way for the recrudescence of the national idea which emerged in the period of the pogroms.[22]

Perez Smolenskin, born in the Russian Empire but publishing his Hebrew periodical *Ha-Shahar* (Dawn) in Vienna, was also a partisan of the national idea. In the mid–1860s, through novels and essays published in his periodical, Smolenskin sharply deviated from the prevailing mood of the times and warned that all Jewish attempts to curry favor with governments and host populations through enlightenment and rapprochement would not result in Jewish equality. He warned those Jews who had so warmly supported the Russian government in its struggle against the Poles that their actions would be for naught—they would not be emancipated. Smolenskin was one of the few Jews in mid-nineteenth-century Europe to raise doubts about solving the Jewish question through emancipation. He speculated that those Jews who had already been granted equality would have their emancipation revoked in the future.

In opposition to Russification, rapprochement and assimilation, Smolenskin sought to effect a renaissance of Hebrew language and Jewish pride.

"You say," said Smolenskin to the assimilationists, "let us be like the other nations. Well and good. Let us indeed, be like the other nations, cultured men and women, free from superstition, loyal citizens of the country. But let us also remember, as the other nations do, that we have no right to be ashamed of our origin, that it is our duty to hold dear our national language and our national dignity."[23]

Smolenskin believed the very preservation of the Jewish people to be inextricably bound up with the Hebrew language, "without which there is no Judaism."

Like Mapu, Smolenskin groped in the direction of Zionism without making a total commitment to it. He criticized Western European Jews for eliminating from their prayerbooks prayers for the restitution of Zion, and in 1872 he wrote that anyone who denied the messianic hope of a return to Palestine was a traitor to the Jewish people. But a clear, unequivocal call for Jewish settlement in Palestine was not voiced by Smolenskin, and he was, therefore, criticized in his own periodical for taking halfway measures that could not possibly resolve the Jewish predicament.

The critic was the young Eliezer Perlman, known as Ben-Yehudah, the foremost proponent of Jewish nationalism in the 1870s. Perlman took Smolenskin's ideas and drove them to their furthest point. For Perlman, the Jews were not a spiritual nation, they were a nation like all the others, and, like the others, they were entitled to a land of their own. He argued that the revival of the Hebrew language was not enough to revive Jewish national consciousness. What was needed was a national center which would allow Jewish nationhood to be resurrected as of old and to nourish the Jewish communities of the Diaspora. To achieve the goal of such a national center, Perlman called upon Jewish literary figures to form a society which would work for the large-scale settlement of Jews in Palestine. Over twenty years before the first Zionist congress, Perlman had formulated the basic outline of what was to be the Zionist program.[24]

Thus in the 1860s and 1870s, Jewish nationalist sentiments were an important element in the thinking of at least part of the Jewish intelligentsia. There is some evidence to suggest that the growing anti-Semitism of the 1870s accelerated this process. Marcus Kagan, a university student in the 1870s, wrote that in the last years of the seventies Jewish students increasingly celebrated holidays with a Jewish national character, such as Chanukah and Purim, and they had begun to express concern for Jewish causes, including settlement in Palestine.[25] The goal of *sblizhenie* still prevailed among secularly educated Jews but by 1879 and 1880 faith in its fulfillment was somewhat diminished. The debacle of 1881–1882 would, for some Jews, shatter this faith completely and forever.

Of course the new stratum of Jews educated in secular schools which appeared in the 1860s and 1870s represented only a tiny fraction of Russian Jewry. The great bulk of the Jewish masses continued to reject completely secular education and government schools. They remained committed to the *heder* and *yeshiva*. The several thousand Jewish students in the gymnasiums and the hundreds of Jewish students in Russian universities and professional schools by 1872 testify to the rapid growth of the new stratum, but the figures also demonstrate its insignificant numbers.

Even within the group of secularized and educated Jews there was considerable heterogeneity. Levanda, Orshanskii, Lilienblum, and Linetski, in their espousal of linguistic Russification, internal reform, and the preservation of Jewish national and communal identity, and Smolenskin, Mapu, and Perlman, with their emphasis on the Jewish national idea and Palestine, spoke for many but most certainly not for all Jews. In Russia's Polish provinces a small number of young Jews educated in Polish assimilated into Polish culture with a passion that transformed them into "Poles of the Mosaic persuasion" who desired nothing better than to abandon all communal and national manifestations of Jewish life. They participated in the Polish rebellion of 1863 against the Russian Empire, and from that time on were indefatigable in manifesting their Polish patriotism and identity. The Polish Jewish weekly, *Jutrzenka* (The Dawn), did not share the concern of the Jewish press in Russia with preserving a Jewish collective identity in the modern age.[26]

In addition to these assimilated Polish Jews, there were other manifestations of heterogeneity. While there were many who subscribed to the ideas advanced by Levanda, Orshanskii, and the other educated Russian Jews for the reform and restructuring of Russian Jewry, a large number of young people were concerned only with their own personal integration into Russian society rather than with any fundamental amelioration of the general condition of Russian Jews. The Russian Jewish press of the 1860s and 1870s, together with a number of Jewish literary figures, particularly Lilienblum, railed against those Jewish graduates of universities and gymnasiums who played down their Jewish origins and severed their links with the Jewish people. The writer Ben-Ami (M.I. Rabinovich) relates that as a student at the university in Odessa he tried to raise money in behalf of indigent Jewish farmers. Unlike the Jewish university student friends of Marcus Kagan, many of the Odessa Jewish students refused to give "on principle": "We will not give anything for a specifically Jewish cause."[27]

There were a number of reasons for this indifference. Some were simply caught up in material pursuits. Others, like Ben-Ami's peers, were so enraptured with Russian culture and a society that seemed to beckon them that Jewish interests seemed parochial and narrow in comparison. Still others were casualties, the "martyrs of enlightenment." They had participated in an ideological war with their more traditional and orthodox elders, a veritable battle, in the words of Jewish contemporaries, "between fathers and sons." The young, educated Jews emerged from the conflict with a profound sense of alienation from the Jewish people and therefore an indifference, if not hostility, to their faith. Many had become indifferent, because, as Levanda portrays so vividly in his novel *Turbulent Times*, they had found, after much suffering, a new home. Russified and secularized, young Russian Jewish students had abandoned their former homes and way of life, and sought eagerly to find comfort and acceptance in another. It was this desperate longing to solve their crisis of identity, to find an answer to the question, "What are we?" and end their loneliness, that led so many educated Russian Jews to embrace fervent Russification and assimilation (*slianie*), and in Russian Poland, Polonization, with such passion that indifference to the Jewish faith and people was the natural corollary.

In a few cases the passion and longing was so great that when coupled with a drive for material gain or professional achievement, they led individuals not only to be indifferent but to abandon Judaism completely, through conversion to the Russian Orthodox faith. Russian Jewry, it will be remembered, was in a transitional legal position. Some but not all of the legal restrictions had been eliminated or eased. While educated Russian Jews had unprecedented opportunities, the full scope of options were open only to those who could show a baptismal certificate. In the 1850s, 1860s, 1870s and beyond, a small number of Jews, some extremely gifted, crossed over into Christian Russia. The distinguished orientalist Daniel Khvolson, who had converted to Christianity, probably spoke for many when he allegedly responded to the question, "Did you convert out of conviction?" with the answer, "Yes, I was convinced that it was far better to live as a Gentile professor than a Jewish *melamed* [a teacher in a *heder*]."[28]

JEWISH REVOLUTIONARIES

One group of educated Jews was much smaller than the others in the 1860s and 1870s, and never shared the belief in an emancipated and brilliant future for Jews in Tsarist Russia. Russification, secularization, internal reform, the entire program of the Haskalah itself were trifles, according to this group, which would not fundamentally alter the position of the Jews in Russia. For the small band of Jewish revolutionaries the only solution to Jewish poverty and to endemic anti-Semitism was a social revolution, the complete destruction of the existing social, economic, and political order and its replacement by a socialist Russia.

The relationship between the revolutionary movement and the Jews dates from the time of the Decembrists' abortive revolt of 1825, which had included one baptized Jew, Gregory Perets. It was the view of Pavel Pestel, one of the Decembrist leaders, that the Jews should either assimilate into Russian society or, preferably, be assisted to immigrate to Asia Minor where they could create a state of their own.

The Jewish factor in the revolutionary movement became more pronounced with the increase in opposition groups' activity during the reign of Alexander II. The movement of Jews into gymnasiums and universities, where they were exposed to new currents of thought, and to increasing anti-Semitism, particulary in the mid-seventies, played a role in creating the Jewish revolutionaries. Revolutionary myths notwithstanding, the bulk of the Jewish revolutionaries in this period did not come from the yeshivot and did not derive their socialist inspiration from Biblical and prophetic teachings. Assimilated, Russified Jews, imbibing contemporary Russian revolutionary themes, and Jews caught up in what they believed to be the revolutionary message of the New Testament, not the Hebrew Scriptures, constituted a majority of the Jewish revolutionaries.

The very first revolutionary circles formed in the late 1850s included Jews. It was, however, not until the 1870s that the Jewish component began to reach larger proportions. As the revolutionaries under the inspiration of Peter Lavrov went out "to the people," a number of Jews joined the journey to the countryside to inform the peasants about socialism and the need for revolution. The primary contribution of the Jewish revolutionaries was organizational and technical. They were more involved in printing, smuggling, organizing escapes, and constructing explosives than in conducting propaganda among peasants or in terrorist acts. Mark Natanson, Pavel Akselrod, Lev Deych, Osip Aptekman, Lev Ginsburg, Lazar Goldenberg, Gregory Goldenberg, and Aaron Zundelevich were the most prominent Jewish participants in the revolutionary activity of the 1870s. It is estimated that in the period from the middle of 1873 to January 1, 1877, the Jews, who comprised about 4 percent of the empire's population, constituted 6.5 percent of all those brought to trial for engaging in propaganda work, 15 percent of those deported, and 7.5 percent of those placed under police surveillance—sixty-eight people in all.[29]

The presence of Jews in the revolutionary movement, and the existence of about four million Jews in the empire, obliged the revolutionaries to devote some attention to the Jewish question. In the decade 1871–1881, immediately prior to the pogroms of 1881–1882, the revolutionaries did concern themselves with the Jews. The attack in Odessa in 1871 upon Jewish artisans and small businessmen perplexed the revolutionaries in the south. A number of them, Jews and non-Jews alike, argued that the violence was triggered by "Jewish exploitation." In the eyes of these revolutionaries, the artisans and commercial elements, who made up a significant percentage of the Jewish population, were indistinguishable from the Christian industrialists and merchants who exploited Russian and Ukrainian workers. In this light many revolutionaries argued that the economic elite, Christian and Jewish, should be smashed, and some viewed the Odessa pogrom from this standpoint. The destruction of the oppressive economic system would also cause the disappearance of all intermediary economic groups such as the Jews, and presumably, anti-Jewish sentiments would disappear.

The Odessa pogrom also stimulated a discussion of the revolutionary inclinations of the Jewish masses. Most revolutionaries became convinced that the Jews, as a nonagricultural people without many manual workers, did not constitute a suitable element for the adoption of socialist principles. The high visibility of a handful of extremely wealthy Jews, such as the Günzburgs, Poliakovs, and Brodskiis, and the fervent patriotism and support for Alexander II in the ranks of the Russified and secularized Jews, led Jewish and non-Jewish revolutionaries to the belief that Jews were either intrinsically reactionary or were just not proper revolutionary material. The idea of allocating personnel and money for the purpose of propagandizing the unenlightened Jewish masses in their own language, Yiddish, was a proposition advanced for the first time in the middle of the 1870s by the Jewish revolutionaries in Vilna, Aaron Lieberman and Lazar Goldenberg. But their idea that there was a revolutionary potential in the Jewish poor was met with astonishment and sarcasm on the part of Russian revolutionaries, Jews and non-Jews alike.[30]

Therefore as the revolutionary movement emerged from the decade of the 1870s it possessed certain notions of the Jews which, when linked with the basic principles and attitudes of Russian Populism, would have a great impact on how the Russian revolutionary movement would react to the Jewish question in the future. The nearly universal belief that many Jews were "exploiters" and reactionaries, and that the Jewish masses were poor revolutionary material, was joined with the populist idealization of the "oppressed peasantry." The final element to be added was the feeling of desperation felt by many revolutionaries at the end of the seventies and early eighties as a result of government harassment and their failure to move the peasants to revolutionary action. Small wonder that the revolutionaries would react to the coming pogroms in ways that did not at all defend the Jews.

THE ECONOMY OF THE JEWS

No discussion of Jewish life in the period prior to the pogroms would be complete without some discussion of the economic position of Russian Jewry. Accurate statistical data is not available before 1897, the date of the first reliable census in Russian history. But it is still possible, on the basis of studies made by nineteenth-century scholars and various government committees, to construct at least a partial view of Jewish economic life.

The key characteristics of the Jewish economy were its diversity and the great poverty which encumbered the vast majority of Russian Jews. Commerce and trade, crafts and industry, day labor and domestic work, transportation, liberal professions and administrative work, military service and agriculture were the chief sources of Jewish livelihood in the nineteenth century. The precise number of Jews in each endeavor changed with the times. The full range of Jewish economic activity is best exemplified by the following list of crafts which attracted Jewish artisans.

Bakers	Locksmiths
Barbers and wigmakers	Musicians and piano-tuners
Blacksmiths	Oven-makers and bricklayers
Bookbinders	Painters
Butchers	Saddlers and harness-makers
Cabinetmakers and joiners	Seamstresses
Cap-makers	Shoemakers
Carpenters	Stocking-makers
Coppersmiths	Tailors
Dressmakers	Tanners
Dyers	Tobacco-cutters
Glazers	Watchmakers
	Weavers[31]

More significant than the diversity was the great poverty which overwhelmed Russian Jewry. The rubrics of "commerce and trade" and "crafts and industry" should not be misconstrued. For the most part they are synonymous with small-scale retail and wholesale enterprises—peddling, leasing, innkeeping, and artisan activity at the lowest possible level. The fate of the great majority of Russian Jews, whatever their occupation, was misery and occasional demoralization.

Shaul Ginsburg, the historian and biographer of prominent Russian Jewish personalities of the second half of the nineteenth century, writes of a case in which a father of seven children was informed in the early morning before he went to work that the youngest child had died. The father registered no reaction and left the house. Before he returned in the late afternoon a small dog came into the family lodging. The man, returning, heard the whining of the dog and mistook it for the child he believed had died. The result was a terrible tantrum by the father, a storm of curses hurled at the rest of the family. It was clear that the father had welcomed the death of the child. One less mouth to feed made the daily burden just that much easier. Normal sensitivity had turned to callousness. Ginsburg's biographies of other Jews born in the second half and third quarter of the nineteenth century are replete with analogous episodes.[32]

What biography has discovered, statistical data and economic research, albeit primitive, have confirmed. In 1849 B. Milutin found that only 3 percent of the Jews possessed any capital, while the rest lived miserable lives.[33] In the 1860s studies of the province of Kovno revealed that it was common for several Jewish families to occupy a single room, and in the province of Grodno a three or four-room house often had as many as twelve Jewish families living in it.[34] The situation in the Ukraine, the scene of the worst pogroms, was somewhat better, but even there, according to a landowner in the province of Kiev, most Jews were poorer than the peasants, a terrible state given the great impoverishment of the peasantry in nineteenth-century Russia.[35] With the passage of time the situation only got worse. Government committees appointed in the 1880s found that 90 percent of the Jews existed as "a proletariat living from hand to mouth, in poverty and under the most trying and unhygienic conditions."[36] By the end of the century it was estimated that nearly 19 percent of the Jewish population was reported to have received some type of charity at the time of Passover.[37]

The causes of Jewish poverty and misery were manifold. The general backwardness of Russia in the nineteenth century insured that Jews, together with Christians, would in the great majority of cases lead a miserable existence. Similarly, Jews as well as Christians suffered greatly during the various economic downturns experienced by Russia, the first beginning in the late 1850s and lasting for a good part of the next decade, and the second in the years from 1873 to 1880.

The emancipation of the Russian serfs also had a negative impact on the economic situation of the Jewish masses. Those Jews that had made a living either as managers or lessees of aristocratic estates found after emancipation that the aristocracy, in a weakened financial position, was inclined to do without them. The peasantry, too, after emancipation made less use of Jewish economic intermediaries. Moreover, the emancipation of the serfs facilitated the movement of peasants away from the countryside into the cities and towns where in a relatively short period of time they began to compete with Jewish artisans and shopkeepers, who already had enough competition from each other.

The progressive industrialization of Russia brought particular hardship to three types of Jewish workers who were already living a marginal existence. The construction of railroads hurt the tens of thousands of

Jewish carters and haulers. The new textile and shoe factories, some owned by Jews, proved, as elsewhere, to be fierce and effective competitors with the artisan class in Russia, many of whom were Jews. Industrialization, of course, created significant opportunities for some Jews. These benefitted enormously, but in the 1860s, 1870s, and 1880s the impact on many segments of Russian Jewry was devastating.

In addition to these objective factors affecting Jewish life adversely, there was the subjective side to the fact of discriminatory legislation. A myriad of legislative acts prevented Jews from entering certain occupations and forced them out of others. Jews were compelled to pay higher taxes. Most significantly, they were kept from leaving the Pale of Settlement for the Russian interior in numbers large enough to have a positive impact on Jewish life.

The case of the artisans is instructive in this regard. According to the 1897 census there were 500,986 Jewish artisans in the empire, 13.2 percent of the total Jewish population.[38] In every province of the Pale of Settlement Jewish artisans constituted the greatest percentage of the artisan class. In backward agrarian Russia they devoured each other through ferocious competition. One solution to this economic maelstrom was to open up the Russian interior to Jewish settlement and provide the artisans with greater opportunities. This was, however, not to be allowed.

In fact, the government of Alexander II clung tenaciously to the Pale even though a large number of government officials and several government commissions called upon the government to increase Jewish settlement in the interior of Russia. At all costs the Russian people must be protected from the insidious and obnoxious influence of the Jews. The law of 1865 which allowed Jewish artisans to leave the Pale was a sham. A Jewish artisan who attempted to take advantage of the new law found that he could not register in his new community and could obtain only a temporary passport. He also confronted a situation in which renewal of residential permits played into the hands of extortionist police officials. What was even worse was that if he were sick or incapacitated he could be deported back to the Pale immediately, and if his children for any reason did not take up artisan work, they too could be forced back into the Pale. In the end, from 1865 to 1881 less than two thousand Jewish artisans out of what must have been a much larger number left the Pale for the Russian interior.[39]

The extremely difficult situation of the artisans, with their terrible competition, was shared by the petty mercantile element among the Russian Jews who, by the end of the century, were still numerically larger than the craft and industrial segment, by 38.5 percent of the Jewish work force to 35.4 percent.[40] These hundreds of thousands of shopkeepers, innkeepers, peddlers, and brokers also desperately needed an end or at least a substantial modification of the residential restrictions on Jews. Since this was not forthcoming, they, and the rest of the Jewish community sought an alternative through migration, primarily to other parts of the Pale of Settlement in Russia, but also in very small but increasing numbers to areas outside of Russia, primarily the United States.

MIGRATION AND EMIGRATION

In the period before 1881, the primary movement of Jews was to the southern provinces in the Pale. Belief that this less densely inhabited region offered better opportunities led a steady stream of Jews to relocate there. By 1897, 13.8 percent of all Jews living in Russia could be found in the southern provinces whereas in 1847 the figure had been only 2.5 percent.[41] But as early as the 1840s there was another much smaller but steady migration of Jews, probably no more than several hundred a year at most, out of the country, primarily to America.

The first fairly substantial emigration stream—the term "wave" is not yet relevant—took place at the end of the 1860s, as Lithuanian Jews fleeing hunger, typhus, and ubiquitous poverty sought refuge in neighboring European states, particularly in Germany. In Memel and Koenigsberg where most of the Jews settled, various assistance committees, composed in many cases of previous refugees, were established to care for the newcomers. Dr. Rulf, the Chief Rabbi of Memel and later an activist in the emigration wave in the early 1880s, took the lead in the formation of these committees.

It was only natural that the Lithuanian emigration would find some echoes in the Jewish press. In 1869 the Russian Jewish newspaper *Dyen* (Day), of Odessa, far from hungry Lithuania, lamented the fact that so many Jews were abandoning their fatherland, but said it was understandable in view of the impossible economic and legal situation the Jews confronted in the Pale. It was the periodical *Ha-Magid* (The Herald), however, published in Lyck in East Prussia but with much of its readership in Russia, that gave the greatest coverage to the emigration issue.

Ha-Magid did not take a consistent position on the question of whether or not America was the place where Russian Jews should seek salvation. One article, by a correspondent in St. Louis, confirmed that the United States was a free country. But the trouble is, claimed the writer, that Americans are not very religious. In St. Louis there are 4,000 Jews but only 2 synagogues, with a combined membership of 230! No one understands the Holy Book, people eat *tref* (nonkosher) food, and the Sabbath is not observed. The writer concludes: "The Jews of Russia and

Poland must not think of leaving their homes and coming here.... The good times when one rakes in the gold have already passed."[42]

Another article against settlement in America gave different reasons: "People observe the Sabbath and keep kosher in America," stated the writer, this time from Memphis, "but there is no need for Russian Jews to come here, now when the holy Tsar has given Jews in Russia equal rights...."[43]

In 1868 *Ha-Magid* published its first article emphatically endorsing settlement in America. The author, Dr. Bernard Felsenthal, a prominent Reform rabbi in the United States, informed the readers of *Ha-Magid* that in America the Jews were equal to all other citizens and that Jews had risen to high and respected places in the country. Earning a living was not a problem in America since the land was prosperous and Jews could enter any profession they wished. "Many who left their homeland with a bitter heart, poor and naked, ... have prospered.... No one wants to return from here to his old humiliating situation."[44]

The articles in *Ha-Magid* are a hint of the great debate that would rage during the wave of pogroms in the early 1880s. The response of foreign and Russian Jewish leaders to the emigration movement of the late sixties and seventies foreshadowed the vitriolic arguments among prominent Jews in Russia, Europe, and the United States. Given the small number of emigrants in the 1860s and 1870s, the debate was muted. In Russia, usually in private conversations and correspondence, prominent and often wealthy Russian Jews vehemently opposed emigration, believing that to advocate it was to dishonor the fatherland. As an alternative, they urged Russian Jews not to lose hope in the imminent redress of their grievances and, simultaneously, they beseeched the Russian government to either eliminate residential restrictions completely or modify them so as to allow large numbers of Russian Jews to leave for the forbidden provinces. Internal migration to the Russian interior was the panacea of Russian Jewish community leaders in the 1860s and 1870s.

It was also the solution advocated by many foreign Jewish leaders. Dr. Rulf, for example, for all of his support for Russian Jewish refugees in Memel believed throughout the 1870s that the best policy was to settle Jews in areas in Russia outside of the Pale. Other European and American Jewish leaders might agree that emigration was a possible way of solving the Jewish question, but they could not agree on where the Jews should go. German and French Jews believed that America was the most attractive place for settlement and in the years 1870 and 1871 the newly formed Alliance Israélite Universelle assisted 528 Russian Jews to go to America. American Jews, however, viewed the question differently; a number of unsubtle statements were issued by American Jewish groups in the 1870s protesting the arrival of Russian Jewish emigrants. Yet all of this was tame in comparison to the fierce and protracted debate over emigration and settlement that was to be triggered by the massive exodus soon to take place in the 1880s as a consequence of the pogroms.

The discussions of community leaders notwithstanding, Jewish emigration continued to grow in the 1870s. Reliable figures are not available since Russian governmental reports do not include the information and the receiving nations also fail to provide satisfactory data. In the United States, for example, it was not until 1899 that immigration data made reference to Jews. In that year the category Hebrew was introduced. Until then, they were registered only according to the country from which they came. Nonetheless, it is possible to arrive at the conclusion that from 1871 to 1880 approximately fifteen to twenty thousand Russian Jews arrived in the United States, an extremely large increase over the preceding decade, and a harbinger of the massive influx to come (see Chapter VI).

THE JEWISH PLUTOCRACY

Poverty, demoralization, and emigration were issues that affected in significant ways the great majority of Russian Jews, but not all of them. There existed in the empire, primarily in St. Petersburg, a very small stratum of extremely affluent Jews who were sheltered from the evils that beset their coreligionists in the third quarter of the nineteenth century. These men, the Günzburgs, Poliakovs, Brodskiis, Zaks, Zaitsevs, and a small number of others, were, like the educated Jews of the same period, creations of a Russian government and society experiencing the first throes of change.[45] The humiliating loss of the Crimean War and the growing sentiment in government circles that modernization and industrialization were necessary for the empire's survival created enormous opportunities for a small group of wealthy Jews. These Jews, many of whose sires had begun their fortunes in moneylending and in the leasing of alcohol concessions from the government or from local landlords, were encouraged by the government to participate in the industrialization of Russia. In the 1860s and 1870s Jewish capital played a substantial role in railroad construction, river transport, the development of oil fields in the Caucasus, sugar refining, and the tobacco industry. The Günzburgs, Poliakovs, and Brodskiis had not only become famous throughout Russia, they also, particularly the first two families, had been permitted to enter tentatively into the highest government circles in St. Petersburg.

This small circle of wealthy Jews, most of whom resided in St. Petersburg, was even more emphatic in its support for Tsar Alexander II and his reforms than was the Russian Jewish intelligentsia. One historian goes so far as to call their patriotism "primitive."[46] The rich Jews not only had no contact with the fledgling revolutionary movement, they also kept their distance from the liberal opposition. Always at pains to display their loyalty to the government, the Jews of St. Petersburg used every opportunity for this purpose. In the aftermath of an aborted assassination attempt on the Tsar's life in 1866, a number of St. Petersburg Jews endowed two scholarships at the government rabbinical school in honor of the Tsar. Horace Günzburg even commissioned the sculptor Anotolsky to create a statue of the Tsar to be placed in front of the synagogue established by the Günzburg family in St. Petersburg. To commemorate the twenty-fifth anniversary of the reign of Alexander II, Samuel Poliakov subsidized the building of a dormitory at St. Petersburg University. The dormitory, which became known as "Poliakov's College," fell prey to the growing anti-Semitism of the early 1880s; its statutes forbade Jewish students from being admitted.

In dealing with the problems of Russian Jewry the Jewish plutocracy displayed a lack of unanimity. In the beginning of Alexander's reign, in 1856, the small number of St. Petersburg Jews subscribed to the notion that rights and privileges should be granted only to the wealthy and educated. "It is necessary to separate the wheat from the chaff," states a petition to the government in 1856, and there was no ambiguity as to the application of the two categories.[47] With time, however, some Jews, particularly Yuzel and Horace Günzburg, extended their concern to the entire Russian Jewish community.

The Günzburgs were probably the most committed Jews within the group. The head of the family, Yuzel, remained an orthodox Jew and his son Horace received a good Jewish education. In the 1860s and 1870s the Günzburgs practiced the traditional Jewish occupation of *shtadlanut*, intervention by rich and powerful Jews in behalf of the Jewish community, for the purpose of extending the rights of the Jewish masses. They fought the slanderous attacks on the Talmud and Judaism which appeared with increasing frequency and strength in the 1870s, as well as the Kutaisi Blood Libel at the end of the reign of Alexander II (see Chapter II). But their most determined efforts were devoted to insuring that the new military conscription law promulgated in 1874 did not exclude Jews nor treat them differently from the rest of the population. Horace Günzburg was a typical representative of this small group, and of the Russified Jews in general, in his belief that Jewish usefulness and willingness to share the burdens of Russian society were the keys to the emancipation of Russian Jewry. Their efforts were successful; Jews were included in the general conscription scheme. Their hopes for eventual emancipation, however, remained unfulfilled, although they were optimistic down to the end of Alexander's reign.

Not all of the wealthy Jews were as committed to Jewish interests as were the Günzburgs. Samuel Poliakov does not seem to have concerned himself very much with Jewish affairs, although, in 1880, with the same idea that Jewish usefulness was a desirable commodity, he took the lead in the formation of ORT, *Obshchestvo Rasprostraneniia Truda sredi Yevreiev* (Society for the Spread of Manual Work Among Jews), an organization, as its name indicates, dedicated to providing Jews with training in manual trades and agricultural work. What united virtually all of the wealthy Jews in St. Petersburg and elsewhere, including those whose relationship to the Jewish community was most tenuous, was the belief that the enlightenment and Russification of the Jewish masses was the surest guarantee of their economic and spiritual regeneration and their political emancipation.

To achieve this regeneration of the Jewish masses, the St. Petersburg plutocracy created the one institution which for contemporaries became synonomous with it and with the Russification impulse of the 1860s and 1870s, the Society for the Diffusion of Enlightenment Among the Jews. It testifies to how small this group of affluent and educated Jews in St. Petersburg really was, that the executive committee of the society in its first decade included, in addition to its Jewish founders, two converts to Christianity, Professor Daniel Khvolson and Dr. I. Berthenson, the court physician.

The aim of the society was stated unambiguously and in a tone reflecting the spirit of the times by one of its founders, Leon Rosenthal:

We constantly hear men in high positions, with whom we come in contact, complain about the separatism and fanaticism of the Jews and about their aloofness from everything Russian, and we have received assurances on all hands that, with the removal of these peculiarities, the condition of our brethren in Russia will be improved, and we shall become full-fledged citizens of this country. Actuated by this motive, we have organized a league of educated men for the purpose of eradicating our above mentioned shortcomings by disseminating among the Jews the knowledge of the Russian language and other useful subjects.[48]

In the period 1867–1881 the society subsidized dozens of Jewish students in Russian institutions of higher learning, and provided grants to Jewish writers whose books, it was thought, would bring enlightenment to large numbers of Jews.

The efforts of the society did not yield anywhere near the rewards that its founders had anticipated. On the contrary, this institution, designed to integrate the Jews into Russian society, a goal of the Russian government in the 1860s, was a casualty of the anti-Semitism of the 1870s, which viewed with suspicion any independent activity exhibited by Jews. Ironically, the society found itself being accused of fomenting Jewish separatism. What was even more significant was that the society was losing the very reasons for its existence and was turning out to be a redundant institution. Increasingly, young Jews were moving into the gymnasiums and universities without the assistance of the society.

Perhaps the saddest chapter of the society's history is to be found in the experience of its Odessa branch, also founded in 1867. Odessa Jewry, a bastion of the Jewish Russification tendency, could be expected to support the efforts of the society and to drive it even further than its St. Petersburg founders had intended. That this was the case soon became evident when the Odessa chapter adopted as its slogan, "The enlightenment of the Jews through the Russian language and in the Russian spirit." The Russification of Jewry was to be facilitated by translating the Bible and the Jewish prayerbook into the Russian language, "which must become the national tongue of the Jews." This was just the opposite of the program of the St. Petersburg branch, which subsidized the translation of books in science and history into Hebrew so as to reach the unsecular and unrussified but educated Jews.

Unfortunately, the fierce assimilationist drive of the Odessa branch received a brutal check from the Odessa pogrom of 1871. The leaders of the local branch, using language that would be employed much more frequently a decade later, could not help "losing heart and becoming rather doubtful as to whether the goal pursued by them is in reality a good one, seeing that all the endeavors of our brethren to draw nearer to the Russians are of no avail so long as the Russian masses remain in their present unenlightened condition and harbor hostile sentiments towards the Jews."[49]

CONCLUSION

It would be wrong, however, to end this chapter on the despondent note sounded by the Odessa society, for it reflects the mood neither of the Jewish plutocracy nor of the new secularized and educated Jews, nor even of the unassimilated and uneducated Jewish masses in the 1870s. For the affluent and educated, the predominant feeling was one of optimism. They sensed that profound changes had taken place, and that more were coming. Neither the Odessa pogrom of 1871 nor the growing anti-Semitism of the last part of the reign seemed to shake their faith in Alexander or the future. Believing in *sblizhenie* or *slianie* and adamantly opposed to emigration, the privileged layers of Russian Jewry believed that if emancipation was not imminent, nonetheless it would come. The Russian Jews at large, on the other hand, bearing the burden of the economic and social changes taking place in the 1860s and 1870s, received few of the benefits of the Era of the Great Reforms. But with the exception of about twenty thousand of them, there was no massive flight from the cruel Russian reality. They remained in their centuries-long state of passivity, biding their time, waiting to see what the future would bring. They would not have long to wait.

II

"The Southern Storms"

THE POGROMS ERUPT AND THE GENERAL ASSAULT UPON RUSSIAN JEWRY BEGINS

On April 15, 1881, the first of a series of violent anti-Jewish disorders in the Russian Empire broke out in the Ukrainian town of Elizavetgrad (now Kirovograd). The violence, which spread quickly across the Ukraine, ended only in 1884, and then erupted again after the turn of the century. The anti-Jewish movement reached its peak in 1881–1882. Within two years pogroms struck over two hundred communities in the Russian Empire, as far west as Warsaw. Hundreds of Jews were killed, wounded, mutilated, and raped.[1] Thousands were made homeless, and damage to property ran into millions of rubles. Virtually all students of Jewish history agree that these excesses set in motion a sequence of events that altered the course of modern Jewish history.

An eyewitness to the violence in Kiev in April 1881 provided readers of the Russian Jewish press with a vivid description of a pogrom.

At twelve o'clock at noon, the air echoed with wild shouts, whistling, jeering, hooting, and laughing. An enormous crowd of young boys, artisans and laborers was marching. The entire street was jammed with the barefoot brigade. The destruction of Jewish houses began. Windowpanes and doors began to fly about, and shortly thereafter the mob, having gained access to the houses and stores, began to throw upon the streets absolutely everything that fell into their hands. Clouds of feathers began to whirl in the air. The sound of broken windowpanes and frames, the crying, shouting, and despair on the one hand, and the terrible yelling and jeering on the other, completed the picture.... Shortly afterwards the mob threw itself upon the Jewish synagogue, which, despite its strong bars, locks and shutters, was wrecked in a moment. One should have seen the fury with which the riff-raff fell upon the [Torah] scrolls, of which there were many in the synagogue. The scrolls were torn to shreds, trampled in the dirt, and destroyed with incredible passion. The streets were soon crammed with the trophies of destruction. Everywhere fragments of dishes, furniture, household utensils, and other articles lay scattered about.[2]

What is left out of this account, horrible as it is, are the sordid details concerning physical assaults on individuals, particularly the rapes of women and girls, some of them ten and eleven years old, and the murder of children, including infants who were often tossed out of windows to be crushed to death on the ground. The perpetrators of attacks on women were not loath to rape mothers and daughters in sight of each other.[3] In addition to the physical violence there also occurred a wave of fires which swept primarily over southern Russia but also beyond into Russian Poland and Lithuania.

There was panic everywhere in Jewish communities in the Pale of Settlement, in Russian Poland, and Lithuania, and in those relatively small Jewish communities in the Russian interior. By reading such Russian Jewish weeklies as *Russkii Evrei* (The Russian Jew), *Razsvet* (Dawn) and *Nedel'naia khronika Voskhoda* (Weekly Chronicle of Sunrise) for the period April 1881 to the autumn of 1882, it is possible to glimpse the tension and trauma of Russian Jews. The pogroms in the cities, towns, and villages were only the most dramatic manifestations of the physical violence directed against the Jews. Every week the Russian Jewish press reported individual cases of murdered Jewish families, Jews beaten, and Jewish women raped.

In those areas such as Lithuania and Russian Poland where pogroms did not occur, Jews often received anonymous letters threatening pogroms.[4] "Living on the top of a volcano" was the way one representative of a Jewish community expressed it.[5] Everywhere there were rumors of impending pogroms, and local Christians, sensing the disquiet of the Jewish population, demanded money and goods, and spoke openly before Jews about dividing Jewish property after the coming disorders.[6] Soldiers sent to prevent violence often treated Jewish entrepreneurs with contempt, taking whatever they wanted without payment.[7]

In addition to pogroms, individual acts of physical violence, rough personal treatment and frightening rumors, various groups of Jews were subjected to more subtle harassment. In the schools, Jewish children were frequently beaten, or, in the case of gymnasium and university students, made the objects of verbal assaults by anti-Semitic teachers.[8] There were attempts to segregate Jewish students in class, and even Jewish converts to Christianity suffered.[9] In one Odessa gymnasium, poorer Jewish students were denied financial assistance and were forced to leave.[10]

Next to physical assault, the most vicious form of attack on the Jews was the "cleansing" (*ochistka*) of Russian society by removing Jews from certain geographic and occupational areas. Local authorities took their lead from officials in St. Petersburg, who, as will become evident in Chapter III, were convinced that Jews constituted a pernicious and destructive element in Russian society. Laws that had not been enforced for years or had been interpreted benignly were now utilized to purge Russia of nefarious Jewish influence.[11]

The government, for example, dusted off old laws restricting Jews from owning or administering pharmacies outside of the Pale of Settlement and promptly closed the fairly large number of them that had appeared in St. Petersburg in the lenient sixties and seventies.[12] Jewish policemen were dismissed in Odessa and in the same city officials of the military-medical office of the War Department prohibited Jewish physicians from examining Jewish recruits on the grounds that people would say that the Jewish physicians were inclined to grant exemptions to the recruits.[13] It was also feared that the Jewish recruits were more likely to attempt deceptions since they believed that Jewish physicians would be sympathetic to their plight. In Kiev, Jewish railroad workers were dismissed.[14]

The cleansing process included the deportation of thousands of Jews from cities and towns beyond the Pale and on some occasions from villages within. In Kiev, Moscow, and St. Petersburg many Jews, including the sick and the elderly, were expelled after police checks discovered they did not fit into the categories of "permitted Jews."[15] Those who were expelled were forced to sell their property very cheaply. One newspaper reported that in St. Petersburg Jewish females at the university were obtaining the yellow card granting certification as a prostitute, a step that would allow them to remain in the city.[16]

The sad plight of these Jews is exemplified by the case of a Jewish soldier, a veteran of the Russo-Turkish war of the early 1870s and a recipient of the Cross of St. George for heroism. He arrived in Moscow to seek work and was expelled after three days. He told a newspaper in the city that he was treated "as if I am a criminal. If belonging to the Jewish people is a crime, then doesn't the blood shed for the fatherland remove from us our criminality? Do I, a bearer of the Georgian Cross . . . have only one exit, to seek my fortune in America?"[17]

What was happening in the large cities occurred in towns and villages as well. The correspondents of the Russian Jewish press reported that local inhabitants often petitioned officials to expel the Jews and in some cases, as even in the provinces of Podolsk and Ekaterinoslav, which were within the Pale, the officials complied.[18] Villagers, according to one writer, used an old law permitting them to call for the elimination of socially disruptive elements.[19] The town *duma* of Orel, outside the Pale, asked for the expulsion of Jews, and hundreds of families left the city.[20] A petition to expel Jews also circulated in Smolensk.[21]

In all areas of Jewish settlement, including those far removed from the pogroms, the economic impact of the disorders was devastating, and not only upon Jews, as will be seen in Chapter III. The fires that raged all over the Pale of Settlement seemed to hit particularly hard at the Jewish sections of the affected cities and towns, perhaps as a consequence of arson, as suspected by local Jews. Fires and pogroms wiped out Jewish businesses, reducing their owners to paupers and generating large numbers of unemployed Jewish workers.[22] From Lithuania a Jewish writer wrote of "workers without work."[23] Even where there were no pogroms, or where violence had come and gone, fear remained, and it acted to stifle commercial activity. There were occasions when Jewish businessmen were reluctant to pick up goods at railroad stations lest they be attacked on the way home. Others emptied their stores and placed the goods in storage at the stations hoping to avoid destruction.[24] Fear also served to diminish the flow of investment capital, Jewish and non-Jewish, Russian and foreign, into the Pale. The result was industrial and commercial stagnation in Minsk, Kovno, Odessa, Berdichev, Uman, and Riga.[25] For Jewish workers in enterprises employing both Gentiles and Jews, harsh economic conditions often led, as it did in Kiev, to tension between members of the two groups and the eventual dismissal of the Jewish workers.[26]

In addition to the violence to persons and property, fires, economic hardship and fear there was another problem that confronted Russian Jews—a dramatic rise in popular suspicion of them. They were blamed for everything. When a peasant disappeared, local Jews were suspected of murdering him.[27] Delay in the delivery of mail was said to be the fault of a Jewish mailman.[28] Jews were even accused of arson for the alleged purpose of collecting insurance money.[29] Jewish physicians in Odessa were prohibited from employing Christian girls as domestics on the grounds that the physicians "demoralized" them.[30] Rumors circulated that Jews not only led Christian domestics away from Christianity but turned them into prostitutes.[31] A speaker at a conference of secondary school teachers in Odessa castigated Jewish students for possessing little religious feeling, for corrupting the morals of Christian students, and for generally exerting a bad influence.[32] The correspondent of the journal *Vestnik Evropy* reported that significant price rises in sugar, attributable to the early frosts in the autumn of 1881 which killed the sugar beets, were blamed on the Jews who, it was said, were deliberately inflating prices so as to compensate themselves for their losses from the pogroms. The same was said about the substantial price rise for firewood.[33]

Taken as a whole, then, the sixteen-month period from April 1881 to September 1882 was a catastrophe for Russian Jewry. Perhaps the most devastating commentary on this general onslaught against the Jews was provided by Rabbi Yitschak Elhanan Spektor of Kovno in April

1882. Officiating at the funeral of a participant in the St. Petersburg conference of Jewish representatives, who had died shortly after making a speech describing the terrible situation of his coreligionists, Spektor reconciled the tragedy of this man's death with the words of the Talmud that those messengers of the community working for the common good will not be exposed to danger. Death in this case, he said, could not be considered a misfortune, since "for a Jew, in present circumstances, death is much better than life."[34]

PERPETRATORS

The pogroms were primarily a Ukrainian phenomenon, in the sense that most of the pogroms occurred in Ukrainian cities, towns, and villages. The usual pattern was of a pogrom beginning in a city or large town and spreading within a matter of days to nearby towns and villages. Riverboats and especially railroads not only spread news of the pogroms to the nearby localities but apparently helped carry the perpetrators of the pogroms across the countryside, where they instigated the local populations' anti-Jewish atrocities. The railroad workers, according to one recent commentator on the pogroms, were especially active in spreading the pogrom outward from its point of origin, both by bringing news of it and by directly participating in further outbreaks.[35]

Although most of the pogroms took place in the Ukraine, the Ukrainians were not the only participants in these excesses. Much evidence testifies to the fact that there was a large Great Russian component among the *pogromshchiki* (the people carrying out the pogroms). Extremely difficult economic conditions in northern and central Russia, as will be explained below, had created a vast legion of migratory workers, the *bosiaki* (the barefoot brigade), who roamed across the Ukraine seeking work. Contemporary observers claimed that they contributed substantially to the outbreak of the pogroms.[36] But the core group of *pogromshchiki* was the *meshchanstvo* or petty bourgeoisie, including shopkeepers, butchers, clerks, joiners, tanners, carpenters, and artisan elements of all types. Together with the local *bosiaki*, day laborers and peasants, they formed the crowds which attacked Jews and destroyed Jewish property.[37]

Contrary to popular belief, the peasantry was not mainly responsible for the pogroms, which were, in terms of origin and severity, primarily urban events. The pogroms began in the cities and only later spread to the villages. Peasant participation in pogroms occurring in nearby towns did take place; but it always came at the end of the pogrom, when the peasants, hearing that Jewish property and goods were being taken by urban mobs, entered the city to gather up booty. In the villages themselves, the pogroms did not take on the same violent overtones as they did in the urban areas. Some peasants even tried to prevent their neigh-

bors from beginning a pogrom, and protected Jews once it was underway. There were cases in which peasants returned property to Jews after
a pogrom was over.[38]

Contemporary observers, as well as later analysts of the pogroms,
discounted spontaneity as a factor in the events and were inclined to
seek a conspiracy behind the turbulence. One who lived through the
period, Simon Dubnow, the great historian of the Jewish people, wrote:
"From above a hidden hand pushed the masses of people to a great
crime. . . ."[39] As the author of a memorandum prepared for the government-appointed Pahlen Committee in 1883, he also concluded that the
pogroms followed a specific plan. "The anti-Jewish disorders were prepared by organized and disciplined persons of those classes of society
that stood higher than the common people."[40] The government or some
extra-governmental organization was considered the most likely source
of the conspiracy.

THE QUESTION OF CONSPIRACY

Some aspects of the pogroms seemed to point to conspiracy. First and
perhaps foremost was the fact that almost everywhere in the first months
of the pogroms police and military units did not act energetically to quell
the disturbances but very often failed to intervene at all. In several cases,
most notably in Kiev, soldiers actually joined the *pogromshchiki* in their
attacks on Jewish life and property. In Odessa, where Jews attempted
to resist, the police intervened and incarcerated the defenders. The Austrian consul in Kiev wrote: "From the behavior of the police we can
conclude that the destruction comes under the protection of the authorities."[41] The consul was convinced that this was evidence that the
pogroms were planned and organized from above.

Another reason for suspecting the existence of a "hidden hand" was
the ubiquitous rumor of a secret *ukaz* (decree) issued by the new Tsar
calling upon the population to "beat the Jews." Furthermore there was
the presence of elements from outside the Ukraine, particularly Great
Russians, at locations where pogroms broke out. In addition, relatively
well-dressed, educated or semi-educated young people had appeared
in various places just prior to the outbreak of pogroms, each instigating
trouble, and leaving just as he had come, on the railroad, even before
the pogroms were over.

There is no definitive answer to the conspiracy charge, but the evidence does not appear to justify it. On the contrary, it would seem that
the pogroms were spontaneous, and not planned. The movement of the
pogroms, for example, suggests spontaneity rather than planning. The
general pattern of the disorders was for pogroms to begin in a large city
or town, and in the next several days to spread to nearby areas. The

pogroms would then stop for several days or even weeks, only to erupt in, and spread from, another large town usually quite far removed from the area of earlier outbreaks. If the pogroms had been organized and planned, one would expect to see simultaneous pogroms in many distant places, or a greater element of continuity, the pogroms shifting from one place to an ever-increasing adjacent area, with no interruptions in timing or continuity. Neither simultaneous outbreaks nor much continuity were present in the years 1881–1882.[42]

The reluctance of the police and military to thwart the rioters, and even on some occasions their assisting the attacks, while confirmed by a veritable mountain of testimony, do not by themselves confirm the conspiracy argument, for there were several reasons for this behavior that have nothing to do with a conspiracy.[43] The idea that high-ranking government authorities, including the Tsar, ordered local police and military officials not to restrain the *pogromshchiki*, or even to join in their attacks, is not supported by evidence. There is, in fact, not a single document that has come to light which comes even close to revealing such government orders or, for that matter, any government involvement in the pogroms. The government was as shocked as everyone else; its immediate response was one of fear that outside forces—revolutionaries—were responsible for the outbreak of violence. Alexander III spoke for most high government officials when he told a Jewish delegation on May 11, 1881, "In the criminal disorders in the south of Russia, the Jews serve as a pretext.... This is the work of anarchists."[44]

If the government did not order the police and the military to stand aside, then why did they do so? The answer to this question can be found in the general inefficiency of the Russian military, and the personal antipathy toward the Jews felt by many high-ranking officials as well as large numbers of the rank and file. Russian military and police units were simply caught by surprise, and were incapable of swift reaction. Accustomed to dealing with rural disturbances, they were unsure as to how to proceed against urban pogroms. Some may even have been convinced that the pogroms were instigated by the government and therefore should not be stopped. Others, probably a greater number, so despised the Jews that they let their animosity overwhelm their sense of civic, professional, or official responsibility. Neither case presupposes the existence of a conspiracy.

The quintessential example of a high official allowing his personal feelings to guide his response to the pogroms is the case of General A. P. Drenteln, the governor-general of the southwestern region. According to General Novitskii, the Chief of the State Police, Drenteln hated the Jews with such passion that the very course of the Kiev pogrom disturbances was affected. Novitskii, who prior to his arrival in Kiev had met with government officials in St. Petersburg and had been told to get Drenteln to stop the pogroms, was unable at first to move Drenteln to action. At their first meeting Drenteln told Novitskii. "It is better to smash them [the Jews] thoroughly in order to halt their impudence and thirst for profit."[45] Novitskii also learned that at the very beginning of the pogrom in Kiev, Drenteln had, in an address to his subordinates, spoken so harshly against the Jews that one of them who later told the story to Novitskii ordered the troops in his detachment not to resort to violence against the *pogromshchiki*. It was only when Drenteln accompanied Novitskii to the Podol section of Kiev, the site of the pogrom, and was attacked by rioters that he became incensed and finally decided to crush the riots.

The belief that the Tsar had issued a special *ukaz* to "beat the Jews" was an important factor in the pogroms, particularly in the villages, but it, too, need not have been the work of a conspiratorial center.[46] It had long been a tradition among the peasants, going back to the time of the first False Dimitri in the early seventeenth century and probably before, to believe all sorts of rumors concerning the alleged wishes of the holy Tsar. Given traditional enmity toward the Jews and the belief that Jews had even been responsible for the assassination of Alexander II (fostered by the presence of a single Jewish member in the assassination team), it was no wonder that many peasants, including those now working in the urban areas, should believe in a Tsarist *ukaz* ordering them to attack the Jews.[47]

The presence of a large contingent of Great Russian *pogromshchiki*, the *bosiaki*, is to be explained by the difficult economic situation experienced by Russia in the last half of the 1870s. All over Russia there was a massive migration of peasants away from their land to the cities and towns in search of work. In the years 1870–1880 the government issued almost thirty-seven million passports as compared to not quite thirteen million for the preceding decade.[48] Since most of this peasant flow was to the south where, in fact, conditions were not much better, the presence of Great Russians among the *pogromshchiki* was only natural and was not a consequence of manipulation by higher authorities in St. Petersburg and Moscow.

The charge that is more difficult to refute, although it is equally difficult to confirm, is that many of the pogroms were preceded by the appearance of well-dressed and relatively well-educated young men who, according to the proponents of this argument, were sent from Moscow and St. Peterburg by unknown individuals, and who stirred up the indigenous population against the Jews.[49] It is possible that these people, if they existed at all (for many accounts of the pogroms do not mention them), were students of gymnasiums and universities caught up in the wave of anti-Jewish sentiment that swept over the country. In Odessa, for example, harsh anti-Jewish sentiments were espoused by university and gymnasium students, as well as by the lower classes that made up the rioting mobs. It is possible that students and young men from the local urban middle class provided the leadership that some authors talk about. They could have done so, of course, without being prompted to act by government officials or anyone else. Nonetheless, mention of such "guests from the capital" and the difficulty of tracking them down leaves the question of conspiracy still open.

In the absence of any evidence indicating government complicity in the pogroms, some analysts have sought to find the "hidden hand" in private or quasi-official organizations. The one that has attracted most attention is the Sviashchennaia Druzhina, the Holy League, which was formally established on March 12, 1881. The documents reveal an organization numbering 729 members, nearly all of whom came from the most privileged strata of Russian society, and 14,672 volunteer assistants whose social origin is not clear.[50] Its goals were both simple and complex. The murder of Alexander II, according to the Druzhina, revealed the impotence of the police in defending the Tsar against revolutionary terror. As a result, the Druzhina was to have as its most pressing task the protection of the Tsar's life on every occasion in which he had contact with the public. The Druzhina was to act as the Tsar's bodyguard.

The second and more complex task was to discredit and isolate the revolutionary movement. To achieve this goal, the Druzhina had a large number of agents in Russia and in foreign countries to infiltrate the plethora of small revolutionary groups and act as *agents provocateurs*. These agents were also supposed to emulate the assassination tactics of the revolutionaries; such prominent members of the revolutionary movement as Lev Hartman and Prince Kropotkin were to be the targets of the Druzhina. In a more subtle move, the Druzhina helped establish "revolutionary" newspapers, such as *Vol'noe Slovo* (Free Word) in Zurich, which the organization hoped would engender ideological and personal conflicts within the revolutionary movement, and therefore weaken its effectiveness. All of these activities, it was believed, would serve to completely isolate the revolutionary movement, weaken it, and restore calm to Russian society.

Its goals, numerical strength, and publishing success notwithstanding, the Druzhina in practice was a woeful, often farcical, organization; a close look at its operations leads one to strongly doubt that it was the conspiratorial center stimulating and guiding the pogroms. V. Smelskii, a member of the Druzhina who many years later wrote the most detailed account of its operations, chronicles a tale of inefficiency, cupidity, and corruption. According to Smelskii, those hordes of agents in Russia and Western Europe achieved as their only accomplishment the squandering of large sums of money. The most strenuous activities performed by these agents were the invention of incredible yarns, the procurement of prostitutes, and the creation of vitriolic quarrels among themselves. Smelskii claims the organization was poorly run, its inefficiency and corruption an open secret in St. Petersburg, where it enjoyed almost universal contempt from government and police officials. When the reactionary and anti-Semitic *Novoe Vremia* (New Times) referred to the Druzhina as "political buffoonery" the Tsar ordered the group's dissolution.[51]

Interestingly, the documents concerning the Druzhina make no mention of the Jews in general or the pogroms in particular. The only time the Jews are mentioned is in connection with membership. The by-laws of the organization stipulated that Jews and representatives from other national groups were not allowed to become members because their interests diverged from those of the primary nationality of the land, the Great Russians.

The picture that emerges, therefore, is that of a poorly led organization whose representatives abroad were paragons of incompetence. The documentary evidence and the memoir literature provide no support for the assertion that the Druzhina played any role, much less a commanding one, in the outbreak of the pogroms.

Yet, there is some evidence that the *druzhiniki* (the members of the Druzhina), if not the organizational leadership in St. Petersburg, did play a role. A number of writers, including the contemptuous Smelskii, make the point that the *druzhiniki* and their sympathizers were well represented in the railroad system as heads of stations and as conductors. Their chief role was to secure the railroad lines from the revolutionaries and to provide a bodyguard for the Tsar when he traveled by train. It is not inconceivable that these railroad *druzhiniki* played a role in consciously spreading news of the pogroms and in facilitating the dispersement of the *pogromshchiki* to far-flung points. They may also have been those individuals who, some accounts say, appeared just prior to the pogroms and left immediately thereafter. This task could also have been performed by younger members of the Druzhina who attended universities and were recruited into the organization for the purpose of maintaining surveillance over the student body. In either case, whether by railroad men or by students, such actions, if they actually did take place, do not necessarily imply a guiding hand. Entrenched agents could have responded to spontaneous outbreaks by joining in without any orders from an ineffective leadership many miles away. On balance, then, the record would indicate that the Druzhina was not the "hidden hand." But the question of individual participation by locally based members and fellow-travelers must still be left open.

THE ANTI-SEMITIC BACKGROUND

Even if it could be proven that there was a conspiratorial center responsible for instigating and guiding the pogroms, such an organization can be regarded only as an immediate cause of the pogroms. A massive movement involving thousands upon thousands of ordinary Russians, Ukrainians and, to a lesser extent, Poles, must have had some deeper underlying causes without which even the most effective conspiracy would have been powerless. The first of such factors, particularly in the 1870s, was the significant growth in government and private circles of vicious anti-Jewish sentiments. This may have penetrated into broader circles of society. There it could be ignited by especially dramatic events such as the assassination of Tsar Alexander II. It is significant that a vitriolic press campaign between March 2, 1881, the day after the assassination, and April 15 of the same year, the date of the first pogrom, fanned popular hatred against the Jews. Furthermore, economic changes taking place in Russian society had a catastrophic impact upon large numbers of Russians and Ukrainians and made them look with envy and anger upon that one particular group of people with whom they were inextricably bound up in peculiar economic relationships. All of these factors must finally be set against the background of the vulnerable legal position that had been occupied by Russian Jews for over a century.

The various manifestations of anti-Jewish sentiment in the reign of Alexander II are easier to treat than are the causes. But beginning in the early 1860s, almost immediately after the legislation that ameliorated the severe condition of Jewish life under Nicholas I, a reaction set in against the Jews which continued to the end of the reign. The Polish rebellion of 1863 seemed to contribute to this, since it generated considerable chauvinism among the Great Russians, along with a corresponding animosity toward all of the national minorities. The rapid strides made by small numbers of such wealthy Russian Jews as the Günzburgs, Poliakovs, and Zaks, also contributed toward anti-Jewish sentiment by increasing the visibility of Jews and by making them seem both ubiquitous and omnipotent. But by the end of the reign of Alexander II it was the growing presence of Jews in the revolutionary movement that spurred on anti-Semitism.

Any discussion of the factors responsible for the rise of anti-Jewish feelings among other Russians in the 1860s and 1870s must pay heed not only to more general factors but also to the role of specific personalities. No one individual did more than Iakov Brafman, a Jewish convert to Russian Orthodoxy, to envenom popular attitudes against the Jews. Brafman was a son of extremely poor parents whose poverty caused the family and later Brafman himself great difficulty with the Jewish community leaders. One Jewish biographer of Brafman claims that his troubles with Jewish community officials began when they, in their customary fashion, chose him and other poor boys as recruits for the army.[52] A worse fate for a Jewish child in nineteenth-century Tsarist Russia could not be imagined; and Brafman fled for his life, sinking in the process into even greater poverty than before.

Whether this led Brafman down the path he was to take is not known for sure, but he eventually became an apostate and very quickly came to the attention of the authorities, who conferred upon him ever more important positions of government employment. His greatest success came in 1869 with the publication of the book *Kniga Kagala* (The Book of the Kahal)—*kahal* being the term, before Brafman changed its meaning, for the executive agency of the local Jewish community, the *evreiskoe obshchestvo*.[53] The *kahal* had control over taxation, internal policing, and the administration of justice for the Jews, but was abolished in 1844 by order of the government. In point of fact, however, the *kahal* persisted down to the end of the nineteenth century.[54] Brafman's book, which incorporated material published by him in 1866 in a series of newspaper articles, established him not only as the leading expert in Russia on Jews but as one of Europe's leading authorities as well.

According to Brafman the Jews do not recognize the law of the land. They constitute a Talmudic Republic, a state within a state. All Jewish organizations throughout the world, even the smallest and most provincial, are part of this Talmudic Republic which Brafman called the Kahal. It was an international secret Jewish organization operating on the basis of the Talmud, with representatives in every land, and that had as its ultimate goal the subjugation of the Christian world to Jewish hegemony and exploitation. No amount of refutation by Jewish and non-Jewish scholars, who showed that Brafman had falsified and misinterpreted Talmudic and other Jewish writings, could serve as an effective counterweight to Brafman's work. *Kniga Kagala* was serialized in newspapers and became mandatory reading for government officials everywhere in the empire. A second edition was published at government expense in 1878 and was soon translated into French, Polish, German, and English. It is not out of the realm of the possible that subsequent publications that purported to be the writings of Jewish cabals, such as the *Protocols of the Elders of Zion*, drew their inspiration from Brafman's work.

Brafman wrote his book without possessing any real knowledge of traditional Jewish sources. He knew little Hebrew and was forced to hire unsuspecting students at the Vilna Rabbinical Seminary to assist him in his research. Perhaps the most revealing testimony to Brafman's lack of erudition is related by the prominent Jewish scholar, Abraham Harkavy, who worked for the State Library in St. Petersburg. Harkavy was once visited by Brafman, who asked him if he could get for Brafman the book entitled *Ibid* or *Ibidem*. Brafman told Harkavy that this must be a very important book because it is cited everywhere. Brafman even complied with Harkavy's request that he write out a book order for *Ibid*.[55]

Erudite or not, Brafman's work contributed to the growing hostility toward Jews, which surfaced in both private and public spheres. Newspapers began to publish articles emphasizing two themes: Jewish exploitation of the lower classes and the growing inundation of Russia by Jews. "The yid is coming" became a battle cry of anti-Semites in the late sixties and seventies. The Jew was a cunning spider whom it was necessary to crush in the name of general security.

In his attacks upon the Jews, Brafman was joined by other, more prominent men of letters. Ivan Aksakov, the famous Slavophile, who early in the reign of Alexander II had made some favorable comments about the Jews, quickly turned against them. "We should not talk about the emancipation of the Jews," he said, "but about the emancipation of the Russians from the Jews."[56] Between 1862 and 1880 Aksakov repeatedly castigated the Jews for exploiting ordinary Russians. He called upon them to renounce their faith, accept Christianity, and enter the world of European civilization.

The new publisher of *Novoe Vremia*, A. S. Suvorin, turned the once prominent liberal newspaper into a fountain of anti-Jewish propaganda. In the middle of the 1870s he wrote in *Novoe Vremia* from Odessa, "a very beautiful city ... but yids, yids, yids."[57] In 1880 Suvorin actually wrote an article for *Novoe Vremia*, entitled "The Yid is Coming" in which he indicted the Jews for leading the revolutionary movement and for exercising a pernicious influence on Russia by their participation in the twin evils of capitalism and socialism. Jewish participation in the gymnasiums and universities was so great that Suvorin feared Jewish domination of the liberal professions and through them control of Russia itself.[58]

The great Dostoyevsky, too, was caught up in the new spirit of anti-Semitism. He hammered at the idea that the Jews were devouring Russia, sucking the peasants dry. Not only in Russia but in all of Europe and the United States, according to Dostoyevsky, the Jews were exercising nefarious influence. The Jews have no respect for Gentiles and humiliate them at every opportunity. They want to exterminate or enslave the non-Jewish populations of the world. Their banks will inherit the property of a world plunged by the Jews into anarchy. Dostoyevsky feared that Jewish triumph on a global scale was totally assured.[59]

The response of Jewish and non-Jewish writers defending Jews against this onslaught was of no avail. Orshanskii and others wrote penetrating analyses of life in the Pale of Settlement which revealed that non-Jews living in the Pale were better off economically than those living outside of it, but this did not alter the perception of Jewish exploitation. I. Bliuch's massive study, *Sravnenie materialnago i nravstvennago blagosostoianiia guberni zapadnykh, veliko rossiskikh i privislianskikh* (A Comparative Study of the Material and Moral Status of the Western Great Russian and Bi-Vistula Provinces) written in the 1880s but dealing with the preceding period, confirms the view that peasants living in areas inhabited by Jews were much better off in many ways than peasants living in areas where there were no Jews. Yet it was not reality but the perception of reality that was important. The periodical *Syn Otechevsta* (Son of the Fatherland) spoke for many when it referred to Jews as that "mass of usurers and hucksters of dubious honesty, who will enrich themselves by exploiting the gullible Russians."[60]

After its initial spurt of beneficial legislation in the late fifties and early sixties, government hostility toward the Jews clearly manifested itself in 1870 with the promulgation of the decree on the municipal *dumas*. In contrast to the rural self-government and judicial reform laws, both promulgated in 1864, which included no restrictions on the Jews, the Municipal Duma Law decreed that only a third of the representatives to the *duma*, the self-governing council for each city, could be non-Christians and that no Jew was eligible to be mayor. Since Jews were disproportionately present in the cities and towns of the Pale, these restrictions bore down heavily upon them.

In the Committee for the Amelioration of the Condition of the Jews, established by the Ministry of the Interior in 1871, the anti-Jewish spirit was evident in the comments and reports of its members. For example, one member, V. Grigoriev, in discussing whether or not to allow Jews to live and work beyond the Pale said that the question was not how the Jews would fare but rather what impact Jewish commercial activity would have on the Russian people. His conclusion was that it would be dangerous to let the Jews reside outside of the Pale because "the plague which has thus far been restricted to the western provinces will then spread over the whole empire."[61] Grigoriev's attitudes were shared by others on the committee who on occasion went even further. Following Brafman's lead, there were a number of harsh attacks by the committee on the pernicious influence of the Talmud.

Brafman's book seems to have influenced another commentator on Jewish affairs. In 1872 the governor-general of Kiev, Prince A. M. Dondukov-Korsakov, submitted a report to the Tsar, in which he related what was by now becoming the customary account of Jewish economic domination and exploitation. The Brafman component appears in the governor-general's statement that "the cause of every last Jew is also the cause of the world-wide Jewish kahal . . . that powerful yet elusive association."[62]

Anti-Jewish sentiment received a tremendous boost from the Russo-Turkish war of 1873–1874. Like the Polish rebellion of 1863, the outbreak of war, this time accompanied by intense pan-Slavism, heightened Russian xenophobia and hostility toward the minorities living within the empire. The war and the diplomatic negotiations that followed it generated a wave of accusations against Russian Jewry. The right-wing anti-

Jewish press featured stories on alleged Jewish corruption, embezzlement, and cowardice. Jews were accused of being responsible for beginning the war. The writer Vsevelod Krestovskii in his novel, *Tamara Ben-David*, maintained that Jews had wanted the war for the purpose of increasing business.[63]

The British involvement in the diplomatic activity that followed the Russo-Turkish War, in which the British prime minister Disraeli (Lord Beaconsfield) played the major role at the Congress of Berlin in paring down Russia's victory, brought discredit to the Jews of Russia. Disraeli's Jewish ancestry was trumpeted in the press in such a way as to place in doubt the loyalty of Russian Jewry to the empire. It was suggested that the Russian Jews had set Disraeli against Russia as an act of vengeance for their lack of civil rights in Russia. That hater of the Jews, Suvorin, linked Russian Jewry and Disraeli in a plot designed to fulfill Jewish national aspirations: "The mind of Beaconsfield is blurred by a tribal disposition for the Turks. The Jews have dreamt for two thousand years about the resurrection of a Jewish kingdom. Isn't this what inspires the Jews toward the resurrection of Turkey?"[64] The attacks on Jews were so fierce that one Jewish community, that of Berdichev, published a declaration in one of the Moscow newspapers that it had nothing in common with Beaconsfield and was loyal to Russia.[65]

The anti-Jewish mood that was exacerbated by the Russo-Turkish War continued unabated to the end of the decade and into the 1880s. In the midst of the frenetic diplomatic activity over the end of war, there appeared in 1876 a new book libelling the Jews, which had significant influence upon the Russian public. The book, *Ob upotreblenii evreiami khristianskoi krovi dlia religioznykh tseli* (Concerning the Use of Christian Blood by the Jews), raised the "old blood libel" accusation, the charge that Jews used Christian blood at the time of Passover for the baking of unleavened bread, the matzoh. The author of the book, Ippolit Liutostanskii, a defrocked Catholic priest who had converted to Russian Orthodoxy, was a better salesman than he was a scholar. He managed to present a copy of the book to the heir to the throne, the future Alexander III, and to receive from him a grateful acknowledgment. The book also seems to have found favor with high police officials who acquired large numbers of copies and disseminated them to police officials throughout the country. Liutostanskii followed his great success by stealing a page from Brafman. In 1879 he published another defamatory work entitled, *Talmud i Evrei* (The Talmud and the Jew), which further stirred up the by now hackneyed charges about the Talmud.[66]

Unfortunately, the pattern established with the Brafman episode was followed here as well. The libelous accounts caused a great stir and were read widely. The refutations by Jewish and non-Jewish commentators pointing out that Liutostanskii, like Brafman, had forged and misinterpreted quotations, did not undo the damage. Perhaps as a consequence of Liutostanskii's publications, a blood libel trial took place at the end of the 1870s in Kutaisi in the Caucasus. Ten local Jews were accused of the death of a girl who had disappeared just before Passover. Fortunately for the accused, defense attorneys were able successfully to challenge the evidence used to support the indictment.

In the few years just prior to the pogroms of 1881–1882 the anti-Jewish press hammered at a new theme, the relationship between Jews and the revolutionary movement. "Everyone knows," commented *Novoe Vremia*, "that these Jews, since time immemorial the representatives of the revolutionary spirit, now stand at the head of the nihilists."[67] The Jewish-revolutionary nexus prompted calls for a *numerus clausus* on Jewish candidates for admission into institutions of higher learning. In 1880 the attempted assassination of the government minister Loris-Melikov by a Jewish convert to Christianity, I. I. Mlodetskii, was followed by even more vituperative press claims of a Jewish connection with the revolutionaries. The Russian correspondent of *The Times* of London was prompted to inform his readers that the reactionary press was making effective and widespread use of Mlodetskii's Jewish origins.[68] Not only would the cry, "Beat the yids" be heard among lower-class Russians, but the more educated classes were bound to be influenced and would soon embrace the anti-Jewish spirit. *The Times'* correspondent's apprehension that "evil days" were returning was an accurate one.

It is, of course, difficult to prove that a cause and effect relationship existed between a growing anti-Jewish mood in some circles of Russian society and the pogroms of 1881–1882. Still, it is reasonable to assume that a decade or more of fervent agitation against one particular group must have had some influence on mass consciousness even in a country where literacy rates were very low. This increasingly hostile view of the Jews could easily spill over into acts of violence on certain occasions, such as the murder of a Tsar. Of equal if not greater probability is that this animosity against Jews was held by government officials both at the center and on the local level, and that the response of these individuals from the very beginning of the pogroms was conditioned by their previous exposure to anti-Jewish propaganda. To be precise, the behavior of government, military, and police officials, which was so strongly criticized by contemporary and later analysts of the events, and which had direct impact on the course of the pogrom disturbances, was very likely to have been affected by the almost hysterical anti-Semitism that preceded the pogroms.

ECONOMIC FACTORS

The anti-Jewish sentiment of the 1870s is only one cause of the pogroms. Another underlying reason can be found in the extremely difficult economic situation of millions of peasants and workers living in the Ukraine in the late 1870s and very early 1880s. For the peasantry throughout the empire the situation was grim; for the peasants of the Ukraine it was even more desperate.

Twenty years after their emancipation in 1861, the condition of the peasantry seemed worse than it had been before their liberation. The peasants received less land after emancipation than they had farmed in the pre–1861 period.

In the south, where the great majority of the pogroms took place, the situation was particularly bad; the emancipatory legislation pertaining to the fertile black soil region had served to benefit the nobility by minimizing peasant landholdings. In Ekaterinoslav *guberniia* (province), for example, in the period before 1861 the peasants had farmed 535,500 *desiatiny* (a *desiatina* equals 2.7 acres), while in the years 1877–1878 peasant plots totaled only 334,600 *desiatiny*.[69] In Poltova, Tavricheskii, Kharkov, Kherson, and Chernigov *gubernii* a similar diminution had occurred.[70] While peasants in several other southern *gubernii*, such as Volinskaia and Kiev, had fairly insignificant increases in total holdings over the same period, the position of the peasants in these areas most likely deteriorated as a consequence of factors that affected the empire as a whole. There had been a general increase in the peasant population, which led to even greater pressure on the land and on peasant households. By the 1870s even the "middle" peasants were struggling desperately to meet their financial obligations, which included a multitude of taxes along with the redemption payments made to the government as a condition of emancipation.

By the late 1870s the position of the peasants throughout the empire was so bad that it was estimated that almost half of the peasants had insufficient plots, meaning that they could not support their families on their allotted land.[71] One result was that in order to survive, the peasants, particularly in the south, began to rent ever more land from their former landlords or to hire themselves out as farm laborers to landlords or to the small group of affluent peasants. At the end of the 1870s peasants in the south had rented twelve million *desiatiny*, almost one-third of the entire land fund granted by the emancipation to ex-serfs in all of European Russia.[72] Unfortunately for the peasants of the south as well as of the rest of the empire, these expedients did not ameliorate their situation: Increases in wages and the price of wheat failed to keep pace with the even more dramatic increases in rental payments for land.

Another device utilized by peasants of the northern and central provinces of Russia was migration southwards to find employment either on farms or in cities. As already indicated, the government issued thirty-seven million passports in the period 1870–1880. Only a small number, however, were able to find permanent work. Of these, a fairly large number found work on the railroads in one capacity or another. The great majority wandered from place to place searching for any kind of work that they could find. They constituted that "barefoot brigade" that was to play such a significant role in the pogroms.

Working long hours under horrible conditions when they did work, the itinerant workers were in an extremely difficult position. Their situation was made worse by the very significant increases in the price of bread and other food commodities which occurred in the 1879–1881 period. In Chernigov *guberniia*, for example, a *pud* (36.11 pounds) of rye flour in 1881 cost one ruble and twenty-nine kopeiks, twice as much as it had cost in 1879.[73]

The result was that there existed in the cities, towns, and villages of the Ukraine an isolated and embittered mass of people who did not receive substantial assistance from anyone. It should come as no surprise that even before the pogroms this large mass of impoverished migrants and peasants had become a great burden especially on the urban areas of the south. There was a definite increase in crime in the period just before the pogroms; and some contemporary commentators believed that people committed crimes just to enjoy the shelter and food that prison offered.[74] Southern Russia was under siege.

The migrants and the peasants were not the only people in the south who had serious grievances. In the cities and towns indigenous manual laborers, artisans, and merchants also had to cope with difficult economic times. Russia was still struggling with the consequences of the pan-European depression of 1873. What is significant for an understanding of the causes of the pogroms is that this urban group, together with the peasants and the *bosiaki*, seem to have associated much of their misfortune with the Jews, a group of people highly visible by virtue of their manifold distinctiveness, with whom Great Russians and Ukrainians interacted in a number of ways, particularly in economic affairs. In the cities, for example, Jewish, Great Russian, and Ukrainian retailers, wholesalers, and artisans competed against each other in an environment that was generally poverty-stricken.

It is difficult to ascertain the mood of ordinary people on any issue, particularly in an age when nearly universal illiteracy was the rule. Nonetheless, in the case of southern Russia at the time of the pogroms it is possible to gain a partial glimpse of popular attitudes toward the Jews. The government, stunned by the pogroms, did send investigators to search out the causes of these events. The most thorough agent of the government in this regard was Prince P. I. Kutaisov, whose investigation involved conversations with hundreds of ordinary people in the villages, towns and cities, and whose report covers several hundred pages. Allowing for Kutaisov's great bias against the Jews, and the attempts of the ordinary people to give ex post facto justification for acts of violence against Jews, there is no reason to doubt that the anti-Jewish views reported by Kutaisov were felt in the period prior to the outbreak of the pogroms.

Kutaisov found an enormous number of complaints against the Jews. Peasants and urban dwellers claimed that Jews exploited them in a variety of ways. The chief form of exploitation was in the sale of liquor: Jews sold the peasants vodka taking their hard-earned money from them. Jews, it was said, speculated in grain and other products, and drove up their price. Jews acquired wealth by trickery: They were charged with selling poor quality goods and giving incorrect weight on various commodities. They stole horses, dealt in stolen goods, and did not fulfill military or tax obligations. Many charged that Jews were incapable of physical labor and lived off of the sweat of Christians. It was believed that Jews diluted vodka and adulterated tobacco that they sold. There were complaints against Jewish moneylending. And there was the broad charge, especially heard among business people, that the Jews took advantage of the ignorance and simplicity of ordinary Great Russians and Ukrainians. The Jews were always taking peasants to court and winning there, according to their detractors, because the peasants did not know the law. On the other hand, the Jews did not fulfill contracts to buy grain from the peasants.

ADDITIONAL FACTORS

Beside economic grievances, there were attacks on the social and even political behavior of Jews. Jews are dirty, Kutaisov heard. They cause epidemics, and they turn their Russian and Ukrainian female servants into prostitutes. Jews make their Christian servants lazy and unfit for work for Christian employers. The Jews in each community have their *kahal* to help them devise ways to bypass the law. The Talmud, Kutaisov was told, creates a mentality among Jews that makes them different from Christians. Jews have no sense of honor. The Jews isolate themselves from the rest of the population. Several people told Kutaisov, "They stand away from us and our social interests." They are concerned only with their own needs. Jewish women, Russian merchants complained, flaunted their clothing and jewelry, and made the Russian women envious, who in turn made life miserable for their husbands. Jewish wealth was especially intolerable, Kutaisov was told, because it did not coincide with the Jewish position in Russian society and because it was perceived by everyone as the fruit of vicious exploitation. It was claimed the Jews led young Great Russians and Ukrainians astray. To many the Jews were "a dark force" that exercised a pernicious influence in all spheres of Russian life.[75]

It is not easy for the historian to evaluate this testimony. To be sure,

Kutaisov's interviewing techniques and sampling defy any rules for mathematical or scientific precision. It is probable, however, that charges of Jewish cheating and exploitation were not without foundation. The competition faced by Jews was fierce not only from other Jews who gathered in such large numbers in cities and towns of the Pale as a result of being forbidden to leave, but also from Great Russians, Ukrainians, Armenians, Greeks, and Germans. Moreover, the frenetic commercial activity was conducted against a background of endemic poverty. The result was not only that some Jews, as well as other people, probably acted in bad faith at times but that as noted above, the economic situation of most Jewish entrepreneurs was marginal.

There were, of course, other factors that contributed to the hostility toward the Jews. The distinctive dress of the Jews, their language, their adherence to a seemingly mysterious and hostile religion could not have endeared them to an unlearned population caught up in its own religious enthusiasms. Their "strangeness" made them objects of suspicion, rumor, and contempt. The inferior legal position of the Jews, casting them into a near-pariah status, most certainly made them vulnerable to attack, since it made Jewish wealth appear anomalous and served as inspiration for the idea that attacks against them were not only justified but mandated by the authorities.

The only thing that one can say with certainty is that the fervor, repetitiveness, and ubiquity of the charges, whatever their source and whatever their veracity, do testify to widespread antipathy in the Ukraine toward Jews. This, coupled with the tragic situation of the migrants, turned southern Russia into a tinderbox waiting to explode.

The explosion was triggered on March 1, 1881, by the assassination of Tsar Alexander II in St. Petersburg, by Russian revolutionaries. One of the participants in the attack on the Tsar was the Jewish woman Gessia Gelfman; the anti-Semitic press capitalized on her ethnicity with such enthusiasm that it provided the final stimulus for the pogroms. On March 2, one day after the murder, the *Vilenskii Vestnik*, published in Vilna, designated the Jews as guilty of the Tsar's death: "This is their affair."[76] In St. Petersburg, *Novoe Vremia* took particular note of the fact that one of the assassins had an "Eastern demeanor and a crooked nose." On March 20, in the *Novorossiskii Telegraf*, published in the south in Odessa, an article reported a rumor that on Easter Sunday people would gather in Odessa and attack the Jews because of their responsibility for the assassination and for the terrible economic situation. The article was couched in language unfriendly to the Jews. The Kiev journal, *Kievlianin*, in a series of articles, the last on April 5, spoke not only of Jewish participation in the assassination but dwelled at length on the great economic harm caused by the Jews and on the "holy necessity" of simple people to struggle against them. In Elizavetgrad, where the pogroms began, the local newspaper after March 1 carried articles accusing the Jews of obnoxious economic behavior; on the eve of Passover it gave prominent space to rumors of ritual murder, the blood libel, calculated to enflame the local population.

Kutaisov concluded that after the first pogrom the journalistic onslaught against the Jews continued and was an important factor in the spread of the disturbances. The *Novorossiskii Telegraf*, according to Kutaisov, was particularly effective in fanning anti-Jewish sentiment, creating the illusion among the public that the authorities would not act to check the pogroms or punish the rioters.[77]

CONCLUSION

The assassination of the Tsar, the press orgy, and the proximity of both to Easter, the traditional time for violent attacks against the Jews, are the immediate causes of the pogroms. The underlying causes are to be found in Russian history and the socioeconomic conditions in Russia in the seventh and eighth decades of the nineteenth century. Impoverished masses of artisans, merchants, peasants, and workers, together with a vast number of migrants, were caught in a situation of rising prices, substantial unemployment, and intense competition. In the heated atmosphere of the post-assassination period they lashed out at a group whose economic behavior was held to be abhorrent and whose very existence was viewed with contempt. Religion, law, and a new secular anti-Semitism combined with economic factors to make the Jews visible, ostensibly contemptible and inferior, and, most significantly, vulnerable. The explosion when it came was spontaneous. The inaction of local civilian authorities, police officals and the military transformed limited violence into pogroms. There was no guidance from above; no "hidden hand" directed the perpetrators of violence. In an autocracy, where spontaneity from any source was viewed as destructive, a phenomenon like the pogroms was not only unexpected, it was also greatly feared. The Russian government would not find it easy to deal with this very significant disturbance of the peace.

III

Government and Society Respond to the Pogroms

The Russian government had been caught totally unawares by the pogroms. Surprised and frightened, the government sought an explanation
for the violence. Its first response, and that of privileged society in St.
Petersburg, was that the revolutionary movement was responsible: The
"nihilists" were turning the lower classes against the traditional enemy,
the Jews, but the ultimate goal must be the overthrow of the existing
order. The fact that just a short time before the Jews themselves had
been accused of being nihilists was quickly forgotten. Ignatiev, the Minister of the Interior, subscribed to this new viewpoint, as did the Grand
Duke Vladimir and a number of governor-generals. So did John W.
Foster, the United States Minister to Russia. The new Tsar, Alexander
III, was persuaded by Ignatiev that the revolutionaries were behind the
pogroms. In May of 1881, in the midst of the turbulence, he told a group
of Jewish representatives in St. Petersburg, "This is the work of the
anarchists."[1]

BLAMING THE JEWS

Yet within a short period of time, the government experienced a change
of heart. By late May and early June its position had tilted strongly
against the Jews. The Jews, the government now claimed, exploited the
peasants in all sorts of ways and, therefore, they were the ones who
must bear the responsibility for the violence. In the words of the Jewish
historian, Dubnov, "They beat you, . . . therefore, you are guilty."[2]

In retrospect, it seems only natural that the government would eventually blame the Jews. There was, after all, a tradition in government
circles of anti-Jewish sentiment, with its concomitant charge of Jewish
"exploitation."[3] Beyond this, however, a number of high-ranking personalities played an important role in the government's change of view.

There was, for example, the brilliant Procurator of the Holy Synod, the leader of the Russian Orthodox Church, Konstantine Pobedonostov. Pobedonostov had been the tutor of the future Alexander III since the middle of the 1860s and, in the words of his biographer, had acquired mastery over Alexander and was able until the end of Alexander's life to shape his views on public issues.[4] Pobedonostov was fervently opposed not only to the revolutionary movement but also to the most tepid forms of liberalism. In March and April of 1881, he waged a successful campaign to persuade the new Tsar to drop Loris-Melikov, Alexander II's Minister of the Interior and one of the most progressive members of the murdered Tsar's government, on the grounds that the constitutional reforms championed by Loris-Melikov would endanger autocratic rule. "Constitutions as they exist are weapons of all untruth and the source of all intrigue," Pobedonostov had declared.[5] He mounted a ferocious attack on the entire reform program of the preceding reign, going so far as to hold the reforms responsible for the upsurge in revolutionary activity which culminated in the March 1 assassination.

When it came to the Jews, Pobedonostov showed the same, if not more, abhorrence. He was convinced, he told Dostoyevsky in 1879, that the Jews "undermined everything.... They are at the root of the revolutionary socialist movement and of regicide; they own the periodical press; they have in their hands the financial markets; the people as a whole fall into financial slavery to them; they even control the principles of contemporary science and strive to place it outside of Christianity."[6] For Pobedonostov the Jews were a "great ulcer." In addition to all these faults they were responsible by virtue of their ownership of taverns for much of the immorality and crime among the peasants.

In 1881 Pobedonostov became convinced that the Jews were responsible for the pogroms. He was now closer to Alexander III than ever before, seeing him two or three times a week and writing him often. The result was that Alexander, too, began to speak of Jewish culpability. Of course, the new Tsar did not need much prodding to accept this interpretation of events. Alexander, not weighed down by much intellectual baggage, and a fervent disciple of Russian Orthodoxy, shared the view of the Jews held by conservative religious elements in Russia. In the 1870s Pobedonostov had introduced Alexander to both Aksakov and Dostoyevsky, and had prescribed for him the reading of their works, particularly the men's journalistic pieces. Since Aksakov and Dostoyevsky were not averse to venting their intense dislike of Jews in public, the heir to the throne was exposed to considerable anti-Jewish sentiment. Given the closeness of Alexander and Pobedonostov, the influence of distinguished authors hostile to the Jews, and his own penchant to revere those who seemed well informed and spoke with confidence and authority, it is understandable that the Tsar's reaction to the pogroms would move in a direction extremely unsympathetic to the Jews. There is no reason to doubt that the opinion expressed by Alexander in 1883, that the "zhidi" are repulsive to the Christians because they exploit them and that this is the real cause of the pogroms, was held by the Tsar as early as the spring and summer of 1881.[7]

Other influences contributing to the government's view that Jewish exploitation caused the pogroms were the presence of Ignatiev at the helm of the Ministry of the Interior and the already mentioned mission of Prince Kutaisov. Prince Meshcherskii, who knew Ignatiev well, maintains that like other landed gentry from the southwestern region of the empire, Ignatiev despised Jews.[8] In a memorandum dated March 12, 1881, Ignatiev wrote to the new Tsar about a powerful group of Poles and Jews who controlled a large segment of the Russian economy and acted, he claimed, in illegal, rapacious, and seditious fashion.[9] Ignatiev's close links to Aksakov and the Muscovite Pan-Slavs was bound to heighten this perception.

More than anything else, however, it was the mission of Kutaisov that influenced the government's attitude toward both the pogroms and the Jews. The mission itself was a consequence of the government's bewilderment and fear. A trusted and capable investigator was needed to ascertain the causes of the spring events and, above all, to find out whether or not the revolutionary movement was responsible. Biased, but nonetheless thorough, Kutaisov traveled through the strife-torn region in July, 1881, and within a short time completed a report totaling several hundred pages that soon came to the attention of Ignatiev and the Tsar. Kutaisov met and corresponded with bureaucrats and local people, most of whom were hostile toward the Jews. He became convinced very quickly that the belief prevalent in government circles in St. Petersburg that the pogroms were the work of revolutionaries was fallacious. He added, however, that the revolutionaries might successfully capitalize upon the disorders.[10] Most important, he became an advocate of the proposition that the Jews bore the guilt for the attacks upon them.[11] Repeatedly he heard testimony by non-Jews, detailed in the preceding chapter, on the malevolent economic practices of the Jews and their taking control of all trade and industry. For Kutaisov, who most likely shared his class' disinclination for commercial and industrial people, the repetition of accusatory statements was enough to persuade him that Jewish economic activity was exploitive, and was therefore instrumental in the outbreak of the pogroms.

On August 21, 1881, Ignatiev reported to the Tsar the findings of Kutaisov. He repeated the prince's belief that Jewish exploitation was the primary cause of the pogroms and that the revolutionaries might use them to weaken the government. He added his own view that the reforms of Alexander II which pertained to the Jews had allowed them to become increasingly harmful to the Christian inhabitants of Russia. As a way out of the crisis, he proposed to the Tsar that special commissions be established in each *guberniia* where there were large numbers of Jews, to discuss the question of how to restrain the Jews' pernicious activities.[12]

The Tsar immediately complied by issuing an imperial *ukaz* establishing the so-called *guberniia* commissions, to be composed of representatives of the local population, both urban and rural, and presided over by the governor of the *guberniia*. In his memorandum of August 25, 1881, to the governor-generals giving instructions on the formation of the *guberniia* commissions, Ignatiev revealed that the commissions were not to labor under the burden of impartiality. He included in the memorandum his own hostile views on the Jews and ordered the *guberniia* commissions to answer a number of questions, the two most important being: (1) Which economic activities of the Jews were especially injurious to the "native" population? and (2) What new legislation would be useful in restraining the harmful activities of the Jews?[13] In other words, the commissions were to assume that the Jews were guilty, that they constituted an evil and dangerous group, and that the task of the local commissions was limited to determining just how the Jews hurt the Christian population and what were the best means to deal with this evil group. The commissions were given two months to conclude their work, a short time, but Ignatiev wanted to act quickly so as to forestall further pogroms and revolutionary involvement.

In most of the *guberniia* commissons one or two Jews were allowed to participate, probably as a means of demonstrating the government's fairness. The internal workings of the commissions and the incredibly difficult position that their Jewish members found themselves in have been described by the prominent Jewish ophthalmologist, Dr. Max Mandelshtam, who was a member of the Kiev *guberniia* commission and who was one of the two Jews sitting among thirty-one non-Jewish members.[14] From the very beginning Mandelshtam and his companion were treated to declarations that reeked of ignorance and bigotry. Commission members, says Mandelshtam, were surprised to discover that there were poor Jews and that their number was far in excess of that of the Jewish rich. Other speakers spoke in a racist idiom, one complaining that the moral corruption of the Jews was in their blood and was passed on from generation to generation. Another commission member, in opposing the idea of allowing Jews out of the Pale and into the Russian interior, stated that this could not be permitted because not only were the Jews immoral but they proliferated like rabbits and would corrupt the whole empire.

Mandelshtam relates that he fought tenaciously in defense of the Jews. It was, he says, like going to Golgotha, but he derived his strength from the knowledge that he was defending those that had no defense, a people whom no one wished to protect and defend, and everyone wished to harm. He attacked the idea that the Jews exploited the local population and were immoral, and maintained that Jews do engage in physical labor. He denounced the existing restrictions on Jews, claiming that these were a medieval vestige shameful for a state claiming to be a member of the family of nations. Dogs, he said, could travel from the Pale into the interior, but not Jews.

In the Kiev commission the difficult Jewish position was exacerbated by the bias practiced by the secretary of the commission and by the governor-general. Both acted to minimize the contributions not only of the Jewish members but of anyone who spoke in defense of the Jews. Speeches favorable to the Jews were shortened in the minutes, or they were not even recorded. Mandelshtam explains that some speeches were distorted. There was even a proposal not to allow the Jewish members to see the previous minutes because they would conspire with the *kahal* for some unseemly purpose. Fortunately, this proposal was voted down by the commission. The governor-general, however, took a position unfavorable to the Jews. He did not participate in discussions but limited himself to summarizing the positions of various speakers for the minutes: According to Mandelshtam, he shortened the summaries when speakers were sympathetic to the Jews.

The Jewish members, in fact, found that they were not always alone and, on a number of occasions, received support from some of the non-Jewish members. The mayor of Berdichev, a city with a large Jewish population, spoke sympathetically of the Jews. He was accused by other members of the commission of being the recipient of Jewish bribes. A police offical from Kiev also spoke in support of some Jewish positions. Most of the members, however, for a variety of reasons, some of which had nothing to do with conviction, voted against the Jews. The bureaucratic representatives had to vote in this way and, Mandleshtam says, so did the delegates from the villages, who were subjected to enormous government pressure. When these were added to those imbued with deep Judeophobia, as it was called at the time, the result was a large majority that voted consistently for an increase in the number of restrictions placed on the Jews, and against amelioration of the Jews' position in Russia.

The workings of the Kiev *guberniia* commission, while typical in some respects, were unusual in others. What is remarkable is that on almost every *guberniia* commission there were non-Jews who argued for a general emancipation of the Jews, and a majority which supported one or more proposals to alleviate or eliminate discriminatory restrictions on Jews. There were, for example, commissions that voted to allow Jews into public schools without a quota, to distill and sell liquor, and to acquire land belonging to peasants and other landowners. About half of the commissions actually voted to allow a larger number of Jews to reside outside the Pale of Settlement. There existed, in short, at least some support for the Jews on these commissions; it is possible that this support might have grown had it received encouragement from the authorities in St. Petersburg.[15]

The *guberniia* commissions were only the first link in a chain designed by Ignatiev to reshape the government's policies vis-à-vis the Jews. On October 19, 1881, even before the commissions had finished their work, Ignatiev had received the Tsar's approval to establish a Central Committee for the Revision of the Jewish Question, which was placed under the jurisdiction of the Ministry of the Interior, with its Deputy Minister, D. V. Gotovtsev, as chairman. The committee was to base its recommendation on the work of the *guberniia* commissions, but it began its deliberations before the commissions had completed theirs. The committee reflected the anti-Jewish position not only of Ignatiev but of even more vitriolic anti-Semites. Brafman's influence is discernible in at least one of the committee's declarations, which spoke of an international Jewish organization, based in Western Europe, established to advance Jewish interests. The committee called for the elimination of the Society for the Diffusion of Enlightenment Among the Jews, since it considered the society a branch of this devious Jewish organization. As could be expected, since Gotovtsev was not only a subordinate but a friend of Ignatiev, and the majority of the committee was composed of bureaucrats, the committee followed the line on the pogroms set by the Minister of the Interior. It subscribed to the idea that the Jews exploited the population and that the Jewish reforms of Alexander II had only served to increase the vulnerability of the Christian population to this exploitation. The outbreak of pogroms in Russian Poland, where the Jews could reside anywhere, confirmed for the committee the wisdom of its belief that the Jews exerted a deleterious influence and that the attacks on them by the local population were a natural response.[16]

For the committee two things were imperative. First, it was necessary to rescind the reforms of Alexander II and return to the policies of Nicholas I, when the Jews enjoyed very little in the way of rights. Second, the government must act as far as possible to separate the Jews from the rest of the local population. The result, in early 1882, was a "Project" of the committee which proposed extremely harsh restrictions on Russian Jewry. In contrast to the *guberniia* commissions, a number of which actually envisioned a broadening of Jewish rights, the committee totally rejected the idea of emancipation, and sought to resolve the Jewish Question through repression.

The Project of the committee called for the following: a prohibition on all Jews' moving from the Pale to the interior of the empire; in the Pale Jews were not to be allowed to settle in the villages; those Jews already in the villages could be expelled by a majority of votes in the village assemblies; Jews were not to carry on any sort of liquor trade in the villages or retail sale of liquor in the towns; Jews were not to purchase or rent land in the rural areas; Jewish businesses were to be closed on Sundays and Christian holidays; and the percentage of Jews in public schools was to equal their percentage in the general population.

The proposals were extremely harsh and would have led to the dislocation of large numbers of Jews by throwing them on the mercy of the neighboring peasants and by restricting Jewish economic activity. But they were not tough enough for Ignatiev. He amended the Project to require complete expulsion of Jews from villages and rural areas of the Pale, regardless of the village assemblies and the nature of Jewish business activity. Ignatiev's proposals, if implemented, would have meant the removal of hundreds of thousands of Jews from their homes in the rural areas of the Pale of Settlement. For the committee, and even more for Ignatiev, there was no doubt as to who was guilty for bringing on the pogroms—the Jews were and they had to be dealt with accordingly.[17]

The harshness of the committee's proposals was matched by the government's callous behavior toward those who suffered as a result of the pogroms. In contrast to previous calamities when the government and the Tsar himself had granted donations to the suffering people, nothing of this sort was forthcoming for the victims of the pogroms. The government even refused to countenance Jewish charitable action in behalf of the victims. Wealthy Jews in St. Petersburg were prohibited from raising money in behalf of their coreligionists in the south. Perhaps most galling to the Jews was the fact that civil and military courts treated the perpetrators of the pogroms very leniently; in most cases that were tried in 1881 the sentences were light. Since the Minister of the Interior had announced during the summer that noxious Jewish economic behavior was the cause of the pogroms, why should representatives of the long suffering *narod*, the people, who had no other recourse than violent attacks on their Jewish exploiters, be severely punished? No wonder that civil and military prosecuters declared before the courts that the Jews were the real guilty ones and that the *pogromshchiki* should be treated mercifully.[18]

The question arises: Did the government's indifference and hostility toward the Jews encompass the idea of expulsion, the forced emigration of all or at least some Jews from Russia? There is contradictory evidence on this matter. On the one hand, there are statements by some officials, including one by Ignatiev in late 1881 that "the western frontier is open" and that Jews were free to leave.[19] On January 16, 1882, Ignatiev met with Dr. Isaac Orshanskii and, by alluding to his statement of the previous year, created the widespread impression that he continued to favor Jewish emigration, that the western frontier was still open.[20] Pobedonostov, in a famous statement, is alleged to have said that the Jewish problem in Russia would be solved in thirds: One-third of the Jews would emigrate, one-third would convert to Russian Orthodoxy, and one-third would die off.[21] There were also statements made in the *guberniia* commissions concerning the growing Jewish domination of Russian society and the inhuman ability of Jews to proliferate. Some commission members speculated that at least some emigration might be a solution to the Jewish problem.

But there is also evidence on the other side. In late January 1882, Ignatiev told Rabbi Drabkin that he would not encourage emigration and that while love for the fatherland could not be forced on anyone, the government would examine Jews very carefully before they were granted permission to leave.[22] He also was quoted in April 1882 by the Jewish plutocrat, S. Poliakov as saying that talk of emigration was encouragement to sedition.[23] Pobedonostov's statements have never been confirmed, and a perusal of the various *guberniia* commission reports reveals that the great majority of members, including those most hostile to the Jews, believed that the Jews, although harmful, could eventually be made into productive Russian citizens.[24] The decades-long belief in eventual assimilation and the positive things that would result from it that reached its zenith under Alexander II lingered on for some time after his death. After Ignatiev's dismissal in May 1882 and for some time thereafter, the issue, as far as the Ministry of the Interior was concerned, was easily resolved. The new minister, Dmitri Tolstoi, on June 25, 1882, published a report directed against the emigration of Jews and threatened reprisals against those who instigated it or assisted it.[25]

Some things are clear, however. One is that whatever the ambivalences in Russian governmental spheres in the capital, officials responsible for granting permits to Russian Jews wishing to emigrate acted speedily in issuing exit visas. Second, government policies, whatever their stated goal, were so harsh, as will be seen, as to drive Jews to emigrate. Finally, a number of Jewish leaders and many ordinary Jews became convinced that the government did indeed desire the emigration of the Jewish population and acted accordingly.

FOREIGN OUTRAGE

In the first months of 1882 the Jewish predicament appeared grim. A new wave of pogroms was expected. In the Balta pogrom of March 1882 the worst fears of Russian Jews were exceeded; this pogrom dwarfed the others in its savagery. The same inability or unwillingness of the police and the military to resist the *pogromshchiki* was evident. Murder and the destruction of Jewish property occurred on an unprecedented scale. Russian Jewry was also aware by this time of the hostile predisposition of Ignatiev and braced itself for the coming legislation, sure to be repressive.

Yet by the spring and summer of 1882 the situation would change for the better. The pogroms would diminish in strength and number and there would soon be a vigorous government response to violence against the Jews. The Project of Gotovtsev's committee, for which Ignatiev sought to gain the approval of the Committee of Ministers, would not be implemented. To be sure, the ensuing legislation would be harsh and would severely restrict Jewish activity in Russia but it was not as harsh as the Project, which, if promulgated, would have had catastrophic effects upon Russian Jewry.

By the late spring, therefore, the worst was over. There were a number of reasons for this, one of which had to do with the growing foreign opposition both to Ignatiev's policies and the pogroms themselves, a sentiment to which the Russian government was becoming increasingly sensitive. The opposition to the pogroms that was expressed by conservative Russian thinkers and journalists, including some ferocious anti-Semites, together with the concerns voiced by Russian business interests, also had a moderating impact on the policies of the government. Finally the Committee of Ministers itself, which still included some liberal carry-overs from the preceding reign, recoiled on moral and pragmatic grounds from the harsh prescriptions of Ignatiev, and increasingly worried over the consequences of continued violence.

News of the pogroms, particularly the horrible details, was not disseminated in Western Europe and the United States until months after the first pogrom in Elizavetgrad in mid-April 1881. The small number of foreign correspondents operating in Russia, as well as the Russian government's censorship significantly delayed making large numbers elsewhere aware of what was taking place. The government, in its desire to avoid embarrassment and criticism, either domestic or foreign, even put the lid on press accounts of the deliberations of the *guberniia* commissions. Yet the news, including the shocking and grisly, did eventually manage to reach other countries and crossed the ocean to America. When it finally came, the news unleashed a response on the part of Jews and Gentiles which in magnitude and vociferousness was unprecedented. The uproar over both the Mortara Affair (a Jewish boy's baptism, abduction, and conversion in Bologna) and the Damascus Blood Libel (the torture of Jews for the murder of a monk) does not compare to that which now developed in Europe, England, and the United States. It heightened Jewish consciousness in the West and served to coalesce Ashkenazic Jews in the face of assimilation and dispersion.

Emigrants huddling in temporary havens in Central Europe related what they had seen and experienced, and this information was occasionally picked up by some of Europe's leading newspapers as well as by a number of Jewish organs. In October of 1881 a group of Russian Jews arrived in Liverpool on their way to America, and they informed British Jewry of the situation in Russia.[26] The Russian press, including government-run papers such as the *Pravitelstvennyi Vestnik* (the Government Messenger) poked a few holes in the censorship screen by printing several articles on the pogroms and on the trials of the *pogromshchiki*.[27]

The main source of information on the pogroms, however, was a small but highly effective group of Orthodox Jews who operated out of Kovno and Vilna in Russian Lithuania. These Lithuanian Jews formed an organization, *Hayay im pipiyot* (Inspire the Lips)—the words taken from a prayer on the Jewish New Year—which gathered information on the pogroms and transmitted it to prominent Jewish leaders in other countries in order to stimulate international protest.[28] By the autumn of 1881, letters from Kovno arrived in London and were soon handed over to Baron Nathaniel Rothschild, a leader of British Jewry. There was no ambiguity in this correspondence. Rothschild was told about the pogroms and the harsh impending legislation, and he was urged to organize a protest movement. The author of the letters and leader of the organization, the already mentioned Rabbi Yitschak Elhanan Spektor, was an orthodox Jew living in remote Lithuania, but he was not oblivious to the politics of protest. The rabbi urged Jewish leaders to make the protest movement a general one, not limited to the British Jewish community. It was a technique that would become a common feature of Jewish protest actions in England and elsewhere.

Rothschild acted immediately. He turned the letters over to *The Times* of London and the information was incorporated into two articles on January 11 and 13, 1882. To twentieth-century readers the articles and the responses evoked by them are not only interesting, they appear remarkable. First, the articles are highly accurate. Laboring under horrendous conditions and confronting obstacles that would have daunted more experienced reporters with greater means, the rabbis in Lithuania transmitted information which has been confirmed by subsequent studies. The mistakes are minor ones. Even more impressive is the tone of *The Times'* articles, a tribute both to their author, Joseph Jacobs, and the period during which they appeared. It was a time when Europeans and Americans were not yet jaded by the incessant horrors of the twentieth century. Journalists and their readers could still be shocked into righteous indignation by reports of murder and rape; and objectivity had not yet come to mean neutrality.

At the very beginning of the initial article there is an example of that style and tone that so electrified large numbers of the English, Jews and non-Jews alike. "Men ruthlessly murdered, tender married women the prey of a brutal lust that has also caused their death, and young girls violated in the sight of their relatives by soldiers who should have been the guardians of their honor, these have been the deeds with which the population of southern Russia has been stained since last April."[29] In subsequent pages the author provided a detailed list of the towns in which pogroms took place, the nature of the crimes perpetrated against the Jews, including some horrible descriptions of attacks against women and children, and the numbers of victims of these attacks.

In Elizavetgrad, the readers of *The Times* were told, a young girl, Pelikoff, was gang-raped by soldiers. In Kiev, the three-year old son of Mordichai Wienarsky was thrown out of a window by the *pogromshchiki* and torn to pieces. The house of the Preskoff family in Kitzkis was burned to the ground and the father and two children "were left to roast in it." According to Jacobs, the year 1881 saw over 160 towns and villages in which brutal attacks on Jews had taken place.

The articles do not spare the Russian government, both central and local authorities, as well as civilian and military personnel. Ignatiev's rescript establishing the *guberniia* commissions is printed in full and is referred to as a "refinement of cruelty," since it appeared in the midst of the pogrom wave and its talk of Jewish exploitation only exacerbated the hostility toward the Jews because it convinced the mobs that the government shared their prejudices. The *guberniia* commissions themselves were viewed as extremely tendentious institutions that were preparing legislation to return Russia to the Middle Ages. The greatest anger, however, was reserved for those officials, especially in the police and in the army, who violated their oath to maintain the tranquility and peace of society and collaborated with those who attacked the Jews.

The Times' articles not only reported the horrors of the preceding months, they analyzed the causes of the violence and issued a prescription for the future. The "barbarous" Russian laws which restricted the Jews and served to distinguish them from the rest of the population were held to be the primary cause of the pogroms. Talk of Jewish exploitation and usury was considered absurd, as the Jews were thought to be "thrifty and hard working." Then, in a statement exemplifying the ideals of nineteenth-century liberalism, the articles conclude with a solution to the crisis and a call for action. "It is the lesson taught by all experience that the only solution of the Jewish Question is the granting of full equality.... The Russian Jewish question may ... be summed up in the words: Are three and a half millions of human beings to perish because they are Jews?"[30]

The articles in *The Times* generated considerable discussion in British society and triggered a series of demonstrations throughout England and Wales, in Liverpool, Manchester, Cardiff, and Oxford. The largest and most important demonstration was held on February 1, 1882, at Mansion House in London under the chairmanship of the Lord Mayor. Even more remarkable than the fact that the demonstration was held in the first place, was that it attracted some of the most prominent personalities in the country, including Members of Parliament, scholars, and leading church officials. It was, in many ways, the prototype of meetings and demonstrations that would be convened repeatedly in behalf of Jewish causes over the next century. Speaker after speaker at Mansion House called upon the Russian government to stop the violence that plagued the Jews. Cardinal Manning, the leader of the Roman Catholic Church in England, delivered a powerful speech in which he condemned not only the pogroms but the degrading legislation which had harassed the Jews for centuries and which had caused them to groan under a terrible yoke.[31] One result of the meeting was the formation of the Mansion House Relief Fund, which soon collected £108,000, a fairly significant sum.

If the Mansion House meeting foreshadowed many similar events in subsequent decades, the immediate aftermath of the meeting revealed the problems which the well-intentioned were to confront in the future. The demonstrators at Mansion House and, for that matter, anyone who wanted something to be done for Russian Jewry, were moving onto dangerous diplomatic terrain; they were attempting to intervene in the domestic affairs of a sovereign state. The Mansion House Meeting, for example, not only passed a resolution that condemned the pogroms as an "offense to Christian civilization," but also expressed the hope that "Her Majesty's government may be able, when an opportunity arises, to exercise a friendly influence with the Russian government in accordance with the spirit of the preceding resolution."[32]

The British government would do no such thing. In the House of Commons, Prime Minister Gladstone did say that the reports of the pogroms had inspired sentiments of pain and horror, but nonetheless the matter was an internal affair of another country, and "it could not become the object of official correspondence or inquiry on the part of a foreign government."[33] Gladstone also refused to transmit to St. Petersburg a petition signed by British Jews and addressed to the Russian government. Officially, then, there would be no approaches to the Russian government by Britain during the era of pogroms. Not even the willingness of the United States to make a joint representation to the Russian government could sway Gladstone from his course.

His refusal was not only based on conventional diplomatic practice, which resisted intervention in the internal affairs of a foreign country, but was also the consequence of strong and bitter Russian opposition to even the most mild foreign diplomatic interference. The harsh Russian reaction, moreover, contained a threat, not to Britain, but to persecuted Russian Jews themselves, and this too must have influenced Gladstone.

The *Pravitelstvennyi Vestnik*, for example, had issued a statement condemning interference in the internal affairs of nations. The government

organ also uttered a threat: "Any attempt on the part of another government to intercede on behalf of the Jewish people can only have the
result of calling forth the resentment of the lower classes and thereby
affect unfavorably the condition of Russian Jews."[34] In short, the Jews
were being held hostage in order to prevent British diplomatic
intervention.

The strong position of the Russian government did not miss its mark.
Before the House of Commons, Gladstone declared that British governmental representation and even Parliamentary debates about the situation of the Jews in Russia were "more likely to harm than to help the
Jewish population." Private and unofficial contacts would influence the
Russian government, which, Gladstone assured the House, shared the
anguish of the people of England over the anti-Jewish disorders.[35]

The strong stand taken by the Russian government had succeeded in
forestalling a British diplomatic initiative. In this sense, it could be argued
that the Russians had won. But the fact of the matter was that the Russian
government could ill afford to antagonize Britain, even if it was only
British public opinion that was affected. With its vast empire, its huge
financial reserves, and its proximity to Europe, Great Britain was a factor
that no European state could disregard. Britain's powerful role in the
recent Congress of Berlin in 1878, a role viewed negatively by the Russian
government, confirmed the importance of Britain in relations among
European nations. Even in this early period of Russian industrial development, it was dependent to a certain extent on foreign investment,
and would suffer if relations between the two countries deteriorated
significantly. All of this meant that somehow the British concern for the
Jews would have to be accommodated. Ignatiev might not be aware of
it; more perceptive Russian statesmen were.

The foreign opprobrium, it should be pointed out, was not limited to
Britain. In the United States, Italy, the Netherlands, and Spain there
were demonstrations against the Russian pogroms. On the Continent
the strongest outcry was heard in France. As early as July 1881, a weekly
bulletin began to appear in Paris to inform the public of the persecution
of Russian Jewry. The pogroms were reported in leading newspapers,
which were highly critical of the Russian government. Victor Hugo and
other prominent French citizens participated in relief work for Russian
Jewry. The most interesting aspect of these public expressions of sympathy was that they did not come from the French Jewish community,
whose leading personalities and institutions tended not to make public
pronouncements. The Alliance Israélite Universelle, perhaps the foremost Jewish institution not only in France but in the world, despite its
important role in providing support for the emigrants, opposed the
convocation of public protest meetings and the raising of the issue in
the Chamber of Deputies. Indigenous French anti-Semitism, together

with increasing speculation in government circles about the need for an alliance with Russia to end France's diplomatic isolation and vulnerability vis-à-vis Germany may have been responsible for this very cautious position. French Jews, then and later, would go to great lengths to demonstrate their patriotism. The silence of French Jews notwithstanding, the declarations of support in France and elsewhere for the Russian Jews were additional factors that had to be reckoned with by Russian statesmen.[36]

DISAPPROVAL AT HOME

Foreigners were not the only ones to express strong disapproval of the pogroms. In Russia, too, there was growing awareness that the violence was getting out of hand. Pobedonostov, for all his loathing of the Jews, was a staunch opponent of the pogroms. He was convinced that the mobs attacking the Jews would eventually turn against the state. A true conservative, Pobedonostov feared popular movements of any kind. In June 1881, he sent a letter to Alexander III expressing his opposition to the pogroms precisely for these reasons. In the first months of 1882 he denounced the Ministry of the Interior for allowing demagogues to instigate riots and demonstrations against the Jews.[37]

Pobedonostov was not the only conservative to take this position. M. N. Katkov, a distinguished Russian journalist whose conservative views on Russian nationalism, the intelligentsia, socialism, and education were widely disseminated, was silent throughout 1881.[38] Yet his newspaper, *Moskovskiia Vedomosti* (The Moscow Gazette), gave space to at least one Jewish letter-writer who condemned the pogroms and defended the Jews against their detractors.[39] In the early spring of 1882, Katkov ended his silence. He was appalled by the Balta pogrom and his paper claimed that "if Attila the Hun had passed through Balta, . . . he could not have done more."[40] Katkov called upon the government to stop this "shameful scandal" which posed a great danger to Russia. The disorders were extremely destructive of the Russian economy, and the pogroms could play into the hands of the revolutionaries.[41] He harshly criticized the government's policy of expelling the Jews from places they had inhabited for decades. The expulsions, together with the government's new policy of interpreting old laws very stringently, left thousands of innocent people homeless and starving. "They ravaged the unfortunates, no less than the violent uproar of the agitated crowd."[42] He particularly lamented the fate of Jewish soldiers who had fought for the fatherland and were now rewarded for their efforts with expulsion.

Katkov went beyond calling for an end to the pogroms. He criticized those who so facilely blamed the Jews for the evils besetting Russia. All of the talk about Jewish innkeepers being responsible for the poverty of the peasants was nonsense. Katkov argued that the peasants of the Russian interior, where there were no Jews, were more inebriated and poorer than peasants in the Pale. There was poverty in the west, Katkov declared, but it was Jewish poverty.[43]

Katkov was no ordinary journalist. He had very close links to the government; and contemporaries saw him as one of the most influential figures in the early years of the reign of Alexander III. He corresponded with Pobedonostov, with Dmitri Tolstoi, Ignatiev's successor in the Ministry of Interior, and with the Tsar himself. Alexander carefully read Katkov's articles in *Moskovskiia Vedomosti*. It is reasonable to believe that his view of the pogroms as dangerous for Russia, and even his sympathetic defense of the Jews, elicited a response in the highest circles of government.[44]

Additional pressure upon the government to do something decisive in the way of quelling the anti-Jewish disorders came from the commercial and industrial classes. On May 30, 1881, I. S. Morozov, a leading Moscow textile manufacturer, wrote to Ignatiev informing him of the harsh economic consequences of the pogroms and the potentially dangerous political ones. The minister was told that the violence in the south was causing commercial elements in the Ukraine, most of whom he claimed were Jewish, to suspend active trading. The various trade fairs were doing far less business than before because Jewish merchants were reluctant to appear. What was worse was that some Jewish commercial people were unable to make payments to manufacturers in central Russia. The result was not only that "patriotic industry and trade" was suffering but that the Moscow producers would soon be forced to cut production, which would lead to an increase in unemployment and possibly to political instability. The government was urged to take all necessary steps, including that of prodding foot-dragging local authorities, such as those in Kiev, to stop the violence.[45]

The Moscow manufacturers did not let the matter drop. In early May 1882, representatives of fifty Moscow firms presented a petition to the Ministry of Finance detailing the great harm that the anti-Jewish disorders were doing to the Russian economy. As an example, the petition stated that at the recent Kharkov trade fair Jewish buyers who constituted a majority of those present purchased only a fraction of the goods they had bought in previous years. The petitioners informed the government that they had extended credit worth tens of millions of rubles to retailers and wholesalers in the south and that dire consequences would ensue if the economic situation in that area did not improve.[46]

The economic and social impact of the pogroms was also noted by diplomatic representatives of the Hapsburg Empire in Moscow, St. Petersburg, and Kiev. Their reports speak of rising unemployment in Moscow and St. Petersburg, as well as of a breakdown of commercial intercourse in the south. In the area where the pogroms were occurring, credit dried up, since the Jews were reluctant to lend more to the peasants, artisans, and small shopkeepers. The resultant slowing of economic activity led to a migration opposite to the direction of the preceding decade's. The Austrian officials noted that the railroad stations in central Russia, including Moscow, were jammed with peasant migrants from the south seeking work. Eventually, the diplomats maintained, the government would have to react harshly and decisively against the violence, if not for the Jews, then for the domestic tranquility and economic well-being of Russian society.[47]

THE MAY LAWS AND THE WINDING DOWN OF THE POGROMS

All of these concerns influenced the fate of the Project of the Committee for the Revision of the Jewish Question, already tightened by Ignatiev, which had proposed, as its core, the total elimination of Jewish settlement from the rural areas of the Pale of Settlement. Ignatiev submitted his proposal to the Committee of Ministers for approval as temporary legislation. By law, the much larger and allegedly more progressive State Council, which had to approve all permanent legislation, should have been the recipient of the proposal. Ignatiev believed he had a better chance in the Committee of Ministers, a smaller body. He therefore bypassed the larger body, using the pretext that he sought only temporary and not permanent implementation of this legislation.

Whatever Ignatiev's reasons were for choosing the Committee of Ministers, he must certainly have been disappointed. Minister after minister denounced the Project. The Minister of Finance, N. K. Bunge, was the most adamant opponent, and spoke against Ignatiev's proposal on a number of grounds.[48] If the proposals were enacted, Bunge claimed, Russia's credit would dry up, since the Rothschilds and other Jewish bankers would refuse to lend money to the state, and this would influence other sources of credit. The very well-being of the state depended on adequate sources of credit; anything that affected Russia's credit adversely would damage the empire. Bunge also pointed out that the Christian population, which had very extensive commercial relations with the Jews, would be devastated. He added that the enactment of the Project would not only have disastrous impact on the affected Jews but would also place enormous burdens on the inhabitants and authorities of the cities and towns of the Pale that would have to absorb the Jewish migrants. He concluded that the contemplated legislation would exacerbate the political situation by creating masses of disaffected people, both Jews and Christians.

M. N. Ostrovsky, Minister of State Domains, spoke of the "sufferings of tens of thousands of individuals, although they may be Jews."[49] The Minister of Justice, D. N. Nabokov, echoed Bunge in claiming that Ignatiev's proposals would create large numbers of dissatisfied people who would be adversely affected, particulary in economic terms, by the forced migration of the Jews. Nabokov also worried about Jewish resistance to displacement.[50] M. Solski, the State Comptroller, was almost as fierce as Bunge in his opposition to Ignatiev. He called on the Minister of the Interior to stop the libelous attacks in the press against the Jews which so stirred up the population. He took Ignatiev to task for the inaction of the police during the pogroms, calling it a scandal, and concluded with a statement that the Jews were also Russian subjects whom the government was obligated to protect from criminal interference against their life and property.[51] The chairman of the Committee of Ministers, M. K. Reutern, opposed Ignatiev's proposals and continued Solski's attack on the Ministry's behavior during the pogroms. Criticizing the police and local officials, Reutern worried that their behavior would set a bad precedent.

Everyone should be defended against infringements of their rights. Today they bait and rob the Jews. Tomorrow they will turn on the so-called *kulaks* [rich peasants].... Then merchants and landowners will take their turn under the gun. In other words, given such inaction by the authorities, one may expect the development in the very near future of the most terrible socialism.[52]

The hostility of the Committee of Ministers forced Ignatiev to back off from the Project. A period of negotiation between the Minister and the Committee followed. There finally emerged on May 3, 1882, the following "temporary decrees" of the Committee of Ministers:

(1) As a temporary measure, and until a general revision is made of their legal status, it is decreed that the Jews be forbidden to settle anew outside of towns and boroughs, exceptions being admitted only in the case of existing Jewish agricultural colonies. (2) Temporarily forbidden are the issuing of mortgages and other deeds to Jews, as well as the registration of Jews as lessees of real property situated outside of towns and boroughs; and also the issuing to Jews of powers of attorney to manage and dispose of such real property. (3) The Jews are forbidden to transact business on Sundays and on the principal Christian holy days; the existing regulation concerning the closing of places of business belonging to Christians on such days apply to Jews also. (4) The measures laid down in paragraphs 1, 2, and 3 shall apply only to governments within the Pale of Jewish Settlement [that is, they shall not apply to the ten provinces of Poland].[53]

It is clear from the legislation that Jews could no longer move from the cities and towns into the villages and rural areas of the Pale, and that they were now prohibited from purchasing or leasing property in the rural areas there. While certainly nowhere near as harsh as the Committee for the Revision of the Jewish Question had wanted—the village assemblies could not evict Jews and Jewish participation in the liquor trade was not prohibited—and certainly not as severe as Ignatiev had proposed, the May Laws had injurious consequences for a growing Jewish population already restricted to the Pale and which now found its residential area constricted even further. In subsequent decades the hardship was compounded by the fact that local officials interpreted the May Laws in arbitrary fashion, most often to the disadvantage of the Jews. There were cases in which Jews already living in villages, who, according to the May Laws, were to be left in place, were not allowed back into their villages if they spent even short periods of time away. This included people who worked for several days in cities or towns. There were cases when local officials acted in the spirit of Ignatiev, but against the May Laws, and followed the inclination of village assemblies that had voted to force the Jews out. In sum, the May Laws were a throttle around the neck of Russian Jewry down to the February Revolution in 1917.[54]

While the "temporary rules," another name for the May Laws, severely constrained Jewish life in the Pale, they had no such effect on Ignatiev. There is some evidence to suggest that just before the Tsar signed the May Laws, Ignatiev had made sure to renew all contracts with his Jewish managers and lessees in his home province of Kiev. Only when he had been informed that these arrangements were finalized did he submit the legislation for the Tsar's approval.[55] Such hypocrisy is consistent with Ignatiev's sense of morality, since there is reason to believe that he, the ferocious defender of the Tsar and his people, was prepared, for a price, to change his attitude toward the discriminatory legislation aimed at Jews. He is reputed to have told Baron Horace Günzburg, "I have heard that the Jews have collected two million rubles for me and have deposited it in your bank." The baron, who was averse to purchasing what he believed to be the legitimate rights of Russian Jews, replied, "I know nothing about it; you are misinformed."[56]

One may wonder how, after the strenuous opposition of the Committee of Ministers to Ignatiev's proposals, it could issue rules that were so extremely harmful to the Jews even if not as pernicious as those advanced by Ignatiev. The anti-Jewish sentiments of some of the ministers may have convinced them that while Ignatiev had gone too far, his and Kutaisov's analyses of the situation were essentially correct: Jewish exploitation was the root cause of the pogroms. Kutaisov's fear that eventually the revolutionaries would use the pogroms for their own purposes may also have convinced the ministers to preempt an anti-Semitic position. It is also likely that the members of the committee were not oblivious to the signals coming from above. The Tsar's intense dislike for the Jews was no secret and his bureaucrats were not about to present him with legislation that relaxed rather than increased pressure on the Jews. The result was the May Laws.

The deliberations of the Committee of Ministers did yield some positive results for the Russian Jews. On the very same day that it issued the Temporary Decrees, the committee declared that attacks against the Jews were not to be permitted. The government, declared the committee, must make it clear that actions against Jews and their property will bring prosecution and that measures will be taken to suppress the anti-Jewish disorders.[57] On May 10 the Senate followed with a declaration to provincial governors which stated that local authorities would be held responsible if the violence continued; officials who failed to deal effectively with the problem would be dismissed.[58] At last the ruling circles had come to the conclusion that continuation of the anti-Jewish attacks was dangerous for the maintenance of state order, and that inefficient, lazy, and anti-Semitic local officials had acted as a spur to the pogroms.

The failure of local officials to deal effectively with the disorders was bound to reflect negatively on Ignatiev and his administration of the Ministry of the Interior. It must be reckoned as a contributing factor in his removal from office, although the major reason for his demise lay in his support for the convocation of a Zemsky Sobor (a consultative "landed assembly").[59] On May 30, 1882, Ignatiev was forced to resign and Count Dmitri Tolstoi was made the new minister.

Tolstoi was no philo-Semite and was considered a staunch reactionary and a fierce champion of autocratic rule. However, he was also strongly opposed to mass eruptions, no matter against whom. Immediately upon assuming office he issued a circular threatening local officials with prosecution if they did not act effectively to prevent disorder.[60] Tolstoi's stringent measures were reflected in the changed character of the trials arising out of the pogroms. In contrast to the Ignatiev period, when local officials refused to bring the *pogromshchiki* to court or passed very lenient sentences when they did, the summer of 1882 saw a number of cases brought to court. The penalties inflicted upon the guilty were quite severe.

The new policy worked with remarkable alacrity. From June 1882 on, the pogroms assumed a sporadic character. According to Dubnov, the next twenty years, until the great Kishinev pogrom of 1903, saw only ten pogroms, isolated phenomena devoid of the epidemic character of the 1881–1882 and 1903–1905 periods.[61] This seems to confirm the assumption that the pogrom wave of 1881–1882 occurred because officials in the capital and on the local level, for whatever reason, refused to take actions to bridle the population. As pointed out in Chapter II, such inaction had the effect of creating the impression among the people that the pogroms were desired by the Tsar and his government, despite the fact that, whatever their feelings about the Jews, they abhorred such spontaneous popular manifestations.

THE PRESS, THE INTELLIGENTSIA, AND THE POGROMS

The violence and destruction of the pogroms were bound to generate a significant response from the Russian press and the intelligentsia. To Jewish contemporaries and to subsequent historians the actions of both press and intelligentsia were shocking, revolting, or, at the very least, disappointing.[62] They were viewed as hostile toward the Jews, or at best indifferent to their fate. A close look at the published material of the period, however, indicates a greater heterogeneity than has been assumed. The Jews did come under ferocious attack but they were not without defenders, although some of the latter displayed an ambivalence in their positions on the pogroms that infuriated many Jewish commentators.

The anti-Semitic press that had been attacking the Jews for years mounted a vituperative campaign against them at the time of the pogroms. Ivan Aksakov's *Rus* saw the anti-Jewish disorders as the "finger of God."[63] The Jews had exploited the Russian people for decades and now the people were rising up in righteous anger against their Jewish oppressors. For Aksakov the roots of the Jewish danger were in the Talmud and the Kahal. The Talmud taught the Jews that they had the right to seize Christian property. The institution which enabled the Jews to do this was the Kahal. All Jews throughout the world, Aksakov claimed, belonged to one international Kahal which had two guiding centers, the Society for the Diffusion of Enlightment among the Jews, in St. Petersburg, and most important, the Alliance Israélite Universelle in Paris. The aim of the Kahal is to subjugate the entire world to the Jews. The Kahal has its own executive organs, and legal institutions, and carries out the death penalty. The Kahal buys and sells Christians and their property without their knowing it. Christians, Aksakov explained, have been transformed into Jewish slaves.

Aksakov rejected any move to alleviate the legal position of the Jews. Russians, he declared, cannot talk about the emancipation of the Jews. Rather, we must bring about the emancipation of Christians from Jewish oppression. "In the Russian land," he claimed, "only the Russian is master, and the Jew is his guest."[64] Aksakov clamored for legislation that would protect Christians from Jewish exploitation. Ideally, the best solution to the Jewish Question was for the Jews to emigrate, he believed. "Do us a favor," he said. "Leave!"[65] He did not shrink from using force to achieve his goals. If the Jews would not leave voluntarily, then it was morally permissible to drive them from Russia.

The same harsh sentiments, with some variations, flowed through the columns of Suvorin's *Novoe Vremia*, published in St. Petersburg.[66] Before the pogroms, it had published the article, "The Yid Is Coming." Now it echoed Aksakov in seeing Jewish exploitation as the cause of the pogroms, and in attacking the Talmud and the insidious Kahal. The pogroms were the only way, claimed the paper, that the peasants could draw attention to their suffering under the "Jewish yoke." *Novoe Vremia*, however, introduced different themes, some of which would be advanced later by anti-Semites in other countries. Russian medical institutions were warned against hiring Jewish physicians lest they do something terrible to their patients. Jewish criminality was discussed at great length; the list of Jewish crimes included fraud, swindling, extortion, the conversion of Christians to Judaism, and the seduction of Christian girls into prostitution.

At the end of 1881 *Novoe Vremia* began to address itself to the debate over legislation affecting the Jews. It argued that the state had the right to protect itself and its citizens from Judaism because that religion had exploitation as one of its dogmas. "We are not the enemies of Jewry," the paper proclaimed, "but are only against equality for the Jews."[67] The Jews must earn the trust of the Russian people before they can become equal citizens of the state. The Jews have to learn to do productive labor and abandon exploitation. *Novoe Vremia* was so adamant on the issue of limiting Jewish rights that it only half-heartedly endorsed the May Laws. The proposals of the Committee for the Revision of the Jewish Question were what it really wanted; it was very disappointed when the Committee of Ministers rejected them. Throughout the pogroms and for thirty years thereafter, *Novoe Vremia* conducted a vigorous anti-Semitic campaign and was regarded by contemporaries, Jewish and non-Jewish, as the most important anti-Semitic publication in Russia.

Rus and *Novoe Vremia* appeared in the capital cities, Moscow and St. Petersburg, respectively. In the provinces the chief purveyor of anti-Jewish sentiment was *Kievlianin*, which stressed Jewish impudence and rapaciousness.[68] It even coined a term for the Jewish exploiter, the *evrei-pomeshchik* (the Jew-landlord) who fleeced and enslaved the Russian peasants. The paper cynically expressed its concern for the Jews by stating, "We grieve about the Jews, grieve that they eat each other up...." The paper proffered the opinion that as long as Jews possessed anti-social tendencies, it was necessary to prevent them from harming others.[69] To ensure the safety of the Russian people, *Kievlianin* proposed the harshest possible interpretation of existing legislation that affected the Jews. The expulsion of Jews from certain areas and occupations was consistently championed by the paper.

Jewish political behavior, particularly the links between some Jews and the liberal and revolutionary movements, also came in for scathing attack. In the summer of 1881, *Kievlianin* pointed to the metamorphosis that had taken place among Jews. "It astonishes us that these same Jews who just two weeks ago flaunted their liberalism and radicalism and were proud of the fact that Lasalle and Karl Marx are of Jewish origin, at the present time have been transformed into such true sons of the motherland and hasten to register in the conservative camp."[70]

In addition to the bona fide anti-Semitic publications which spewed hatred against the Jews, there were other journals which did not have a reputation for attacking Jews but did display during the time of the pogroms bursts of hostility toward them. *Russkii Kurier* (The Russian Courier) published an article depicting Jewish thievery and the alleged Jewish penchant for dealing in stolen goods.[71] *Sovremennyia Izvestiia* (Contemporary News) noted that the government had made a terrible mistake in educating Russian Jews, for education had given the Jews the ability and the power to exploit the Russian people.[72] According to *Sovremennyia Izvestiia*, "the basic idea of Judaism is the desire for gold."[73] The Jews have no history, no religion, and no fatherland. They were, therefore, the most suitable material for socialism.

Not even liberal journals were immune to occasional manifestations of harsh anti-Jewish sentiment. Perhaps the most liberal periodical published legally in Russia during this period was *Otechestvennyia Zapiski* (Patriotic Notes). It did not devote much attention to the Jews or to the pogroms for most of the period, but in its May 1882 issue there appeared a thirty-five page article focusing attention on the exploiting and rapacious activity of the Jews. The author suggested that this type of behavior was the root cause of the pogroms.[74]

Liberal coolness and hostility toward the Jews were not restricted to the pages of periodicals and newspapers. In Odessa, students and professors who inclined to liberal and revolutionary views believed that the Russian people had risen against their oppressors and that "the awakening of popular consciousness" was a good thing.[75] By late 1881 and early 1882, as will be seen in Chapter V, Russian Jewish periodicals were receiving letters from gymnasium and university students who also testified to the indifference and hostility of liberal students and professors. For Jews such attitudes were taken as acts of betrayal and caused considerable anguish.

The virulence of the anti-Semitic press was not matched by equal fervor in defense of the Jews from periodicals and newspapers that opposed the pogroms. Liberal, moderate, and even conservative publications—Katkov's for example—spoke out against the pogroms, in some cases from the outset. Their opposition, however, was hedged with a certain ambivalence that often manifested itself in a degree of hostility to the victims of the very pogroms they were condemning.

The reason was that many educated Russians, including the liberals, were weighed down by considerable political and intellectual baggage in relation to the Jews. More important, the press lacked familiarity with Jewish life. Many Russian writers shared the reactionary view that the Jews were all petty bourgeois and did, in fact, exploit peasants and workers. Linked with this conception was the belief, shared by liberals and revolutionaries, that movements from below, from the *narod*, were intrinsically good and should be treated by progressive people with sympathy. Some liberals combined both views and came to the conclusion that the pogroms were legitimate efforts by the masses to throw off exploitation. This explains the anomaly of liberals and revolutionaries not only approving but encouraging and inspiring violence against a people who were themselves the victims of oppression.

The immediate reaction of the moderate and liberal press was that the pogroms were a consequence of a peculiar economic and legal situation. *Golos* (The Voice) declared in May 1881 that the Russian people misconstrued the legal disabilities of the Jews.[76] The Jews were seen as a pariah people against whom one was free to act. The root cause of the pogroms lay in this and in the Jewish exploitation of the Russian peasantry. The Jews had been taking advantage of poor and ignorant Russian peasants for decades; and the peasantry was now beginning to settle accounts. Nonetheless, proclaimed *Golos*, seconded by *Moskovskii Telegraf*, the Jews are Russian citizens and are therefore entitled to the full protection offered by Russian law.[77]

That the cause of the pogroms lay in Jewish exploitation but at the same time the Jews ought to be protected was a common theme in a number of periodicals.[78] In the beginning of 1882, however, some publications became more strident in their defense of the Jews and in their call for an end to the pogroms. *Golos*, for example, stopped mentioning Jewish exploitation and began to publish articles demonstrating the poverty of the Jewish masses and the fact that the overwhelming majority of Jews were hardworking citizens of the Russian state.[79] More important, *Golos* called for an end to the legal disabilities of the Jews, claiming that only if the Jews possessed full legal rights could they be transformed into productive citizens. As things stood now, *Golos* maintained, Russia was being deprived of four million useful citizens.

Strana (The Country) echoed *Golos* by publishing long articles on the sufferings of the Jewish poor and cataloging the different types of hard labor performed by Jews.[80] *Svetoch* (The Lamp) mentioned Jewish exploitation as a cause of the pogroms but quickly commented that it was the abnormal situation of the Jews, their being penned up in the Pale and their unfortunate legal position, that led them to exploit others.[81] The answer to the Jewish Question, according to *Svetoch*, was that Jews must be given the right to settle all over Russia.

In March of 1882, *Novosti* (News) made the most critical remarks to date concerning government policy. The newspaper confronted Ignatiev directly by claiming that his charge to the *guberniia* commissions and the actual work of the commissions exacerbated an already difficult situation. They justified violence against the Jews in the eyes of the Russian masses.[82] The same straightforwardness appeared in *Moskovskii Telegraf* at almost the same time; the paper demanded that the government either provide the Jews with full civil rights or else expel them from the country, a step that the paper regarded as barbaric and one that no government could even contemplate much less take.[83]

With the coming of new pogroms in the spring of 1882, the pro-Jewish and anti-pogrom position of the moderate and liberal press reached its apogee. *Moskovskii Telegraf* published a long article detailing the contributions of Russian Jews to the fatherland, including the sacrifices made by Jewish soldiers in the recent war against the Ottoman Empire. It concluded with the statement, "Yes, Russia also belongs to the Jews."[84]

It was the pogrom in Balta in the last days of March that stunned certain segments of the Russian press. *Golos* was appalled: "Everything pales before Balta!"[85] Over a period of several weeks it gave detailed analyses of the pogrom. Articles appeared which depicted the terrible suffering of the Balta Jews and their enormous losses of property. Coverage was given to the trials of people accused of raping Jewish women and girls. The paper dwelled upon the shortcomings of the military, police, and local civilian authorities who failed to prevent the pogroms and did not quickly suppress them.[86] *Golos* drew two important conclusions from the Balta pogrom. The Jews had to be made equal with other citizens so as to lessen their vulnerability and the government had to take the firmest possible measures to stop the pogroms.[87] *Golos* speculated that, if the pogroms were not halted, the violence would spread from attacks on the Jews to other groups in society leading to a breakdown in order culminating in anarchy.

The era of good will for the Jews lasted into the early summer and in some cases beyond. *Novosti* proclaimed that the Jews were as much a part of the indigenous population as any other group, including the Great Russians.[88] *Zemstvo* stressed the hardships of Jews expelled from various cities and towns, and *Russkii Kurier*, which had occasionally castigated the Jews, now spoke of the harm that the pogroms were doing to Russia's image in Europe.[89] The May Laws did not calm the moderate press; a number of periodicals, particularly *Novosti*, saw them as discriminatory and counterproductive for the goal of achieving social peace.[90] Tolstoi's circular to the provincial governors, on the other hand, was viewed as most helpful and long overdue.[91]

The very success of Tolstoi's policy and the rapid winding down of the pogroms stimulated the appearance of recidivist impulses in some periodicals, which reverted to the earlier ambivalence or even hostility toward the Jews. They testify to the lingering unease felt by many educated Russians in dealing with the Jewish Question. *Golos*, for example, published in early July an article which once again focused attention on the Jews as the cause of the pogroms. "Where there is smoke, there is fire," said the paper, and it accused the Jews of holding themselves apart from the Russian people.[92] The Jews were a special nation that does not consider itself fully Russian and this antagonized ordinary Russians. Only if the Jewish intelligentsia led Russian Jewry in the direction of Russificiation could the Jews gain equal rights.[93]

It would be inaccurate and unfair to claim that all liberal and progressive elements in the Russian empire held such ambivalent attitudes toward the Jews and the pogroms. There were some whose support for the Jews was unequivocal. The Russian Jewish press published occasional letters from Christians regretting the pogroms and offering assistance to the Jews. One letter-writer to *Razsvet* not only offered sympathy to the Jews but also proposed to organize like-minded Christians into a committee that would disseminate correct information about the Jews and that would also help them to defend themselves. Interestingly, and probably correctly, the writer claimed that there were many Russians who sympathized with the Jews and wanted to do something in their behalf but refrained from doing so because they, like all Russians, were accustomed in civil matters to act only according to a *prikaz* (a decree from the government.)[94]

There were also some Russian writers, to be sure not too many, who spoke out in defense of the Jews and against the pogroms. N. B. Shelgunov, in the journal *Delo* (Cause), in 1881 criticized both the reactionary and liberal press for their attacks on the Jews. Shelgunov rejected all "projects" proposed by these publications and government officals to solve the Jewish Question. He offered in their stead a solution which he claimed would be beneficial to Jews, Russians, and all inhabitants of the empire: a proclamation by the government creating freedom of conscience, freedom of thought, and full freedom for the development of individual personality.[95]

An even stronger statement from the novelist and historian, D. L. Mordovtsev, appeared in *Razsvet* in early 1882 under the title, "Letter from a Christian Regarding the Jewish Question." Mordovtsev wrote of the shame and guilt he felt during the previous years' rampant anti-Semitism and pogroms, since he "together with all of Russian society had in a way taken part in this Godless affair." For Mordovtsev, the Jewish Question was the "most accursed of accursed questions" and he declared that it was the sacred duty not only of Russia but of all civilized humanity "to make impossible forever a recurrence of this shameful affair which has taken place before our eyes." He boldly criticized "those leaders unseen yet known to all, who are directing the movement of

the wild masses . . . from their publishing houses and luxuriously fur-
nished editorial offices, whipping up lead articles for sale at retail."[96]

Mordovtsev went so far as to offer the Jews a solution. He advised
them, in the event of more pogroms, to immigrate to the United States
or Palestine. He believed that the government would be frightened of
this mass departure and would make concessions to the Jews. At last
"Jews would cease to be considered as outside the law." His belief in
ultimate concessions by the Tsarist government in the face of large-scale
Jewish emigration was, as time would show, naive. But what was important from Mordovtsev was not his advice but his righteous indignation and his expression of sympathy for beleaguered Russian Jewry.

The most notable expression of support for the Jews came from one
of the giants of nineteenth-century Russian literature, the great novelist
Saltykov-Shchedrin. In earlier writings he had, together with other Russian writers, most notably Nekrasov, displayed a loathing for the Jewish
plutocracy, but now under the impact of the pogroms he took an unequivocal position in defense of the Jews. His article, "A July Breeze,"
appeared in the August 1882 issue of the same liberal journal, *Otechestvennyia Zapiski*, that had often been cool and disdainful toward the Jews.
Saltykov-Shchedrin sought to stir the conscience of the Russian intelligentsia:

History has never inscribed on its pages a problem more grave, more inhuman
and oppressive than the Jewish problem. The history of humanity is in general
an endless martyrology but at the same time a continued enlightenment. While
in the sphere of martyrology the Jewish people occupy first place, in the sphere
of enlightenment they stand aside, as if the bright perspectives of history do
not involve them. There exists no more heart-rending tale than this endless
torment of man by man.[97]

In the same article, Saltykov-Shchedrin criticized those who held all
Jews responsible for the faults of a few. He argued that even those who
did act wrongly often did so because they were under pressure from
the authorities. He appealed to Russian writers to become acquainted
with the Jews, and in what is a stark commentary on Russian literature's
ignorance of the millions of Jewish subjects in the empire, he could
recommend to interested Russians only one literary work on the Jews
which he thought valid, the short story "Mighty Sampson" written in
1877 by the Polish writer Eliza Orzeszkowa. "Those who wish to know
how much goodness lies concealed in tormented Jewry, and what an
inexpressible tragedy hangs over its existence, should refer to this story
whose every word breathes the painful truth."[98]

Friendly articles and letters to the Russian Jewish periodicals notwithstanding, the overwhelming majority of liberal Russians and the

bulk of the Russian intelligentsia remained indifferent, hostile, or only ambiguously supportive of the Jews. The greatest figures in Russian literature, Turgenev and Tolstoi, had nothing to say in connection with the pogroms.[99] Such indifference and hostility could only hurt the Jews. In late nineteenth-century Russia the intelligentsia had enormous influence upon society. Not even government circles were immune to it. An opportunity was abandoned to move public opinion both in and out of government in a positive direction by a strong condemnation of the pogroms and by appeals to the conscience of Russia. Russian Jewry, particularly those of its sons and daughters who had sought with such fervor to merge into the intelligentsia, was sorely disappointed in the latter's deportment. Their hurt over the behavior of the intelligentsia was rivalled only by their even more bitter feelings about the course taken by the Russian revolutionary movement during the period of the pogroms.

IV

The Bridge to Revolution

The relationship between Russian Jewry and the revolutionary movement in Russia was a strained one in the period before the pogroms.
As pointed out in Chapter I, many revolutionaries, including some Jews,
had become convinced that the Jews were exploiters of the people, as
despicable as the *pomeshchiki* (landlords) and the Tsar. They considered
anti-Jewish pogroms an effective means of generating, first, a revolutionary mood among the peasants, and then the revolution itself.

By the middle of the 1870s, the *zhid* had taken his place among the
oppressors of the Russian people; he would be destroyed in the coming
revolution. One revolutionary of Jewish extraction complained of this
anti-Jewish sentiment among his comrades: "They make no distinction
between Jews and gentry, preaching the extermination of both."[1]

THE PEOPLE'S WILL

By 1881 the Narodnik or Populist movement had begun to weaken.
Neither in the period 1873–1874 nor in 1876 did the young revolutionaries, going "to the people" to establish rapport with the peasants and
convince them of the need for revolution, have the anticipated results.
On the contrary, the Populists' activities had failed, and in many cases
brought about disastrous consequences for them. The peasants were
frequently unable to understand what the revolutionaries had to say,
and in some cases even assaulted them or turned them over to the police.
Many were arrested and exiled or imprisoned. The attempt to create a
new, more centralized revolutionary organization, Land and Liberty
(Zelmlia i Volia), foundered on the question of whether or not to resort
to terror and assassination. The frustrations felt by some of the young
people had led many of them to endorse violence as a political tactic.
In 1879 Land and Liberty had dissolved; in its place appeared two or-

ganizations, Black Partition (Chernyi Peredel) and the People's Will (Narodnaia Volia). Black Partition, rejecting terror, favored the continuation of propaganda work among the Russian masses. In practice, it was an ineffective organization but one that was to play an important transitional role in the revolutionary movement. Its leaders, Georgy Plekhanov and Pavel Akselrod, left Russia for Switzerland, where they created a small organization known as the Emancipation of Labor, the first Russian Marxist organization. Of greater importance, at least in the short term, was the other organization, the People's Will, whose adherents espoused the use of terror as much through desperation as on theoretical grounds. It was members of this group who assassinated Alexander II on March 1, 1881, the event that was to trigger the pogroms.

The People's Will, through the proclamation of its Executive Committee and the columns of its newspaper, *Narodnaia Volia*, provides the clearest expression of revolutionary support for the pogroms. Yet it is clear that sympathy for the pogroms extended beyond the People's Will into most corners of the revolutionary movement. In the spring and early summer of 1881, the revolutionaries viewed the attacks on the Jews as symptomatic of a ripening revolutionary consciousness and a sign that the people had at last risen, after centuries of slumber. It was believed that the pogroms were but the first blow of the coming revolution, which would overthrow all exploitation and oppression; they were a bridge over which the masses would pass en route to the final revolution.

On July 22, 1881, three months after the beginning of the pogroms, there appeared in the first issue of *Listok Narodnoi Voli* (Bulletin of the People's Will) a detailed analysis of the pogroms.[2] The author of the article, which was entitled "Iz derevni" (From a Village), allegedly wrote from a village in Kiev *guberniia*. He considered the anti-Jewish movement the most important development in recent Russian history, and felt it would clarify the role of the masses in the revolutionary movement. He lamented that city people, including members of the intelligentsia, did not understand the psychology of the peasants and the working people who participated in the pogroms. This was not an inebriated mob bent on pillage but an oppressed people striking out against its exploiters. To better their lives, the villagers realized that it was necessary to attack the Jews. As for the latter, the writer stated, they contributed to their own misfortune, not only by exploiting the peasants but also by acting tactlessly, by spying on them, by interrogating all new arrivals in the village about pogroms elsewhere, and by linking themselves closely to local police officials.

The most important development in the village, in the view of the writer, was the gigantic step taken by large numbers of villagers in the development of their "social philosophy." At first, only the more enlightened peasants and working people understood that the anti-Jewish movement was only the first step, and that a more general revolt was necessary if the position of the peasants was to improve. Gradually, however, large numbers of villagers had begun to see that Jews were only a part of that plutocratic coalition that oppressed and exploited them and which had to be destroyed. Curiously enough, then, the Jews played an important role in the peasants developing a more sophisticated social philosophy. By huddling close to the landlords and the local officials, and by constantly harping on the idea that they would only be the first to be attacked and that the *pomeshchiki* themselves would be the next target, the Jews contributed greatly, according to the author, to the peasants' awareness that there was a whole coalition of wealthy oppressors.

The writer went on to argue that the Jews performed a further service by their claiming that the socialists were the instigators of the pogroms; this had the effect of raising the latter's prestige in the eyes of the people. Equally, the rumors in the Ukraine that the pogroms in the south had been instigated by students from Moscow and St. Petersburg made the peasants aware that there existed an organization in the capital whose goal was the amelioration of peasant life. The writer was convinced that a transformation of popular thinking had taken place and that this augured well for the forthcoming revolution. The people were beginning to realize that the revolutionaries were, after all, their defenders and saviours. The old notion of the Tsar-Benefactor was being replaced. The rapid dissemination of the new concept, contended the author, would determine the course of the revolutionary struggle.

The most emphatic and probably most controversial declaration from the People's Will was an Executive Committee proclamation issued in Ukrainian on July 31, 1881. The composition of the committee by now differed drastically from the original 1879 committee. Government persecution, especially after the beginning of March 1881, had taken its toll; most of the prominent original members of the Executive Committee had been arrested or had fled abroad. The result was that less important members, some of whom felt great antipathy toward Jews, were able to influence events. Thus it was the relatively insignificant G. Romanenko who actually drafted the proclamation. Three short paragraphs demonstrate its inflammatory nature:

Good people, honest Ukrainian people! It has become difficult for people to live in the Ukraine, and it's getting worse all the time. You cannot find the truth anywhere. Corrupt officials beat you, the landlords eat you alive, and the Jews, the useless Judases, rob you.

From Jews most of the people in the Ukraine suffer. Who has gained control of the land, the forests and the taverns? The Jews. From whom does the peasant, sometimes in tears, ask access to his field...? The Jews. Wherever you look, whenever you come closer, the Jews are there. The Jew yells at the peasant, deceives him, drinks his blood. You cannot live in the village because of the Jews....

The poor peasant groans and sometimes curses the hour and day his mother bore him, and the landlords are with the Jews and the officials, and they don't care![3]

The appearance of the proclamation generated enormous tension within the revolutionary movement in general, and in the Executive Committee of the People's Will in particular. The sources agree on only one point. Vera Figner, a member of the Executive Committee who was in Odessa at the time and therefore had no role in the decision to publish the proclamation, refused to distribute it and, in fact, destroyed copies in her possession.[4] The question of dissemination, however, is an open one; some writers claim that very few copies of the proclamation were in fact distributed, while others maintain that not only were many distributed but that the proclamation was even reprinted in at least one city, Elizavetgrad, in the spring of 1882.[5]

Narodnaia Volia continued to adhere in subsequent issues to the positions advocated in the first *Bulletin* and in the proclamation. On October 23, 1881, in the section "Vnutrennee obozrenie" (Internal Survey), the journal carried a diatribe against the Jews, who once again were blamed for the pogroms because of the exploitative nature of their economic activity. Statements by members of the intelligentsia concerning the poverty of the Jewish masses were dismissed. The Jew as the exploiting innkeeper, merchant, and usurer was said to be replacing the anachronistic *pomeshchik* as the object of popular wrath. The author, borrowing from the anti-Semitic *Kievlianin*, described the "audacious and mocking" behavior of the Jews, who "have got control of all commerce.... It will soon be impossible for a poor man to live in town.... And still they give you short measure and weight, and short-change you...."[6]

In the view of both the *Kievlianin* and the *Narodnaia Volia* writers, it was the alleged exploitation by the Jews, not their religion, which created the intense animosity toward them on the part of the Ukrainian populace.

The perpetrators of the pogroms were hailed by the writer: They were the sans-culottes of the Russian revolution that would spread from the cities and towns of the south to the rest of the Russian Empire. The revolutionaries were exhorted not to be repelled by the violence and cruelty of the *pogromshchiki*. The French Revolution of 1789 had been violent too, but leaders such as Robespierre and Danton had perceived the centrality of violence to the movement and had been quick to use it in the service of their goals. Similarly, the Russian revolutionaries must not reject the obligation imposed by history.

The manifestation of a revolutionary movement depends on the world view of a specific class or society, but its results are conditioned by the degree of its consciousness. And its guiding force is the leading, more energetic and more conscious revolutionary group. In France during the revolution, the Jacobins were such a group for a long time; in Russia it is the Executive Committee. We do not have the right to relate negatively or even indifferently to a purely popular movement; we are obligated to express a general formula for all the forces that are justifiably discontented and actively protesting, and to consciously direct these forces.... We will not, of course, reject the role of being the leading fighters.[7]

Narodnaia Volia constantly reiterated these themes well into 1883. Jewish exploitation continued to be singled out as the cause of the pogroms. As late as the summer of that year, after numerous Jewish lives had been lost, the writer of an article, "Po povodu evreiskikh bezporiadkov" (Concerning the Jewish Disorders) could still take the government to task for using force against the *pogromshchiki*: "In Ekaterinoslav the people's blood was shed. This fact is disturbing both in its cruelty and its injustice, and is just as illogical as everything else now being done by the government, which wants to show that it is strong and, particularly, that it is intelligent."[8]

The diminution in the strength and frequency of the pogroms did not shake *Narodnaia Volia's* faith in the coming revolution. The writer took heart from disorders in Moscow and Baku. He was convinced that the people now linked the Jews with the landlords, bureaucrats, and the Tsar, and would destroy all of them. For those readers who had begun to doubt the validity of *Narodnaia Volia's* analysis, the precedent of the French Revolution was repeated, and a new source of authority, Karl Marx, was utilized to make the point:

Regarding what will happen in the future, we will inform our readers when the time comes, but now we will only remind them that even the great French Revolution began with the beating of the Jews (Taine). This is the sort of sad fate that is unavoidable. The Jews, as Karl Marx explained so well, being an historically unfortunate people and long oppressed, have become a highly nervous and impressionable people; they reproduce in themselves as if in a mirror ... all the vices of the surrounding milieu and all the evils of a specific social structure, so that when the anti-Jewish movements begin one can be assured that they conceal a protest against the entire order, and that a much more profound movement is begining.[9]

Only in 1884, after the disorders had ended, did the People's Will reverse itself. The pogroms were now viewed as a "mistaken formula"; the people had chosen a path that could not ameliorate their situation. *Narodnaia Volia* admitted that the revolutionaries' judgment had also been fallacious. Russian Populism had finally ridden itself of the "socialism of fools."

ALTERNATIVE REVOLUTIONARY VIEWS

The earlier attitudes expressed in *Narodnaia Volia* were in any case not representative of all Russian revolutionary circles, whether internal or in exile. In Kiev in 1881, the Alliance of South Russian Workers (P. Orlov, N. Shchedrin, E. Kovalskaia-Solntseva, and others) issued a proclamation with interesting nuances on the themes in *Narodnaia Volia*. The Alliance did not deny the fact that some Jews were exploiters, but it called at the same time for an end to religious animosity and for sympathy on the part of Christian working men for the poor Jews:

Brother workers! You beat the *zhidy* but you don't examine why you do it. You should not beat a *zhid* because he is a *zhid* and prays to his own God—after all, there is but one God for all—but because he plunders the people and sucks the blood of the working man. In all fairness, any of our merchants or manufacturers plunders and ruins the worker more than the *zhid*, sucks the last drops of juice from him and amasses capital for himself.... But the other *zhid*, who earns his slice of bread through hard work no more easily than we do, by some trade or labor, should we plunder him too?... If so, then we must also beat any thieving *kulak* ... and beat all the authorities who ... fire at the people on behalf of some miserable millionaire Brodsky and kill innocent people.... [10]

A similar ambivalence was displayed by Black Partition, the organization which had broken with the People's Will in 1879 over the use of terror. In the September 1881 issue of *Chernyi Peredel*, an article entitled "Pisma s iuga" (Letters from the South) revealed sentiments analogous to those in *Narodnaia Volia*. The writer claimed that "the basis of the popular protest against the Jews is the ruthless exploitation of the popular masses by the latter," and concluded with the then common expression of faith that a "pogrom against the Jews is the prelude to the more serious and expedient movement of the people."[11]

Black Partition was, however, inconsistent in its views. Another of its journals, *Zerno* (Grain), published an article reminding the workers that there were poor Jews as well as rich Jews and that the revolutionary struggle demanded an alliance of the oppressed: "Not all Jews are rich, nor are all *kulaks* ... Why were the poor hovels of the Jewish tradesmen destroyed?... Renounce hostility toward those of other peoples and faiths. Remember that all workers to whichever faith or nation they may belong, must unite to fight the common foe."[12]

The *Zerno* article and the refusal of a number of *narodnovoltsy* to distribute Romanenko's proclamation support the thesis that there were exceptions to the general trend of support for the pogroms in the revolutionary movement. Among Jewish revolutionaries, opposition to the pogroms was even more pronounced. Revolutionaries such as I. Kaminer in Kiev and G. Gurevich, an émigré in Zurich, renounced their revolutionary affiliations, and began to urge migration to Palestine as the solution to the Russian Jewish question.[13] Jewish student revolutionaries in Russian universities at first saw the pogroms in the same light as their Gentile comrades; however, in the face of the anti-Jewish sentiments of the "socialist-minded" Russian students and "liberal" professors—which were directed against the Jewish students as well as the Jewish masses—a number of them rapidly abandoned the revolutionary movement and returned to the Jewish fold. They began to play a leading role in organizing the growing emigration movement aimed at settling Jews in America and Palestine. (See chapter V.)

AKSELROD AND HIS COLLEAGUES IN EXILE

Discomfort over the pogroms appears to have been more widespread in émigré circles than in Russia. In February 1882, leaders of the Russian revolutionary community in Zurich—Lavrov, Plekhanov, Akselrod, and Stepnyak—expressed their opposition to the anti-Jewish movement, and agreed on the publication of a pamphlet condemning the pogroms and the sentiments expressed by *Narodnaia Volia*.[14] Attempts to publish this pamphlet failed, however, as each of the non-Jewish leaders subsequently claimed he had neither the time nor the data to write the required pamphlet. It fell to Akselrod, the lone Jew in the group, to draw up a manuscript. Plekhanov promised to publish the pamphlet, after its approval by him and his colleagues, in the name of a "Group of Socialist Revolutionaries" as proof that several leading socialists, and not just a Jewish revolutionary, opposed the pogroms and the attitude toward them of so many Russian revolutionaries.[15]

Akselrod's decision to devote his efforts to writing about the pogroms demonstrates the depth of agitation felt by Jewish revolutionaries as a consequence of the turn taken by events. The son of poor Jewish parents, Akselrod had received a traditional Jewish education. But by 1872, under the influence of such writers as Dobroliubov, Borne, and Lassalle, he had lost interest in Jewish affairs and become involved with the cause of socialist revolution. He became convinced that

there is, in fact, no Jewish problem, only the question of liberating the working masses of all nations, including the Jews. With the victory of socialism, even the so-called Jewish question will be solved. Was it not senseless and criminal to devote one's energies to the Jews who are no more than one of the component parts of the vast population of the Russian Empire![16]

Akselrod's initial response to the pogroms was, in fact, quite remarkable by the standards of the Russian revolutionary movement. In the period before he committed his ideas to paper, he had given serious consideration to the possibility of solving the Jewish Question in Russia through the transfer of Russian Jews to Palestine. Under the influence of his friend Lev Deych (Leo Deutsch) and others, he soon rejected the idea.[17]

Akselrod's pamphlet, *O zadachakh evreisko-sotsialisticheskoi intelligentsii* (The Tasks of the Jewish Socialist Intelligentsia), was not so much a protest against the pogroms as an attempt to explain and understand them, and also to provide a guide to action for Jewish revolutionaries. Akselrod explained Russian hatred of the Jews in terms similar to the conventional revolutionary socialist interpretation of events. He, too, saw the root cause of the anti-Jewish disorders in the peculiar economic position of the Russian Jews, who were primarily occupied in non-productive occupations. They were, in his view, "bourgeois parasites" who exploited the peasants and working people.[18]

The problems confronting the Jews were made even more acute by the fact that they were in conflict not only with the peasants but with virtually all spheres of Russian society: "It is evident that if with respect to the peasantry and working people in general the Jews are one of the most conspicuous elements exploiting [their] labour, then with respect to the Christian-bourgeois population they are very unpleasant competitors, precisely in the area of exploiting the people's labor."[19]

The petty-bourgeois group, the *meshchanstvo*, despised Jews for their competitiveness in the whole range of artisan, small trading, and leasing activities. Professional people feared Jewish competition in the universities and minor government posts occupied by, for example, physicians and lawyers. Finally, the big Christian bourgeoisie engaged in fierce competition with Jewish manufacturers, bankers, and railroad builders.

Akselrod's analysis of the pogroms differed in tone and substance from that of the *narodnovoltsy*. While he subscribed to the view that the Jews were often found in intermediary, non-productive occupations, which led to their exploitation of the poor, he did not neglect to make it clear that these positions were occupied by Jews because they had been excluded for centuries, in Russia and elsewhere, from all productive labor. Akselrod depicted with genuine sympathy the poverty of the Jewish masses and recalled his own humble origins; simultaneously, he insisted that the term proletarian ought not to be applied exclusively to Christians, since the Jews were almost as impoverished as the Christian poor. Akselrod denied, however, that Jewish exploitation was the cause of all hatred of the Jews in the empire. The peasants and laboring poor could legitimately condemn Jewish exploitation, but professional people, petty bourgeois elements, and the big bourgeoisie could not. Their hatred of the Jews was rooted in Jewish competition and not exploitation, although, Akselrod cautioned, propertied Christians were inclined to conceal their class interests and motives behind hypocritical phrases pointing to a Jewish threat to popular and national well-being.

The most significant divergence from *narodnovoltsy* thinking on the pogroms is found in Akselrod's assessment of their revolutionary potential. Rather than viewing the pogroms as the first wave of a general revolutionary upheaval that would sweep away all exploiters, including the *pomeshchiki* and the bourgeoisie, he saw them as playing into the hands of the government and the propertied classes. The government was using the pogroms as a means of deflecting popular discontent. Akselrod was convinced that "agents of the government and various elements of the Christian bourgeoisie not only directly supported the anti-Jewish movement, but in many places directed it...."[20]

Akselrod also differed from the conventional revolutionary wisdom on the role of Jewish revolutionaries. It had been assumed by Jews and non-Jews alike in the revolutionary movement, including Akselrod himself, that Jewish revolutionaries ought to sever themselves from the Jewish masses and their concerns, and dedicate themselves wholly to the task of fomenting revolution among the indigenous population. In the midst of the wave of pogroms, however, Akselrod changed his mind: "For Jewish socialists the first concern must clearly be the interests of the lowest classes of the Jewish population...."[21] He assigned two tasks to the Jewish socialist: to work toward the transformation of the non-productive Jewish masses into a class of physical laborers, and then to establish links between the Jewish poor and the impoverished Christian masses.[22] The Jewish workers must be made to understand that they had more in common with Christian working people than with their own capitalists. Simultaneously, Christian socialist revolutionaries should systematically agitate among Russian and Ukrainian workers to eradicate anti-Semitism. Akselrod hoped that agitation conducted by Jewish and Gentile revolutionaries would lead to a merger of the Jews and the indigenous population.[23]

Akselrod's pamphlet remained unfinished and unpublished. Despite the fact that no one in the émigré community had seen the manuscript, the knowledge that Akselrod was, apparently, working on a defense of the Jews and a condemnation of the pogroms unnerved a number of prominent Russian revolutionaries based in Zurich. Even Lavrov, always sympathetic to the Jews, succumbed to the contemporary interpretation of the pogroms and wrote Akselrod on April 14, 1882, warning him that a condemnation of the pogroms and their perpetrators would greatly complicate matters for a revolutionary party whose objective was to raise the people against the government.[24] In a postscript to Lavrov's letter, Lev Deych, Akselrod's colleague on *Chernyi Peredel* and himself a Jew, expressed total agreement with Lavrov, explaining that the revolutionaries had to remain silent: To criticize the pogroms would serve only to provoke the hatred of the peasants against the revolutionaries. The party was in a difficult situation but it had no choice. Deych added that it was difficult for him to take this position but since the party demanded it, it had to be done.[25] In a further letter on May 26, Deych pointed out to Akselrod the regret of his revolutionary colleagues that he persisted in his efforts to publish the brochure.[26] Finally, Akselrod capitulated. Apparently, the opposition of his colleagues, coupled with the difficult financial straits which beset the revolutionaries, rendered the project unfeasible.[27]

DRAGOMANOV AND THE JEWS

By the mid–1870s a fairly large Russian émigré community resided in the two Swiss cities of Zurich and Geneva. Oppositionists of all stripes published their literature and worked for the cause of revolution. In addition to exiled Populists, there were representatives of the various movements of national liberation which had arisen in the Russian Empire in the third quarter of the nineteenth century. Among these was Mikhail Dragomanov, a founder of the Hromada group in Kiev, and the outstanding spokesman of the Ukrainian nationalist movement.

Dragomanov espoused a mixture of liberalism, socialism, and Ukrainian nationalism, and fervently opposed Russian political centralization, which, he believed, led to the subjugation and eventual destruction of minorities. On the other hand, his nationalism was moderate in tone, and he even extolled nineteenth century Russian literature. He rejected separatism, and argued that a federalized Russia, with cultural and national autonomy for all Slavic nationalities, would best serve the interests of those peoples. The rural self-governing council, or *zemstvo*, would be the predominant political institution of the autonomous regions. On economic matters, Dragomanov subscribed to the agrarian socialism current among nearly all political exiles from the Russian Empire.

By the early 1880s, Dragomanov enjoyed a reputation which extended well beyond the small band of Ukrainian nationalists in Switzerland. He was an acknowledged historian of the *zemstvo* movement, he had edited the works of Bakunin, and had published the correspondence of Turgenev, Kavelin, and Herzen. Invited in the autumn of 1881 to contribute to, and later edit, a new Russian newspaper in Geneva, *Vol'noe Slovo* (The Free Word), as noted in Chapter II, actually secretly subsidized by the Druzhina (The Holy League), Dragomanov used the paper for two years to articulate his views on the future of the Ukraine, the Russian Empire, and the Jews.

Before the pogroms of 1881 Dragomanov and Lavrov were virtually the only social revolutionaries, besides Lieberman, Zundelevich, and a few others, to see in Russian Jewry a revolutionary force which could be mobilized by propaganda. Like Lavrov, Dragomanov was highly regarded by Jewish revolutionaries and, in fact, played a major role in the creation of the Group of Socialist Jews in Geneva in 1880. When the Group appealed to radical Jewish youth to conduct propaganda in Yiddish among the Jewish masses, Dragomanov not only provided financial support for the publication and distribution of the appeal, but also added a short postscript.[28]

In this postscript, in conversation with other émigrés and in at least one public meeting, Dragomanov advocated support for the program advanced by Aaron Lieberman several years earlier. Like Lieberman, Dragomanov stressed revolutionary propaganda among the Jewish poor in their own language. He viewed the Jews as tools of the Russian government which the latter utilized for its own cultural and economic purpose, to the disadvantage of the Ukrainian nation. The Jews of the Ukraine, in Dragomanov's view, were a Russified and Russifying element which undermined Ukrainian culture. It was preferable, he argued, that the Jews develop their own language rather than learn Russian.[29]

Dragomanov believed that only revolutionary propaganda in Yiddish would impel the Jewish workers to join forces with the Ukrainian masses in a general revolutionary struggle, and in an attempt to bring these ideas to fruition in January 1881 he published a Yiddish newspaper, the *Arbeter Tsaytung*, of which one or two issues appeared. Thus, Dragomanov, through his role in the creation of the Group of Socialist Jews in Geneva and his fervent advocacy of the use of Yiddish in revolutionary propaganda, was partly responsible for the widespread use of the Yiddish language in the Jewish workers' movement and the subsequent success of the movement itself.[30]

Moreover, Dragomanov took an unpopular position on the issue of anti-Jewish attitudes and activities among the peasants. At a public meeting in Geneva in the summer of 1880 he vehemently opposed violent manifestations of anti-Semitism, declaring that the Ukrainians would have to learn to live with the Jews who, after all, had inhabited the Ukraine for centuries. In response to Zhukovsky's protest that peasant violence against the Jews was a natural reaction against exploitative forces, Dragomanov replied, "I do not believe in violence.... I believe in a union of nations."[31] One observer of the discussion noted the coolness of the response to Dragomanov's speech.

The ambivalence of Dragomanov's views on the Jewish Question becomes evident upon considering his articles of 1881–1882 and several of his private conversations. Some ideas he had earlier expressed were reformulated in greater detail but were given a new twist as he drew several harsh new conclusions. In his "Historic Poland and Great Russian Democracy, 1881–1882," Dragomanov asserted that the struggle against the Jews was a fundamental part of the struggle for a free Ukraine. The Jews, he affirmed, were not only aliens in the Ukraine and distinguished by strange customs and a peculiar religion, they had also acted from earliest times in the interests of those whose aim was the destruction of the Ukrainian people:

The Muscovite authorities distributed the Ukrainian lands to their Ukrainian servants and to aliens, they enserfed the peasants, introduced taxes and army recruiting, destroyed practically all the schools, and in those that remained prohibited teaching in our language. They imposed on us government-appointed unelected priests, and let loose on us once again Jewish leaseholders, innkeepers, and usurers, whom the Cossacks had seemingly driven out. And they even gave only our land to these Jews as forage, forbidding them to live on Muscovite land. . . .[32]

Dragomanov maintained that the Jewish problem in the Ukraine was rooted in the character and behavior of the Jews themselves. He told the Jewish writer Ben-Ami that the Jews were an unenlightened, ignorant mass of people whose only aim was to acquire money, while in "The Jewish Question in the Ukraine," he put forward the thesis that the Jews' traits of false pride, arrogance, and passion for rewards had been shaped by their unfortunate history of persecution. Of all the characteristics of the Jews, their haughtiness and sense of moral and cultural superiority with regard to the Ukrainians were the most obnoxious.[33] It was for these reasons that virtually all Ukrainians hated the Jews passionately.

The most important cause of hatred for the Jew in the Ukraine, and ultimately the major factor in the outbreak of the pogroms, was, in Dragomanov's view, the economic behavior of the Jews: "The most important aspect of the position of the Jewish nation in the Ukraine is its class essence. . . . It may be considered as proven that the Jewish nation in the Ukraine represents in its majority not only a class, but even, to a considerable extent, a parasitical class."[34]

Statistics from Russian government publications were introduced to demonstrate that Jewish lease-holders, innkeepers, merchants, and manufacturers held the Ukraine in a stranglehold, and were the primary exploiters of the peasants: "There are areas, especially in the villages, where Jew and capitalist, exploiter and his assistant, have become synonymous for the Ukrainian population (as for the Romanian, Belorussian, and Polish). In such areas, the notion of exploiter and zhid have become synonymous in popular language."[35]

The pogroms, Dragomanov contended, were a revolt against age-old oppression, and it was the right and obligation of the Ukrainians to continue their traditional struggle against their Jewish oppressors. In the preceding twenty-five years alone, the Ukrainian maintained, numerous peasant assemblies had petitioned the Tsar to expel the Jews, and in 1871 the people of Odessa had struck at their Jewish oppressors. Dragomanov took pride in the fact that the Ukrainian people had been the first to attack Jewish exploitation.[36] He shared the belief of the *narodnovoltsy* that the pogroms were only the first wave of the coming Russian revolution. So closely linked were the Jews to the government—Dragomanov believed they collected the government's taxes—that the peasants and workers, after first smashing the Jews, would move inexorably against their protectors, the Tsar and his officials, and the long-awaited revolution would finally be at hand.

Dragomanov did not lack sympathy with, or even a certain admiration for, the Jews. He was convinced, he told Ben-Ami, that Jewish national regeneration was a real possibility—but not in the Ukraine. There, the Jews were to disappear.[37] His ideal solution was intermarriage with the Ukrainians. He conceded that the Jews were a more intelligent people than the Ukrainians, whose simplemindedness he often ridiculed. A merger of the two peoples would raise the cultural and intellectual level of the Ukrainians to the point where they would become an important historical people.

Dragomanov assigned the task of achieving this integration to the educated Jewish youth, repeating a statement he had made in the summer of 1880, calling upon these young people to agitate among the Jewish masses in Yiddish, to draw them closer to the Christian laboring population by separating them from the Jewish capitalists, and to prepare the ground for the total fusion of Jews and Ukrainians.[38] Whatever differences Dragomanov may have had with Russian and Polish revolutionaries on questions of revolutionary tactics and the future structure of the Russian Empire, on one point there was total agreement: The Jews had no future as a separate, alien, exploiting class, in the eastern part of Europe.

There was an essential consistency in Dragomanov's thought that links his pre-pogrom ideas on the Jewish problem with those expressed in 1881–1882. He had always maintained that his attitude toward the Jews was dictated by a profound sense of Ukrainian nationalism. If Jewish revolutionaries would form groups to agitate among the Jewish poor in Yiddish, this would serve the interest of Ukrainian nationalism. However, if this same nationalism was to be spurred on by the pogroms, then so be it.

CONCLUSION

The views of the *narodnovoltsy* and Dragomanov demonstrate that both the Russian establishment and the revolutionary movement were inclined, much as were political groupings in Central and Western Europe in the second half of the nineteenth century, to use anti-Semitism as a political weapon. The silence over the pogroms on the part of Akselrod, Deych, Lavrov, and Plekhanov, none of whom could be accused of harboring anti-Semitic sentiments themselves, testifies to the efficacy of that weapon. However, the existence of real anti-Semitic sentiments above and beyond the demands of political expediency cannot be denied. The vitriolic stance taken by Romanenko and other members of Narodnaia Volia, the fierce hatred of the Jews felt by such revolutionaries as Zhelyabov, and the frequent use by Dragomanov of such words as *zhid*, *zhidochka*, and other pejorative terms, leads one to the conclusion that anti-Semitism was a prism through which a number of revolutionary analysts viewed the Russian scene.

But it is more likely that political desperation and expediency accounted for the position held by the bulk of the Russian revolutionary movement. Having failed to spur a peasant revolt against the government in the 1870s, and confronting a ruthless crackdown in the aftermath of the assassination of Alexander II, the revolutionaries clutched at straws. The pogroms seemed to these desperate men and women the first sign of that revolution for which so much had been sacrificed.

The pogroms did not make as significant an impact on Jewish revolutionaries as might be expected. While it is true that some Jews left the revolutionary movement and worked for the immigration of their people to America or Palestine, this was not true of most. According to E. Tcherikower, the most perceptive analyst on the subject of Jews in the revolutionary movement, faith in "socialist cosmopolitanism" remained strong among radical Jewish youth, and the Marxist and Populist movements were replenished by Jewish recruits in the second half of the 1880s.[39] For many in the Russian Jewish intelligentsia and for the Jewish masses, however, the behavior of the revolutionaries was additional proof of Jewish isolation.

With the passage of time the revolutionaries' initial perception of the pogroms proved to be mistaken. The anti-Jewish disorders did not result in a general revolution. Indeed, when the Tsarist government was finally overthrown, the revolutionary dynamic bore no relation to the scenario advanced by the Populists. The populace did not move from the Jews to the landlords to the Tsar. Moreover, rather than hastening the coming of the revolution, the involvement of the revolutionary movement in the pogroms of the early 1880s contributed to the creation of a pervasive anti-Semitism that was exploited by the Black Hundreds (the mobs of *pogromshchiki*) in the first years of the twentieth century. In fact, the pogroms strengthened the hand of the Tsarist government in deflecting popular dissatisfaction. One hundred years after the events in question, it is difficult to draw any other conclusion than that the behavior of the revolutionaries during the pogroms constitutes one of the most dismal chapters in the history of the Russian revolutionary movement.

V

Jewish Responses to the Pogroms

In the aftermath of the March assassination of Alexander II, Jewish communities throughout the empire demonstrated intense nervousness. There was a fearful expectation of coming events. The Russian Jewish periodical *Razsvet* in St. Petersburg sensed that, "A squall is coming, thunder is breaking, lightning is flashing and everything in nature is as if it is standing still.... Everyone is touched by one feeling; everyone has one impression.... For the present everyone is hiding, lapsing into silence ... until the deep echo of the bursting storm gradually dies down."[1]

Once the storm actually did break, in the Elizavetgrad pogrom on April 15, the Jewish communities were seized with terror and a feeling of hopelessness. Even in those areas, such as Lithuania, White Russia, and Poland, which did not experience the shock of the first wave of pogroms, there was great consternation. These sentiments were expressed by the local correspondents of *Razsvet*, and the other major Jewish periodicals: *Voskhod*, *Russkii Evrei*, *Ha-Melits*, and *Yidisher folksblatt*. One of the *Razsvet* correspondents was impelled to use Biblical language to describe the feeling of his coreligionists. "In the morning you wait for the coming of evening, in the evening for the coming of morning; you tremble before the movement of the leaves, and you do not believe in your life.... This is the situation of our Jewish population at the present moment."[2] The signs of demoralization and fear were everywhere and they continued unabated throughout the period 1881–1882.

DISILLUSIONMENT

Those students and intellectuals who were close to Russian culture and the Russian intelligentsia were hit particularly hard by the violence.

Their hopes of rapprochement leading to acceptance by Russian society and to their own emancipation, were at least temporarily shattered. One member of the Jewish intelligentsia wrote:

When I remember what has been done to us, how we have been taught to love Russia and Russian speech, how we have been induced and compelled to introduce the Russian language and everything Russian into our families so that our children know of no other language but Russian, and how we are now repulsed and persecuted, then our hearts are filled with sickening despair from which there seems to be no escape. This terrible insult gnaws at my vitals. It may be that I am mistaken, but I do honestly believe that even if I succeeded in moving to a happier country where all men are equal, where there are no pogroms by day and "Jewish commissions" by night, I would yet remain sick at heart to the very end of my life, to such an extent do I feel worn out by this accursed year, this universal mental eclipse which has visited our dear fatherland.[3]

Chaim Khisin, a gymnasium student in Moscow, was also stunned and transformed by the turn of events. On February 10, 1882, he wrote in his diary:

Until these pogroms began I myself had thrust aside my Jewish origins. I considered myself a devoted son of Russia. I lived and breathed a Russian life and every new Russian scientific discovery, every new creation of Russian literature, every victory of Russian imperial power, everything Russian filled my heart with pride. My passionate desire was to devote my strength to my fatherland, to carry out all the duties of a good and honest citizen.... Then, suddenly, with no warning, we were shown the door and were told flatly: "The Western frontier is open to you." I am continuously haunted by the cruel, pointed question: "Who are you? Identify yourself—if you can".... I answer: "Of course, I'm a Russian." But I feel this would not be sincere. What true basis do I have for such an answer? Really, just my feelings and my dreams. But, lunatic that you are, don't you see that the Russians respond to this passionate love with the coldest and most offensive contempt?... Yes, whether I wish it or not, I am a Jew.[4]

Jewish university and gymnasium students encountered indifference and hostility, in some cases for the first time. In Odessa, Jewish students were told that the peasants were acting justly against the Jews who exploited them. Similar confrontations with anti-Semitism were reported from other cities. As a result, a number of students acted in ways that would have been unthinkable for them in the years before the pogroms. They returned to their people. On January 18, 1882, a day of public prayer and fasting was called by the leaders of Russian Jewry to petition both divine and government intervention on behalf of the Jewish community. Gymnasium and especially university students were conspicuous in their participation.

In Kiev, they participated in the prayers offered in the synagogue. What was even more startling was that they offered their services to the members of the congregation numbed by the violence in Kiev. They wrote songs, delivered speeches, and gave encouragement to thousands of Jews gathering in and around the synagogue. In St. Petersburg, too, students who had not only refused to have anything to do with Jewish life but had so often exhibited contempt toward it, appeared at the main synagogue to participate in its prayers and meetings.

The Odessa Jewish students took the lead in the formation of Jewish self-defense organizations. It was not an easy task. Rich Jews sought to dissuade them on the grounds that the authorities would become angry. The police said such activity was superfluous; the local constabulary together with the military would handle matters effectively. The fear of the Jewish masses themselves was also a problem, as was the procuring of weapons. Eventually the students succeeded in catalyzing for action groups of butchers, carters, and sellers of fruits and vegetables, and they managed, in May 1881, to defend some of the poorest Jewish streets against the *pogromshchiki*. These defense efforts would have been even more successful had the police and the military not stood aloof from the fighting. The latter further contributed to the weakening of Jewish defense by arresting some of the defenders on the grounds that they were the ones provoking the pogroms![5]

It was not only gymnasium and university students that demonstrated unexpected zeal for suffering Jewry. Newspaper accounts record the presence in the Choral Synagogue in St. Petersburg on January 18, 1882, of fashionably dressed businessmen, doctors, civil servants, and members of the Jewish intelligentsia. *"Pora domoi"* (It is time to go home) had become the slogan of many affluent and assimilated Jews who wanted to link themselves to the suffering ordinary Jew.[6]

PROVINCIAL JEWS AND EMIGRATION

Fear, demoralization, a turning inward, and occasional acts of self-defense do not exhaust the reactions of Russian Jews. In the areas directly affected by the pogroms, Jewish community leaders, rabbis and well-to-do business people vigorously countered the harsh attacks on Jews that came from the press and from the mouths of local citizens. Kutaisov reported that Jewish representatives were unanimous in rejecting Jewish exploitation as a cause of the pogroms.[7] He was told that Greeks, Armenians, Germans, and Tatars were also accused of exploitation, but there were no attacks against them. It was the inferior legal position of the Jews, the fact that they appeared as aliens to ordinary citizens of the empire, that made them vulnerable to pogroms. As a result of legal discrimination, claimed the Jews, all Jewish activity is seen as illegal and

Jewish wealth is viewed as ill-gotten. The Jews also denied the existence of a conspiratorial Kahal and declared that it was absurd for those unfamiliar with the Talmud to condemn it.

The provincial Jewish leaders were not content to defend the Jews against what they perceived as slander. They boldly argued the proposition that the government bore some responsibility for the pogroms because it had not effectively opposed the first ones in the spring of 1881. Christian businessmen, said the Jews, incited the pogroms to rid themselves of Jewish competition, and the anti-Semitic press contributed in no small measure to the outbreak of violence. The government must act decisively to crush disorders as soon as they appear. The Jews maintained that the only way out of the crisis was to end the legal discrimination against them and open up the Russian interior to Jewish settlement. Reconciliation and economic well-being would be the rewards of such a policy.

The most significant and consequential Jewish reactions, however, were not those of the students and intellectuals or even of provincial Jewish leaders but of the masses of ordinary, mostly poor Jews who had found themselves bearing the brunt of the pogrom hurricane. Their plight was a terrible one. Robbed of property, physically assaulted, their womenfolk on occasion violated, they were mute and powerless. Most remained immobile, too stunned to do anything. The more traditional attended the prayer services and fasted, or simply resigned themselves to yet another manifestation of divine will. For hundreds and later thousands, however, neither prayer, resignation, nor inertia was the answer. These people, on the contrary, believed in movement; they abandoned their former homes to find safer refuge somewhere else.

Some sought succor in larger cities and towns, and the urban areas of the Pale began to swell. Others, however, sought salvation not in the Pale and not in Russia, but overseas in America, Western Europe, and Palestine. The Russian Jewish emigration movement now began. It was carried out not by wealthy Jews living in St. Petersburg—they strenuously opposed it—and not by the members of the Russian Jewish intelligentsia—although in many cases they did support it—but by ordinary nondescript Jews who in their mundane fashion believed with no theoretical elaboration that the Jewish possibilities in Russia were played out.

An article in *Razsvet* comparing Jewish life in the provinces with that of the capital city, St. Petersburg, maintained that in terms of vitality and dynamism, leadership was passing to the provinces. There, people were thinking how to solve the Jewish problem; thought did not, as it so often did in the capital, lead to a paralysis of will. In the provinces, in contrast to the capital, people were both thinking and acting. Jews in the provinces were on the move.[8]

Wherever one went in the Pale talk of emigration was in the air. Groups, clubs, and informal circles were created to discuss the possibility of emigration and to facilitate it. The Hovevei Tsion (Lovers of Zion) movement, composed of tens, then later hundreds, of small circles, was established to focus attention on Palestine. Emigration reached dramatic proportions in early 1882 after Ignatiev's famous meeting with Orshanskii (see Chapter III). Regardless of what he really said or meant, Ignatiev led Jews to believe that the frontier was still open to Jewish emigration. In Kiev, a student wrote to the Jewish socialist Akselrod, in Switzerland, "Jews are now ready to emigrate anywhere."[9] In early 1882, *Razsvet* reported: "Our poor class lives only with the hope of emigration. Emigration, America, here is the motto for our brothers.[10] A letter to the periodical *Russkii Evrei* from Zhitomir declared that the drive to emigrate was so strong among the Jews of the city, that people hesitated to order garments made, and all credit was suspended.[11]

The desire to emigrate was not restricted to the poorest segments of the Jewish community; middle-class elements were also represented. It was very often university students, in most cases from the middle class, who provided leadership for the potential emigrants, articulating their aspirations and demands and championing emigration in general. Jewish university students at Novorossisk University in Odessa wrote to *Razsvet* in 1882, "Emigration—this is the only way out from the present situation, an escape not dictated by the intelligentsia to the people, but by the people to their spokesmen."[12] The common people, according to the students, looked to the intelligentsia for assistance, for information about America and Palestine.

Students in Kharkov also wrote to *Razsvet*, "Here is the only way out for Jews from their present situation. Emigration, boldly forward."[13] From Nikolaev, Bobrints, Warsaw, Minsk, Elizavetgrad, Kremenchug, Berdichev, Balta, Kherson, and other cities and towns students, teachers, and simple Jews bombarded the Russian Jewish periodicals with letters supporting emigration as a solution for the Jewish problem. They also called upon intellectuals and wealthy Jews, particularly the Jewish plutocrats living in St. Petersburg, to assist the emigration movement by providing it with adequate funds, information on potential places of settlement, and above all with organizational skills so as to end the chaos in the movement and bring to it some order.

In St. Petersburg, Jewish students actually met with Baron Horace Günzburg in early 1882 and asked him to lead a public committee which would organize and assist the emigration movement. After Ignatiev's statement, they told the baron, it was clear that the Jews were not wanted. Therefore, the Jews had to leave. The students were convinced that the pogroms were organized by the government and that there would be no relaxation of pressure. It was a criminal waste of time to delay. The students warned Günzburg and the other notables in St. Petersburg "in the name of the young generation that has not yet lost its self-respect, which loves its people, weeps for the injury done to it, and fears for its future, and in the name of all the House of Israel now given over to plunder and spoilation, abuse and shame," that the notables would be damned forever if they did not act to assist the emigration.[14] As will become clear, the students argued in vain.

INTELLIGENTSIA SUPPORT FOR PALESTINE

The murder, rape, and violence of the pogroms, and the repeated cries from the Pale for assistance, especially for emigration, forced the Russian Jewish intelligentsia and its publications to react. They first addressed themselves to detailed accounts of the pogroms and then, as much as the censors would allow, discussed their causes. The centuries-long legal and social discrimination against the Jews, which created the impression that this people was outside the law, a pariah people, was held to be responsible for the "events in the south." Soon, however, the masses of Jews streaming across the Pale, some toward Brody in the Austro-Hungarian Empire as a preliminary to immigration to America, coupled with large numbers of letters to the periodicals, compelled the Russian Jewish press to address the major question of the day, to emigrate or not to emigrate, and if to emigrate then where to go? For those intellectuals who believed in emigration there were only two possible places: America or Palestine.

Every one of the Jewish periodicals published in Russia lent its columns to the intense debates that raged over these questions. Generally, it can be said that *Razsvet* in Russian and *Ha-Melits* in Hebrew took a stand on emigration that soon had the aura of what was then called Palestinophilism, "Zionism" not yet having been coined. *Voskhod* and *Russkii Evrei* adhered for the most part to an anti-emigration position. However, the various periodicals were very democratic in their publication policies. The editorial board's position notwithstanding, each of the newspapers opened its columns to partisans of the opposing viewpoints. This was a tradition carried over from the 1860s and 1870s, when the Russian Jewish press published contrary views on the then-pressing issues of Russification and assimilation.

The pro-emigration forces were most notably displayed in the pages of *Razsvet*, although this periodical was initially ill-disposed toward the idea of emigration. The old belief in assimilation and emancipation was hard to abandon even after the first shock of the pogroms. Not long after the Elizavetgrad pogrom, *Razsvet* rejected emigration as a viable solution for the problems faced by the Jewish people. This was based in part on the old assimilationist patriotic sentiment. How could Jews "leave the sky unto which they were born, the land where they are buried.... The Jews will remain in Russia. Russia is their fatherland, the Russian land is their land. The sky of Russia is their sky."[15] Beyond sentiment, to emigrate was to accept the charge of the anti-Semites that the Jews were not loyal to Russia. By 1882, anti-emigration spokesmen from the Jewish plutocracy would play mightily upon this theme.

In the ensuing weeks and months, under the impact of the pogroms and the reports of its own correspondents in the provinces, *Razsvet* abandoned its earlier position and became a strong advocate of emigration. "We ... consider it [emigration] in the present moment to be the only measure which corresponds to the material interest of the unfortunate mass and to the moral interests of all Russian Jewry which is now in a condition of the most shocking moral oppression."[16] Its pages featured articles by writers supporting immigration either to Palestine or to America. But by late 1881, *Razsvet* had moved definitely into the camp of the "Palestinians." In June 1882 it was demanding that immigration to Palestine be made "a national, holy task."[17]

As supporters of migration to Palestine, the writers and the editors of *Razsvet* feared that if Jews went to America one of two things would happen to them: They would either vanish through assimilation or, if they competed successfully with the Americans, there would be created new soil for anti-Semitism and pogroms.[18] The *Razsvet* writers were particularly concerned with the question of how to ensure Jewish physical survival and at the same time protect against assimilation. They came to the conclusion that for the Jews to remain in Russia or even in Europe was to doom them to perpetual suffering—anti-Jewish sentiment was not, they believed, a temporary phenomenon. To avoid this suffering and to successfully preserve their national culture, the Jews needed "a Jewish corner of land," and where better than Palestine.

The strongest and perhaps most articulate supporter of immigration to Palestine who appeared in *Razsvet* was Moshe Leib Lilienblum. Lilienblum, it will be remembered, had been a moderate Russifier and a zealous partisan of religious and educational reform in the 1860s and 1870s. The pogroms traumatized him, shook him to his very core and sent him with great passion in another direction. Simply by looking at his diary notations for 1881 one can see the metamorphosis. In March he worries about the rumors of coming violence against the Jews. He is shocked, "the heart fails," at the first news from Elizavetgrad. In May he speaks of his own condition, of being under siege, of courtyards being barred up, of constant peering through the grillwork of the court gates to see if the mob is coming. He worries about saving the children if a pogrom takes place, and he laments: "Terrible, terrible! How long, O God of Israel." When the pogrom finally does come in early May he expresses gratitude not only that the *pogromshchiki* were soon frightened away by nearby soldiers but because he has, for the first time in his life, had the opportunity of feeling what his ancestors had felt every day of their lives.

More important, the pogroms changed the direction of Lilienblum's life. He writes:

In September I discontinued my studies at the gymnasium. Those intoxicated with Haskalah, of whom there are still many among us, will taunt me with my letter of August 4, 1877, in which I said: "I solemnly swear . . . to the last drop of blood in me that I must complete some course of studies. Even if the doctors tell me because of all the work involved I will come down with tuberculosis, and that within two days after completing my studies I will die—I still will not stop." And now I have abandoned the cause—for no apparent reason, out of what the "enlighteners" would regard as womanish timidity. But I say to them: In 1877 I thought, "My life is meaningless; for I cannot live like a human being if I lack high culture and formal education." At the end of 1881 I was inspired by a sublime ideal and I became a different man full of a sense of purpose and spiritual satisfaction even without secular schooling.[19]

For several months, Lilienblum pondered over the phenomenon of the pogroms. He wrote in his diary, corresponded with friends, and finally in *Razsvet* on October 9 and 16 of 1881 in articles entitled, "The General Jewish Problem and Palestine," he permitted his ideas to appear publicly.[20] Lilienblum placed the pogroms within the full context of Jewish history. The anti-Jewish sentiment that was surfacing in Russia and the rest of Europe was not a temporary episode, not an aberration. Hatred of the Jews had deep roots in European history. So deep, in fact, that Lilienblum was convinced that anti-Semitism will always be present in European civilization. The core of the problem, according to him, was to be found in the universal antipathy to strangers.

Lilienblum argued that just as a family is suspicious of strangers in its midst and grows to despise the stranger even more if he competes with members of the family or displaces them, so, too, within a nation do members of the nation resent and grow to hate strangers that compete with its natives. The crucial question, of course, was in the determination of who was a stranger and who was a native. In the Middle Ages it was not difficult to make such a differentiation. Christians were the natives, the legitimate sons of the political or social entity, and the Jews were the strangers. The result very often was that the Jewish strangers were forced to enter into occupations and trades that Christians either did not want or were prohibited from practicing. When the Jews enjoyed success this only infuriated the Christians even further.

Russia, in Lilienblum's view, was still in its medieval period, and, as a result, in the minds of many Russians, the Jews were still considered strangers because of their religion, or were resented on economic grounds. What was depressing to Lilienblum was his belief that not even increasing modernization would eliminate anti-Jewish sentiment. He looked at Western Europe and, like Moses Hess before him and Yehuda Leib Pinsker and Theodor Herzl after him, he perceived that in nineteenth-century Western and Central Europe it was still possible to label the Jews as strangers. But now the exclusion rested not on religious nor even economic grounds but on national ones. The new nationalism, with its strong dosage of racism, did not include the Jews. Germans did not view Jews as Teutons; Russians and Poles did not view them as Slavs; Hungarians did not view them as Magyars. The Jew, therefore, was still a stranger. No matter what the Jew may have thought of himself, he was still a stranger, an outcast, a competitor. Lilienblum drove his argument to its harsh and logical conclusion. As long as the Jews remained in Europe, there was no way of avoiding tension, conflict, and pogroms. No change of place or trade within Europe would solve the Jewish Question.

Lilienblum likewise rejected total assimilation as a viable alternative. For the individual it was cowardice beneath contempt, and for the nation it was an act of suicide. Prophetically, Lilienblum stated that assimilation would not work because no nationality would accept even assimilated Jews; they would still be considered strangers.

There was one way out. The Jews must find a place where they "could exist as masters and not as aliens."[21] Jews, in short, must leave Europe no matter how long it might take. But he rejected America as a place of settlement because in time the Jews would be considered strangers there too. The only place was Eretz-Yisroel (the Land of Israel) to which the Jews "have a historic right which was not abolished and not lost by us along with our [lost] independent rule of the country."[22] No people of the Balkans had lost its rights to lands when it no longer ruled over them and neither should the Jews. The alternative to settling Palestine was humiliation, loss of self-respect, and possible catastrophe.

By 1882, Lilienblum's articles supporting Palestinophilism were appearing in journals other than *Razsvet*. He had become the most articulate spokesman of the cause and a fervent combatant against those who either opposed Palestine as a place of settlement or, while accepting it, gave primacy of place to other problems and issues. In April of 1882, in *Ha-Melits*, he published an article attacking the position of another important figure in the Russian Jewish intelligentsia, Yehudah Leib Gordon, who had expressed his views in the article, "Our Redemption and the Saving of Our Lives." In this article Gordon accepted in somewhat qualified fashion the concept of small-scale Jewish settlement in Palestine but continued to adhere to the old *maskil* view that reform and modernization of the Jewish way of life were the chief needs of the time. As will be seen below, Gordon's real passion was neither for Palestine nor for reform but for mass migration to America.

It was in order to refute not only Gordon but others, including those in the orthodox camp, who were beginning to debate the nature of the future of Jewish settlement in Palestine with such fervor that the entire cause was being jeopardized, that Lilienblum wrote his short essay, "Let Us Not Confuse the Issues" for *Ha-Melits*. For Lilienblum, religious reform, the place of Orthodoxy in Jewish Palestine, and even economic issues were all secondary. There was only one question worth talking about. "Are the Jews to be a living people or not? In the face of this question all others pale into insignificance."[23]

Since the continuation of the Jews as a people was, for Lilienblum, tied up with their restoration in Palestine, it was necessary that the curse of Jewish life in the Diaspora, the constant and harsh feuding between different schools of thought, be moderated. Supporters of Palestinophilism in Russia and settlers in Palestine must substitute cooperation for conflict. Otherwise the whole enterprise would come to naught. He appealed for tolerance and projected a future Jewish community in Palestine that would be composed of all the different shades of opinion that made up the Jewish people.

The nation as a whole is dearer to all of us than all the divisions of a rigid orthodoxy or liberalism in religious observance put together. Where the nation is concerned there are no sects or denominations, there are neither modern nor old fashioned men, no devout nor heretics, but all are children of Abraham, Isaac, and Jacob! Any one of the Jewish seed who does not forsake his people is a Jew in every sense of the word. It has been well said that, just as people do not have identical faces, so are they not of one mind. There is no logic in any desire for all of the future settlers in the ancestral land to belong to the exact same sect. Let each man there follow the dictates of his own conscience; let the *Hasidim* there put on two sets of *Tephillin* [phylacteries] and let the more liberal recite the *Shema* and say the prayers where they will without *Tephillin*; let the orthodox send their children to the *Hedarim* they will establish in the image of the *Hedarim* of Lithuania and Poland, and let the *Maskilim* set up schools patterned after the secular schools of Europe. But let no man oppress his fellow. Within our autonomous political life everything will find its place.[24]

Lilienblum appealed to the orthodox Jews to recognize that all Russian Jews, unbelievers and orthodox alike, were holy. All Jews were suffering, were being humiliated, were laying down their lives for the "Sanctification of the Name." The Jews were living in fear and yet had not betrayed their origins nor lost courage. "Is this not self-sacrifice for the Sanctification of the Name? Is not our entire community holy? Let the Orthodox see that we are one with them in travail."[25]

He also cautioned the *maskilim* not to divorce themselves so radically from Jewish tradition. They must not introduce the forbidden foods nor do away with the ritual bath. If they did these things, a terrible disunity would be introduced into the Jewish community in Palestine. The orthodox would refuse to eat in their homes or to marry among them. Moderation on all sides was Lilienblum's answer to the long-existing divisions among Russian Jews. Moderation would lead to tolerance and tolerance would lead to peaceful relations, a state of mind among Jews that was so desperately necessary at this critical time. Only through submerging all divisions and unifying all forces could the salvation of Israel be assured.

Lilienblum was not the only prominent *maskil* to be affected by the pogroms. Lev Levanda, that passionate advocate of *obrusenie* who in the 1860s had declared that "under the flag of Russification we shall receive a fatherland," was stunned by the violence in the south. In his case, however, the turnabout was neither so sharp nor quick as it was with Lilienblum. Throughout 1881 and early 1882, Levanda, hurt and troubled though he was, had difficulty in abandoning his former belief in Russification and confluence. In 1881 Levanda, in relatively objective fashion, commented on the growth of the pro-Palestine movement, particularly among Jewish intellectuals. It was a consequence, he felt, of the great despair that was experienced by these people following the apparent failure of Jewish assimilation. In the past thirty years the best among the new Jewish generations had supported the idea of confluence for the sake of which they were ready to surrender all their traditions. Levanda was convinced that the mental and physical suffering generated by the pogroms was responsible for the increasing talk about Palestine and that if conditions improved such talk would vanish. "Let our circumstances change somewhat for the better, let us cease to feel that the ground is shaking under us and disappearing from under our legs and— we are certain—that the dreamer who so picturesquely depicts for us a picture of an independent Palestine, that galvanized mummy, will sing, together with many other Russian Jews, 'I am a Russian and I love my home.' "[26]

In early 1882, Levanda was still standing apart from the emigration movement. To those who demanded that both financial and organizational assistance be given to the emigrants, Levanda preached the principle of non-interference—"Laissez-faire, laissez-passer." Subsequent pogroms, however, particularly the one in Balta, rocked Levanda back on his heels. Experiencing what seems to have been a profound spiritual crisis, he finally abandoned his former beliefs and became convinced of the inevitability of the Jews' leaving Russia and the need for a resurrection of the Jewish nation in Palestine. *Razsvet*, in the second half of 1882, became the sounding board for the new Levanda. He wrote that

a black cat (the pogroms) had come between Russians and Jews. Levanda
had no doubt as to who had pushed the cat forward and for what reason.
The most important thing was that the cat had left physical and moral
consequences which would not disappear for decades. There was only
one solution for Russian Jewry, a mass exodus. But Levanda warned
Jews that they must be careful where they go lest they be turned into
gypsies. No matter what country they chose they would somehow,
someday be forced to leave. Levanda's pessimism derived from his belief
that Judeophobia was not a temporary or accidental phenomenon but
a historical constant. What was even worse, in Levanda's eyes, was the
direction being taken by European civilization. It had progressed as high
as it could and was now about to plunge into a rapid descent, a new
wave of barbarism would descend upon Europe.[27]

The Jews, according to Levanda, needed a "new, real, true and not
an imaginary or perfidious land," a land with a Jewish nationality and
Jewish flavor. Only Palestine could serve this purpose. With the passion
and sincerity of the true convert, Levanda lashed out at his opponents,
the partisans of his former ideals. He ridiculed the Jewish intelligentsia
for its foolish hopes in assimilation and Russification. What had they
gotten in return? He castigated the Jewish intelligentsia, the Jewish
bourgeoisie and the rabbis for opposing immigration to Palestine, the
only salvation for the Jewish people. About Palestine, "we must now
think day and night, when we arise and when we go to sleep."[28] The
Palestinophiles had another articulate spokesman.

It would be a mistake to view the movement in support of immigration
to Palestine as emanating only from the Russified members of the Jewish
intelligentsia and from *Razsvet*. Talk of recreating a Jewish polity in the
ancient homeland was bound also to attract and stir the hearts of the
old-style *maskilim*, progressive and secularized men of letters who wrote
and conversed in Hebrew, and even of more orthodox Jews who were
not oblivious to contemporary events and patterns of thought. The He-
brew-language periodicals such as *Ha-Melits* and *Ha-Magid*, particularly
the former, published a myriad of articles in support of immigration to
Palestine, although here, too, a democratic policy of opening the newspaper columns to dissident voices was practiced. In March and April of
1882, Alexander Tsederbaum, the editor and publisher of *Ha-Melits*,
wrote that at the Passover Seder, Russian Jews, facing the reality that
there was no alternative to emigration, had to decide whether to say,
"In the coming year may we be in Jerusalem," or, "May we in this
coming year be in America." The Russian government had decided that
there was no place in Russia for the Jews. It had told them to get out.
"We are like stunned creatures and do not know where to go or where
to turn."[29]

Tsederbaum attempted to analyze the personalities of the two types of potential emigrants. One is so enamored of nineteenth-century ideals and culture that he can find satisfaction only in modern metropolitan centers, where there are great activity and vitality, railroads, steamboats, and telegraph: They will go to America. There are others, however, infused with religious fervor and love of their people, who would rather spend one hour in the Holy Land than all of their lives in the lands of the dispersion: For them there is only Palestine. Tsederbaum, to preserve a cohesive Jewish people, rejected America as a place of settlement, for it would mean, if the Jews settled in the various states of that large country, their dispersal and eventual assimilation. The sense of Jewish peoplehood would disappear. Only settlement in the ancient homeland could preserve the Jewish people. There and only there could the Jew toil without fear of enmity and at the same time preserve his national consciousness.

Ha-Melits did not shrink from criticizing the leaders of both Russian and European Jewry for their disinterest in immigration to Palestine. Zalman Epstein and Chaim Vitkin, the first a Hebrew essayist, the second an educated merchant and writer, both exclaimed: "Where are our great men when it comes to the issue of Jewish settlement in Palestine." Rabbis and Jewish financiers, particularly the Rothschilds, were called upon to respond to the distress of millions of their people.

Open your treasures and purchase alms and vineyards for us in the Holy Land, build houses there in which we may dwell and sheepfolds for our sheep. Let your choices be heard in all the publications that you are ready to make available a piece of property and a vineyard for each Jewish family and immediately from North, South, East and West your brethren will fly like eagles.[30]

The heads of Jewish organizations were asked to mute their enthusiasm for America and, instead, to raise the flag of Zion.

America was played down as a place of settlement in Ha-Melits. Readers were told that only earlier immigrant Jewish groups, from Hungary and Austria, had enjoyed success in the country, but that for Russian and Polish Jews the situation was grim. "They live like birds that go searching each day for a bit of bread. This bit is getting less each day as the number of poor immigrants increases with new arrivals."[31] The situation was so bad that "they cursed the day they came to America." Even if economic conditions improved, settlement in America was dangerous. The Jewish soul would still be in jeopardy. Anti-Jewish feeling might also one day present a problem. Only in "the land of our fathers" would prosperity and freedom from hatred and insults be the lot of the Jewish people.

One of the most perceptive series of articles to appear in Ha-Melits was written by Dr. Herman Schapira, the future founder of the Jewish

National Fund. Schapira, in contrast to most of the Palestinophiles, did not lament the fact that so many Russian Jews were going to America and other places besides Palestine. From wherever they went and prospered, they would support the settlement of Palestine and influence their governments in its behalf. The Diaspora was indispensable for the successful colonization of Palestine. Moreover, since settlement in Palestine was bound to be extremely difficult, it was perhaps more advantageous for the ultimate success of the enterprise that masses of immigrants did not come at once.

It is much better for us that the foundation which we will establish in our ancestral land shall be with people who have chosen to live there, not because they are forced to but because they have chosen this path freely out of love for their people and their homeland and because of their sincere desire to labor in the Holy Land with greatest enthusiasm. Such people are prepared to make the fullest sacrifice of their means and might.[32]

Curiously, it was not *Ha-Melits* and *Razsvet*, not Lilienblum and Levanda, not even Smolenskin—who under the impact of the pogroms finally moved from cultural to political nationalism and endorsed the idea of a Jewish state in the ancient home—that had the greatest influence on the movement in support of Palestine as the Jewish homeland.[33] Nor was it Joel Linetski or Shimon Frug. The former, the author of the extremely popular *Dos Poylishe Yingel*, in the 1880s participated in the debate over America and Palestine by warning about the perils of assimilation in America and calling for preparation for settlement in Palestine. But his series of short pamphlets on the subject did not seem to have the impact that his earlier novel did.

Frug, who in the late 1880s and 1890s became the great poetic spokesman for the nationalist and Zionist aspirations of his people, whose words tugged at their heartstrings, was making his first public appearance as a poet in 1881 and 1882. He began in February 1881 by publishing tender poems about his beloved Russia, the "Second Zion." The pogroms turned him around; his rapture for Russian fields and meadows was replaced by a fervent call for exodus and return. One of his poems, which appeared in *Razsvet* on January 5, 1882, elicited an enthusiastic response. Frug cried out to his people:

Why have you stopped in the middle of the road
And lowered your gray head?. . .
March ahead through the peoples and the centuries
Across the abyss of suffering and the chains of misfortune. . . .
Forward under the sounds of the old song!

The future is calling...
And the thunders are crying to us: Rise again!
The storms are singing hymns to us!...
Forward! Forward!!...[34]

Yet it was only later that a more mature and sophisticated Frug became a great and influential literary figure espousing the cause of Jewish nationalism.

PINSKER

It was left for a middle-aged Jewish physician from Odessa, Yehuda Leib Pinsker, who had spent virtually his entire adult life endorsing Russification and moderate assimilation as the solutions for the Jewish questions in Russia, to stir the imagination of his coreligionists. It was also Pinsker who began the process of organizing the movement to the point where it could be said that Russian Zionism was an active and at least partially successful political movement during the ten years before Theodor Herzl convened the first Zionist congress in Basle in 1897. This is all the more remarkable since Pinsker's seminal work, *Auto-Emancipation*, was published for the first time outside of Russia and in German. Even more incredible is the fact that Pinsker's little book deliberately refused to endorse Palestine as the place for Jewish settlement and salvation. Nonetheless, he was the catalyst, the man who more than any other deserves the title of founder of Russian Zionism.

For Pinsker, the contemporary position of the Jews was derived from the fact that they were considered by everyone and every nation as aliens, strangers. "They are everywhere as guests and are nowhere at home."[35] No matter what the Jew did, no matter how much the Jew renounced his own nationality, he never succeeded in being recognized by his fellow citizens as of equal rank. This, of course, was if the Jew was lucky. If he was unlucky, then his fellow citizens did not merely regard him as being unequal; they viewed him with hatred and contempt and, on occasion, lashed out at him with fury and violence. The pogroms of 1881–1882 were such an occasion.

The strangeness of the Jew, the fact that no one accepted him and many hated him was, for Pinsker, a natural development, because it was rooted in the human psyche. All human beings at all times and in all places have a fear of ghosts. It was an inborn mental trait. The tragedy of the Jews was that they appeared as ghosts to the Europeans among whom they were living. The Jews had lost both their fatherland and their independence and, consequently, had fallen into decay. But even after their state had been crushed in full view of all humanity, they did not cease to exist as a spiritual nation. The result was that in the eyes of the world the Jews took on "the uncanny form of one of the dead walking among the living ... no longer alive and yet moving among the living."[36] The ultimate result, given the natural fear of ghosts, was Judeophobia.

While this was the primary cause of anti-Semitism, it was not the only one, although the other one stressed by Pinsker was closely related. Pinsker saw the Jew as the stranger par excellence, the most alien of all foreigners, who can make no claim on any nation's hospitality. This characteristic of the Jews was a consequence of the fact that the Jew has no fatherland. The foreigner can claim hospitality because he can repay it in the same coin. The Jew, devoid of a fatherland, can make no such promise and, therefore, has no claim to hospitality. "He, the Jew, is more like a beggar and what beggar is welcome? He is rather a refugee, and where is the refugee to whom a refuge may not be refused?"[37]

The Jews were aliens who had no representatives to defend their interests, because they had no fatherland. Nothing could alter this alienation of the Jew, not even the fact that he himself and his ancestors were born in the country where they lived. The Jew is always a stepchild, the Cinderella, never is he considered a legitimate son of the fatherland. The contempt for the Jewish alien, moreover, is heightened when the Jews compete with the natives, often successfully. Charges and complaints of Jewish exploitation abound. In sum, "For the living the Jew is a dead man, for the natives an alien and a vagrant, for property holders a beggar, for the poor an exploiter and millionaire, for patriots a man without a country, for all classes a hated rival."[38]

In Pinsker's eyes, it was necessary to confront this reality honestly and with courage. It was necessary, above all, to recognize that Judeophobia, hatred of the Jews, was a two-thousand-year-old hereditary and incurable disease, peculiar to the human race and based in the final analysis on aberrations of the human mind. The enmity toward Jews was, therefore, a natural antagonism; it would not disappear. It was time to abandon the old illusions. The legal emancipation of the Jews might or might not be a crowning achievement of the nineteenth century but it most certainly had not led to social emancipation. In their heart of hearts the great majority of Europeans continued to despise Jews and no amount of legislation emancipating them could alter this.

A rise in the educational level of the Russian and Ukrainian masses would not solve the problem. Pinsker referred to the editors and publishers of Russian newspapers and periodicals who vied with the peasants and workers in expressing anti-Jewish sentiments. Likewise, vociferous manifestations of patriotism on the part of the Jews would avail them nothing since the Jews would always be reminded of their Semitic descent.

The crucial thing for Pinsker was that Jews draw the right conclusions.

The natural and very human antagonism toward them meant that the Jews must change their tactics if they were to survive. There was no sense in continuing to struggle against what were inevitable and natural impulses. Polemics and appeals to decency, morality, and international law were and would be of no use.

We must reconcile ourselves, once and for all, to the idea that the other nations, by reason of their eternal, natural antagonism, will forever reject us. We must not shut our eyes to this natural force, which works like every other elemental force; we must take it into account. We must not complain of it; on the contrary, we are in duty bound to take courage, to rise and see to it that we do not remain forever the Cinderella, the butt of the peoples.[39]

The answer for Pinsker was simple and straightforward; the Jews had to have a land of their own. The Jews must receive what the Serbs and the Romanians had received. Surely, asked Pinsker, do not the Jews have the right to have similar aspirations? His answer was that since both Jewish contributions to history and Jewish suffering at the hands of humanity exceeded that of the Serbs and Romanians, the Jews were certainly capable and worthy of possessing a homeland. When that happy day arrived, the time of the Jewish parasite, exploiter, alien, and ghost would have passed. In its stead would come even greater Jewish contributions to humanity than before, and a recognition of the Jews as equals.

It was a day, Pinsker conceded, that would be long in coming. Nonetheless, since the alternative was the present oppression and humiliation, work toward the goal had to begin. The obstacles were imposing. Jewish Orthodoxy, with its belief that the dispersion was an act of Providential Will in response to Jewish sin, and its promise that only the Messiah could bring about the resurrection of the Jewish people, generated a sense of passivity. The daily struggle for existence also took its toll. Caught in a battle to avoid extermination, individual Jews had fought alone the hard and unequal struggle for a little oxygen and a morsel of bread. The Jews did not succumb in this virtually hopeless struggle, but the peoples of the world had succeeded "in destroying in us the feeling of our national independence." Religious teaching and a miserable existence, wrote Pinsker, had combined to create a situation in which "the people without a fatherland forgot their fatherland."[40]

Once it was recognized that a land of their own was needed, the Jews had to start the process of selecting such a land. It was imperative that the Jews themselves take the first step; there must be no waiting for divine intervention. Believing in the precept that God helps those that help themselves, Pinsker was convinced that both divine and human persistence would be forthcoming once the project was underway. Auto-emancipation, self-help, was the key to success. Pinsker himself did not have one particular place in mind, although he was in fact inclined against settlement in Palestine and leaned in the direction of North America. As long as the Jews, wherever they went, took with them their most sacred possessions from Judea, which they had carried over the centuries, the Bible and the idea of God, they would be guaranteed their cohesion and uniqueness. "It is only these which have made our old fatherland the Holy Land, and not Jerusalem or the Jordan."[41]

The actual process of selecting a land was to be the task of a national congress or directorate composed of the leaders of the various Jewish societies throughout the world, as well as the best elements from the Jewish people—financiers, scientists, and statesmen. Once a land was chosen, the directorate would facilitate the creation of a stock company composed of great Jewish capitalists from Western Europe which would act to purchase the land in question. In addition to the money received from the most affluent segments of world Jewry, the directorate was also to conduct fund raising among the millions of ordinary Jews throughout the world. The final step would be gaining the assistance of the leading statesmen of Europe, for Pinsker was convinced that without such help the goal could not be accomplished. The most important thing, Pinsker urged again and again, was timing. It was now or never for the Jewish people. The time was ripe; many Europeans, both Jewish and non-Jewish, were convinced that only a land of their own could save the Jewish people. Time was also running out for the Jews in that anti-Semitism was growing rapidly, not only in Russia, but in the more enlightened countries of Central and Western Europe. "Woe to our descendants, woe to the memory of our Jewish contemporaries, if we let this moment pass by."[42]

In retrospect, Pinsker's views as expressed in *Auto-Emancipation* appear naive and somewhat lacking in perception. There was even something banal in the work, since most of the ideas had been advanced before by others, especially in Russia where Lilienblum had said earlier some of the same things. Pinsker's analysis of Judeophobia would be regarded as deficient by modern scholars because he paid insufficient attention to the Christian roots of the anti-Semitic impulse. The Jews may indeed have appeared as ghosts and aliens to contemporary Europeans, but this flowed from earlier Christian views of them. Similarly, Pinsker barely hints at other factors behind the rise of the "new anti-Semitism" in the second half of the nineteenth century—the rise of nationalism, the development of the racial conception of history, and the impact of industrialization on European society. But he was right, whatever the reasons he gave for it, on the fundamental issue, the humiliation and danger facing Jews if they remained within the European states. Not even he, however, could envision the apocalypse that would descend upon European Jewry in the twentieth century.

Whatever the analytical value of *Auto-Emancipation*, the ideas expressed in it generated passionate discussion even before the book appeared, and most certainly after. Before he began to write, Pinsker traveled through Central and Western Europe as well as England, to test his ideas out on various Jewish leaders. He received very little support. One of the prominent leaders of Central European Jewry, the Chief Rabbi of Vienna, Dr. Adolf Jellinek, a close friend of Pinsker's father, made it clear to Pinsker that he was dead wrong. "You exaggerate the importance of anti-Semitism," Jellinek said. "This poisonous plant which sprouted on the banks of the Spree will wither faster than you can imagine, since it has no roots in history."[43] Only in England was the response a bit more positive. A Jewish member of Parliament, Arthur Cohen, agreed with Pinsker's analysis and encouraged him to put it into writing and present his case to the public. It was after this meeting that Pinsker returned to Berlin to write *Auto-Emancipation*.

The reaction to the published book itself was equally lukewarm as far as areas outside of Russia were concerned. German Jewish newspapers attacked Pinsker for his pessimism and for his desire to reverse the course of history. The forward march of history, they claimed, meant that emancipation would some day come to backward Russia as it had already come to Germany and France. Moreover, they asserted that since Jews had been fully integrated into society in many parts of Europe and shared the same national consciousness as did their compatriots, it was foolish to expect them to march backwards and resurrect a sense of Jewish nationalism. Virtually all of the rabbis of Germanic Europe, the Chief Rabbi of Meml, Isaac Rulf, excepted, were either indifferent to or opposed the views set forth in *Auto-Emancipation*.

In America the response was much more muted. There, Emma Lazarus, herself of German Jewish origin, and, therefore, presumably able to read the book in the original, expressed support for Pinsker. In November, 1882, she wrote in one of her *Epistles to the Hebrews*, "With his fiery eloquence and his depth and fervor of conviction, this anonymous author could scarcely fail to enkindle the imagination of his Jewish readers, even if he stood alone."[44]

It was, however, in Russia that the book elicited the most discussion and the greatest support. Its author almost overnight became one of the great heroes of Russian Jewry in the last two decades of the nineteenth century. It was after all in Russia that the situation was grimmest and there that talk of emigration was loudest. The Hovevei Tsion groups which endorsed immigration to Palestine and America were sprouting up in the Pale. Pinsker helped the movement along by being so concise and straightforward in his analysis and appeal. The thirty some pages analyzing the causes of anti-Semitism and the only viable remedy for it contrasted favorably to the wordy and more ambiguous statements made by others earlier. The fact that he, a Russian Jew, wrote in German before a foreign public seemed to enhance his position in the eyes of Russian Jewish intellectuals. In this as in so much else Pinsker fore-shadowed Theodor Herzl.

There were some problems, however. Many of those who rallied to him in Russia shared his belief in the necessity of emigration and the need to create a Jewish homeland but disagreed with him sharply on the question of where the homeland ought to be. For them, the only place for the resurrection of the Jewish people was the ancestral home-land, Palestine. From late 1882, when Pinsker returned to Odessa, until 1884, he was subjected to a voluminous correspondence from supporters of Palestinophilism, particularly Lilienblum and Levanda, who at-tempted to persuade him to accept Palestine as the place of settlement. They also wished to capitalize upon his great popularity by placing him at the head of an organization, Hibbat Tsion (Love of Zion), which would unify all the small circles supporting immigration to Palestine. Pinsker yielded to the pressure to place himself at the head of Hibbat Tsion but to the end of his life, while he remained a passionate advocate of emi-gration, he did not particularly believe that Palestine should be the national home. He steadfastly refused, despite repeated appeals, to re-write *Auto-Emancipation* in this vein. Nevertheless, from 1884 until his death in 1891, Pinsker was the universally accepted leader of Hibbat Tsion.

RUSSIAN JEWS IN PALESTINE

With all of the talk and writing about the desirability of settlement in Palestine one would have expected a veritable wave of migrants to that land. This was, however, not the case. For the period 1881–1882 the total number of Russian Jewish immigrants to Palestine did not exceed several hundred. And for the entire decade, in fact, there were only several thousand Russian Jewish immigrants to the country. There were several reasons for this state of affairs. First of all, not one of the major Jewish organizations in or outside of Russia endorsed the idea of a return to the Holy Land. This was most notably true of the Alliance Israélite Universelle, the largest, wealthiest, and best known of all the Jewish organizations. Charles Netter of the Alliance wrote the *Jewish Chronicle* (London) on March 24, 1882, that Palestine was too poor, the land too barren, and the population too hostile. It could not possibly absorb large numbers of immigrants.[45] The reluctance of the Ottoman Empire to allow Jewish settlement in Palestine because of the fear that such settlement would lead to a call for an independent Jewish state, a precedent that would be very dangerous for that multinational empire, also led the Alliance to downplay the Palestinian option. As will be seen in Chapter VI, the Alliance was much more optimistic concerning the possibility of mass settlement in America.

The poor prospects for settlement in Palestine were not unknown to the Russian Jewish public. For decades, if not for centuries, Russian Jews, like all Jews in the Diaspora, were accustomed to providing *haluka* (charity) for the small Jewish community in Palestine. The poverty of this community and the general backwardness of the area were common knowledge. Nothing that came back from Palestine, in the letters from those who migrated there in early 1882 or in articles in various Jewish periodicals, was likely to change the minds of most prospective Jewish emigrants from Russia. And, there was always the pull of the other option, America. Knowledge of the free, dynamic, wealthy nation burgeoning overseas was penetrating into the nooks and crannies of the distant Pale. For most emigrants it was a far more attractive choice. The appeal of America, and the backwardness, hardships, and absence of organizational sponsorship of settlements in Palestine were not conducive to a return to the ancient home of the Jews.

Nonetheless, in spite of all the obstacles, there was a small but steady stream of Russian Jewish immigrants into Palestine. It was the beginning of what in Zionist history is referred to as the First Aliyah, the first "going up" to Palestine. Its small numbers and its modest achievements notwithstanding, these first immigrants and those that followed them in the later 1880s laid the foundations of the Yishuv, the modern Jewish community in Palestine. The subsequent creation of the State of Israel is inconceivable without them, and therefore this small episode in the Russian Jewish emigration movement of 1881–1882, minor in comparison to the mass exodus to America, deserves attention.

Among the few immigrants to Palestine in 1882, the ones that attracted the greatest attention, both at the time and afterwards, belonged to the small group that took as its name the acronym Bilu, the Hebrew initials for *Beit Yaakov Lekhu ve-nelkah*: "House of Jacob, come ye and let us go" (Isaiah 2:5). The *biluim*, as they were called, originated among university students and middle-class Jews in Kharkov in February 1882. Beginning with only fifty people, the Kharkov *biluim* campaigned for support in other cities; within several months the membership had risen to 525 members.

The *biluim* were greatly influenced by the intellectual ambiance of late nineteenth-century Russia. Since most of them were from the middle classes, and therefore literate and educated, they were not oblivious to the emphasis of Russian Populism on the importance of personal sacrifice, agricultural labor, and socialism. Accordingly, the *biluim* envisioned establishing in Palestine farming communes where there would be no private property and in which members would dedicate all of their means to the well-being of the commune. The commitment to the cause meant that members were also to postpone marriage for an indefinite period of time.

These agricultural communes were to be the seeds of the subsequent restoration of the Jewish homeland. In the spirit of Russian Populism and its "going to the people" movement, which saw the Populists or *narodniki* as the inspirers of the people, the communes were to be the leavening agents for the coming massive immigration to Palestine. The residents of the communes, the most dedicated *biluim*, were to be the spiritual guides and teachers of the future Yishuv. Jewish society in Palestine was to be based on social justice, the absence of exploitation, Jewish labor working in agriculture and industry, and most important, the recreation of Jewish political independence after centuries of Diaspora dependency and vulnerability. Zeev Dubnov, brother of the great historian Simon, and one of the first members of Bilu actually to settle in Palestine, wrote of the primary aim of the organization:

The final goals or *Pia Desideria* are with time to possess Palestine and to return to the Jews the political independence of which they were deprived over two thousand years ago. Do not laugh, this is no chimera. The means for the achievement of these goals can be: the construction of agricultural and artisanal colonies in Palestine, the construction of different types of factories and plants, and their gradual expansion—in a word, to strive to place all of the land, all of the industry in Jewish hands.... Then will come that splendid day the coming of which Isaiah foretold.... Then the Jews ... will in a loud voice declare themselves masters of their old homeland.[46]

The history of Bilu was not limited to expressions of great hopes and aspirations. Disappointment, defection, and discord are the main themes running through the organization's history, although, to be sure, there were some small successes. From the very beginning, Bilu was plagued by problems. Expectations of a substantial influx of funds from wealthy Jews did not materialize. The opposition of the Turkish government to Jewish settlement led to further demoralization and a decline in the ardor of many members for immigration to Palestine. Defections from Bilu, both in Russia and Palestine, became widespread from the middle of 1882 on. There was also considerable disappointment among members when their faith in Lawrence Oliphant, one of the first so-called "Gentile Zionists" turned out to be misplaced. Oliphant, an Englishman, had written and spoken in behalf of a Jewish return to Palestine several years before the pogroms. In 1882, while visiting Jewish refugees in Brody and Lemburg in behalf of the Mansion House Relief Fund for Russian Refugees, Oliphant again spoke of the desirability of Jewish settlement in Palestine and was acclaimed by the Palestinophiles, some of whom came to view him as a new Messiah. Perhaps carried away by the adulation, Oliphant encouraged those who wrote to him for assistance, including a number of *biluim*. A few of the latter actually visited him in Constantinople and asked him to intercede with the Sultan for permission to settle in Palestine. When Oliphant failed to gain such an agreement, the ranks of the *biluim* began to thin out.

The problems of the *biluim* were not confined to Russia and to Oliphant. Even among the faithful, who did not abandon the idea of settlement in Palestine, there was tension and disagreement over tactics. Anticipating Zionist debates fifteen and twenty years later, some believed that the only way to achieve success for the enterprise was to continue negotiations with the Sultan that would lead to an agreement permitting mass settlement in Palestine. Others argued that it was unnecessary and undesirable to wait for the Sultan's approval of mass settlement: The *biluim* should proceed to Palestine immediately and begin the process of settling the land. Even very small numbers of settlers, they claimed, would be a step in the right direction.

The result was that a split occurred among the eighteen *biluim* in Constantinople and only fourteen of them left for Palestine. The difficulties they experienced are poignantly depicted in their letters to relatives and friends remaining in Russia. Possessing no money, the fourteen young *biluim*, including two women, were forced to hire themselves out as laborers in the only Jewish agricultural settlement in Palestine at that time, the Mikveh Israel agricultural school. Unaccustomed to hard physical labor, the young people had a difficult time adjusting to a work day that began at five o'clock in the morning and ended at approximately the same time in the afternoon. There were also problems with the manager of the enterprise, an Alsatian Jew, who, like so many Western Jews, had nothing but contempt for his coreligionists from Eastern Europe. Finally, the by now familiar curse of discord and squabbling among the *biluim* arose once again. Several of them, particularly those who had been leaders of the organization in Russia and Constantinople, considered physical labor beneath their status, and occupied themselves with conducting "negotiations" with the *biluim* that remained in Constantinople. The ordinary *biluim* did not react kindly to this.

What had begun as a movement with such great idealism and fervor in early 1882 had by the end of the year little to show for all its enthusiasm, hope, and hard work. By December 1882, in all of Palestine there were approximately thirty *biluim*. They had not managed to establish a single settlement of their own and would not do so until December 1884 when they finally settled in Gedera, the eighth Jewish settlement founded in modern Palestine.

Yet, for all of their disappointments and failures, the *biluim*, especially those who settled and suffered in Palestine in 1882, left their mark on the history of Zionism and Israel. It was the *biluim* that became a symbol for later generations of Jewish immigrants to Palestine. They established and propagated the mystique of the *chalutzim*, the pioneers, who tilled the soil, fought the heat and the insects, and sacrificed everything— personal comfort, security, marriage, family, property—for the cause of a Jewish Palestine. It was a legend that became embellished as the years passed. The *biluim* were given credit for things they had not done. The symbol was to be transformed into a myth, and unreal though it may have been, it served as an inspiration and guide for subsequent gen- erations of settlers who would be called upon to make even greater sacrifices for the sake of that cause.

The *biluim*, for all of the attention paid them, constituted only a very small number of those Jews who entered Palestine in 1882. There were several hundred Yemenite Jews and much smaller numbers of Russian and Romanian Jews who immigrated to Palestine in 1882, in addition to the *biluim*. These Russian Jews differed from the *biluim* in a number of ways. While they were ideologically committed to the idea of a na- tional resurrection in Palestine for the Jewish people, they were not ideologues who belonged to organizations espousing specific goals. They came as individuals. They were not enraptured with their own theories, and were therefore not vulnerable to ferocious and enervating internal conflicts. They did not carry with them the socialist baggage of the *biluim*, which was only an additional burden for those experiencing the difficult problems of settlement in a harsh land. Most important, many of these immigrants were family people; husbands, wives, and children. The presence of dependents generated a diligence and practicality that was conducive to successful settlement. By August 1882, under the leader- ship of the very capable Zalman David Levontin, the representatives of thirteen families established south of Jaffa one of the first Jewish settle- ments of the 1880s, Rishon le-Zion (The First in Zion), the first Jewish settlement established in modern Palestine by immigrants. The *biluim*, the Yemenites, the Romanian Jews, and the other Russian Jews, small in number even when added together, were by late 1882 establishing a toehold for Jewish settlement in Palestine. It was not the exodus that the Palestinophiles had imagined, but it was a beginning. The modern Yishuv was in the process of creation.

INTELLIGENTSIA SUPPORT FOR AMERICA

The large number of Russian Jewish intellectuals calling for a rebirth of the Jewish nation in its ancient homeland and the attention given to settlers in Palestine should not mislead us. America, too, had its cham- pions and while they do not seem to be as many or as prestigious as those of the Palestinophiles, they, better than the latter, reflected the mood of the overwhelming majority of the emigrants. The passage of time would witness growing intellectual and journalistic support for settlement in the United States, although most apparent only in the years after 1882. It should also be noted that the *biluim* did not have a monopoly on ideology. Among the supporters of immigration to America there were small numbers of young men and women who, like the *biluim*, carried the intellectual baggage of late nineteenth-century Russia. Their Zion, however, was the fertile corn and wheat fields of the North American continent, not Palestine.

One of the most stirring calls for immigration to America came from Yehudah Leib Gordon, the veteran *maskil* from the 1860s and 1870s. Gordon, it will be remembered, had been an adamant supporter of Russification. His poem, "Awake My People," had urged, "Be a man abroad and a Jew in your tent," a passionate plea for secularization and Russification in the land that was supposedly opening its gates to the Jewish people. Several years later he was lamenting the rush toward assimilation in another poem, "For Whom Do I Toil," but he remained a believer in the ability of Russian Jewry to stake out an appropriate position in Russian society; there would be moderate assimilation and, at the same time, Russian Jews would preserve the essential characteristics of Jewishness, an enlightened Judaism, and knowledge of the Hebrew language.

Under the impact of the pogroms Gordon experienced a dramatic change of heart. In a poem entitled "Mahalat Hazikoron" (The Malady of Memory) he spoke of the Haskalah, the enlightenment that he had expected would save Russian Jewry: "That blessing was turned into a curse and the golden cup of which we drank was flung into our faces."[47] Within a short time Gordon's disillusionment with Russia led him to declare that it was necessary for the Jews to emigrate. Perhaps some day they would return to their ancient homeland, but since this was unlikely in the foreseeable future, the Jews must "sleep over in another hotel." If "Awake My People" had been the reveille for Russification in the 1860s, now in 1882 Gordon sounded the call for immigration to America in his poem "Ahoti Ruhama" (My Sister Ruhama). To the "daughter of Jacob," the Jewish people disgraced and humiliated by the son of Hamor (the Russian government), Gordon declared:

> Arise, let us go to a place where the light of freedom
> Will shine on everyone and will illuminate every soul;
> To a place where every human will find grace
> No matter what his nation or gods.
> There the foe will not oppress you.
> There you too will not be disgraced, my sister Ruhama.[48]

In the Jewish press, both in Russian and in Hebrew, there appeared articles advocating immigration to America, although the editorial boards of virtually all Jewish periodicals either supported immigration to Palestine or opposed the idea of emigration altogether. In *Russkii Evrei*, A. Socher, in the article, "To America or to Palestine," argued that only America would do. Palestine, to be sure, was the home of Judaism, but old memories, cold gravestones, and the Wailing Wall constituted merely debris from the past greatness of Israel. "It is capable of calling forth memories but it cannot inspire.... These rooms from the past of our people cannot give it what it needs, what it is missing."[49] Socher did not spare the Jews living in Palestine: He called them religious fanatics who had become accustomed to surviving on charity. Palestine was an unhealthy and unsuitable environment for the masses of Jews desperately seeking salvation there.

America—rich, bountiful America, wrote Socher, where the Jews would be equal to everyone else, was the place for Russian Jewry to plant itself. In America there was no need to worry about the ravages of assimilation. In America the Jews would be free to form religious and philanthropic organizations. Most important, there would be no coercion on the part of the government to distribute the Jews in small groups throughout the country. The Jews would be free to live near each other and to form a cohesive mass that would protect them from assimilation.

In *Razsvet*, too, particularly in 1881 before it began to espouse Palestinophilism, articles frequently appeared in favor of America. The young Simon Dubnow began his public career with an article, "Vopros Dnia" (Question of the Day), in which he proclaimed America as the new fatherland of the Russian and German Jews.[50] When a writer in *Razsvet* defended the choice of Palestine as the place of settlement in view of the traditions that were associated with it, "Amerikanetz" (a supporter of immigration to America) replied in a sharp rejoinder: "The Jews do not now need dreams, they need a quiet corner in which they can gradually develop their strength, to resurrect their situation, which has been shattered at the base."[51] Only in America, claimed the author, was this possible.

Two men who later became Hovevei Tsion passed through an intermediate stage in which they supported immigration to America. Yehudah Leib Levin, a socialist of the 1870s and one of the first writers to introduce socialist themes into Hebrew literature, as a consequence of the pogroms despaired of a socialist solution to the Jewish Question. In a letter written to *Ha-Magid*, the Hebrew weekly published in East Prussia but aimed at readers in the Russian Empire, Levin advocated America over Palestine as a place of settlement and restoration. The enlightened population, rich land, and free institutions of America Levin compared to the hardships of life in Palestine. In the Holy Land the Jews would always be slaves to the Sultan and the Pasha, and would have difficulties with the indigenous population. Levin rejected the possibility of destructive assimilation occurring in America because he believed, mistakenly, that the Constitution of the United States allowed any group of settlers, numbering at least sixty thousand, the right to establish a separate state with its own governors, ministers, and constitution. Agents from steamship companies spread this rumor and many Jews, like Levin, believed it.[52] The ability of the Jews, therefore, to lead their lives in accordance with their own beliefs was guaranteed by law. Levin, unlike some of the supporters of America, did not ridicule Palestine. "The eloquence of the Bible, the piteous spectacle of the bereaved daughter of Zion, the emotion aroused by our ancient memories, all these speak for the land of Israel."[53] But at that time Levin was convinced that America was the place for mass Jewish settlement. His strong feelings for Palestine, however, are attested by his joining the Hovevei Tsion group in Kiev shortly after writing this letter, thus shifting his position: He now wrote in behalf of a return to Palestine.

The young Ludwig Zamenhof, the future inventor of Esperanto, experienced an analogous evolution. In 1881 he was studying medicine in Warsaw; when the pogrom hit the city in December, the apolitical Zamenhof became rapidly politicized. He participated actively in the debate over where to go. In an article entitled, "What Finally Should Be Done?" published in *Razsvet*, Zamenhof, under the pseudonym Gamzephon, argued for America. Like Levin and others he mistakenly assumed that the American Constitution would provide a separate state for Jewish immigrants, thus protecting them from assimilation and anti-Semitism. He too was not hostile to the idea of Palestine as a possible place of settlement, and he authored the interesting and prophetic notion that if, in the end, it was necessary to settle Jews in Palestine, the existence of a large Jewish community in America could only enhance this endeavor because it would increase the overall strength of the Jewish people. Zamenhof was willing to accept the possibility that America and Palestine would constitute the two national homes of the Jewish people.[54] Within a year, however, he, like Levin, became an active Hovev Tsion.

Just as the Palestinophiles did not have a monopoly on support from the Russian Jewish intelligentsia as articulated in the Jewish press, so they also did not corner the market on idealism. Bilu had an analogue in the organizations that grouped themselves under the rubric Am Olam (The Eternal People). The name was taken from the title of an essay written by Smolenskin in 1872. Like Bilu and the emigration movement in general, Am Olam sprang from the people, in some cases university students, in other cases ordinary workers; but in no case was it the result of leadership or inspiration by prominent Russian Jewish intellectuals operating in the larger cities of Russia and publishing in the Jewish periodicals. The founders of the movement were two obscure teachers, Moshe Herder and Monye Bokal, the latter being generally recognized as the leader and chief inspiration of Am Olam.[55] It was Bokal who formed the first group in Odessa right after the May pogrom in that city, and it was Bokal who traveled through the Pale, speaking, writing letters, collecting funds, and organizing many affiliated groups. The social composition of the Am Olam movement was heterogeneous. In nearly every group there were students, teachers, small tradesmen, artisans, common laborers, and even some well-to-do merchants. There was even a former revolutionary, Pinkhas Shukean, who had been a member of Narodnaia Volia and now headed the Vilna Am Olam group. As was to be expected, such differences in education, status, attachment to Jewish culture, religion, and future aspirations generated tension and conflict. Gradually, perhaps inevitably, given their knowledge and articulateness, students and intellectuals began to act as leaders for the various groups.

The social diversity in Am Olam was matched by differences in ideology which flowed from the various groups, although there were ideas that were shared by all. The common thread was the belief that it was both possible and desirable for the Jewish people to establish a home in the United States. Some of the groups actually believed, as did some of the intellectuals writing in the Jewish press, that it was possible to create an autonomous Jewish state or canton in America. The best known of the precepts adhered to by all of the Am Olam, and the one that became synonymous with the movement was that Jewish economic life in America was to be based on agriculture. The members of Am Olam were children of their time. They were influenced by Haskalah ideas on the necessity of making the Jews a "productive" and "normal" people. It was imperative, according to this view, that the Jews eschew "unproductive" occupations such as business and even the professions, and engage in various forms of manual work. Even before the pogroms, it will be remembered, such ideas had motivated a number of Jewish plutocrats to establish ORT, the Society for the Spread of Manual Work among Jews.

For Am Olam, also influenced by Russian Populism and Tolstoyan anarchism, the most desirable manual work, the kind that would uplift the Jewish spirit and refute once and for all the anti-Semitic notion that Jews do not like to perform hard physical labor, was agriculture. Hence, the aim of Am Olam was Jewish colonization on the soil of America. "Our motto," said an *am olamka*, "is a return to agriculture, and our aim the physical and spiritual rehabilitation of our people. In free America, where many people live closely in peace and amity, we Jews, too, shall find a place to lay our heads; we shall demonstrate to the world that we are capable of manual labor."[56]

For some members of Am Olam, those most influenced by the Russian revolutionary movement, the centrality of agriculture in the movement's program was not enough. It had to be agriculture that renounced private property and was based on communal principles. The Odessa group, which in November 1881 sent the first Am Olam contingent to America, drew up plans to establish such an agricultural community where all would work and where all would receive from the common treasury what they needed. The surplus was to be set aside for settling additional Russian Jews in similar settlements.

From November 1881 to the end of 1882, from Vilna, Kiev, Odessa, Minsk, and various other Rusian cities and towns, groups proclaiming the Am Olam philosophy left Russia and came to America. Wherever they went they unfurled their flags emblazoned with a picture of a plow, the words "Am Olam," and then, depending on the group, either the Ten Commandments and the statement "Eternal People arise from the dust, cast off the scorn of the nations, for it is high time," or the rabbinic saying, "If I am not for myself, who will be?" Some marched, as did those from Odessa, in the name of socialism, while others, such as the Kiev Am Olam contented themselves with the aim of simply establishing Jewish farms. Whatever the aspirations, America, agricultural labor, and social harmony proved to be subjects that the passionate idealists of Am Olam would have difficulty mastering. Idealism, either in Palestine or America, was not enough to insure success.

JEWISH OPPOSITION TO EMIGRATION

Immigration to America or Palestine, and Am Olam and Bilu, did not monopolize the attention and support of the Jewish intelligentsia. There were many educated Russian Jews that, for a variety of reasons, opposed the idea of emigration altogether. Three periodicals, *Russkii Evrei*, *Voskhod*, and the latter's weekly supplement, *Nedel'naia khronika Voskhoda*, led the anti-emigration movement. Throughout 1881 and 1882, *Russkii Evrei* carried a series of articles expressing the anti-emigration views of its editorial board.[57] Nothing could shake the views of these gentlemen, not letters to the editor from the towns and cities of the Pale begging for assistance in the matter of emigration, not the supposed statement of Ignatiev to Orshanskii that "the frontier is open," not even the resumption of pogrom violence in 1882.

Russkii Evrei did not believe that emigration would be the salvation of Russian Jewry. Some Jews could emigrate and they should be the recipients of Jewish philanthropy, but there must be no organization of a massive emigration. The Jew is a citizen of Russia, trumpeted *Russkii Evrei*, and he must remain and fight for the equality that is his due. For *Russkii Evrei* the pogroms had, in fact, been caused by the unequal status that had been the lot of the Jews for centuries. This inequality had created the impression in Russian society that the Jews were pariahs and could be beaten with impunity.

Russkii Evrei ridiculed the Russian Jewish intelligentsia which always believes it has found a new key to the Jewish Question. Yesterday it was *obrusenie*, *sblizhenie*, or *slianie*; today it is emigration. Great disappointment in the former had led to even greater enthusiasm for the latter. But this call for emigration was not only inconsistent with the fact that the Russian Jews were Russian citizens, whose forebears had already lived in Russia for centuries, it was detrimental to the Jewish people. In the minds of the editors of *Russkii Evrei*, and of other Russian Jews as well, beyond the ranks of the intelligentsia, talk of emigration played into the hands of the "Judeophobes," the anti-Semites who claimed that the Jews are cowards who "flee from the field of battle" and that Jewish emigration was proof of Jewish disloyalty to the Russian motherland.

Russkii Evrei counseled the Jews that they must not despair, that the spirit of the Great Reforms would return to Russia and the progressive march of humanity would resume. Sooner or later a bona fide emancipation of Russian Jewry would take place. *Russkii Evrei*, however, did not limit itself to a campaign against emigration. The paper actually conducted a two-front war, the first against emigration and "the new exodus," and the second against the rabid assimilationism of the type that had been preached by a fairly large segment of the Jewish intelligentsia in the empire at the end of the 1870s. *Russkii Evrei* suggested: "Educate your children as citizens of Russia and as Jews, inspire in them love and respect for their people and acquaint them with its past, with its literature. . . ."[58] The Russian Jew should preserve his Jewish self-consciousness, and his children should be taught Hebrew in order to ensure that this took place. In 1881 and 1882, *Russkii Evrei* proclaimed that emancipation and equality were the natural rights of Jews. Moreover, the Jewish people constituted a nation that was inferior to none, one that had contributed and would contribute much to humanity, a nation that had survived two thousand years of persecution. In the Russia of the future, the Jews would not only be free, they would be a cohesive national organism within the Russian state.

The same opposition to emigration was voiced by *Voskhod*, a monthly published in St. Petersburg, the only Jewish periodical to be published without preliminary censorship, and by its weekly supplement, *Nedel'-naia khronika Voskhoda*. After an initial flirtation with emigration in mid–1881, *Voskhod* shifted gears and became a consistent opponent, using some of the same arguments as *Russkii Evrei*. Emigration would play into the hands of the anti-Semites, who would immediately proclaim that faced with the slightest adversity the Jews not only flee but their best people encourage them in every possible way to emigrate. The alleged statement by Ignatiev to Orshanskii that the Jews were welcome to leave, which fanned the emigration fires in *Razsvet* and throughout the Pale, only strengthened *Voskhod*'s belief that emigration would not be the prudent thing to do.

   Voskhod and its weekly supplement did not merely echo *Russkii Evrei*. Adolf Landau and the editorial boards of the *Voskhod* journals were made of different stuff from that of the people associated with *Russkii Evrei*, or, for that matter, any of the Jewish periodicals. No Jewish paper in Russia defended Jewish interests or condemned the opponents of the Jews with the passion and skill of Landau and his co-editors.

   Landau was virtually alone among Jewish journalists in his insistent call for Jewish self-defense. *Russkii Evrei* was too timid to speak of it and *Razsvet* and the Hebrew papers were much too engrossed with emigration. This was the great issue of the moment, proclaimed Landau, and the attention of all must be focused on it. No matter that, with the first manifestations of defensive activity by the Jews, the *pogromshchiki* would intensify their beatings. Jewish self-defense would deter attacks in the future. A guiding principle, announced *Nedel'naia khronika Voskhoda*, was that force could be countered only by force.[59] After the Balta pogrom, an event which Landau said, "makes the blood congeal in the veins," he lashed out at the Jews of Balta for their "unpardonable cowardice."[60]

   Just as insistently, the *Voskhod* papers demanded that the Jews be granted equality by the government. While *Russkii Evrei* spoke to Jews of their need to struggle for equality, *Voskhod* and *Nedel'naia khronika Voskhoda* directly addressed the government. Despite the fear of censorship, they criticized the government for not making the Jews equal citizens and for its failure to quash the pogroms.[61] To be sure, the criticism of the government was veiled but it was there, and in this respect *Nedel'naia khronika Voskhoda* was unique.

   What were not concealed were Landau's ferocious attacks on the anti-Semitic press. He did not shrink, either, from attacking the most important segments of his readership, the extremely affluent St. Petersburg Jews. He castigated them repeatedly for their indifference and, when they did act, for their submissive behavior toward the government. It was no longer appropriate, said Landau, for Jewish leaders to go hat in hand with petitions to the government.[62]

   Perhaps the sharpest barbs were reserved for the Russian intelligentsia and the liberal press, whose actions, in Landau's eyes, were sorely deficient. Jews were being murdered and raped while the press and intelligentsia talked about the economic causes of the pogroms, the danger to order and stability at home, the damage to Russia's image abroad, and the need of the Jews to assimilate into Russian society. To be sure, the Jews were not without defenders; Landau's own papers made sure to cite them. But Landau wanted a torrent of articles that unequivocally condemned the attackers and defended the victims. A colossal injustice had been perpetrated; what emerged from the liberals and moderates, he felt, was too little, too mild, and too late.

Landau pointedly noted that only after protest meetings had taken place in England, Western Europe, and the United States did there occur any protest in Russia. Moreover, when it finally did occur, from whom did it come? Not the intelligentsia but the Moscow industrialists, who, afraid for their economic well-being, cautioned the government about the necessity to put an end to the pogroms. Where was the Russian intelligentsia, that great repository of morality, whose moral interests were suffering a thousand times more than the interests of the commercial-industrial class? Apparently, the needs of the pocketbook were more compelling than moral imperatives.[63]

Landau believed that Russian "society" was a fiction and that Russian social thought and consciousness did not exist even in embryonic form. The silence of the intelligentsia was contrasted to the uproar in the 1850s, on the occasion of the anti-Semitic remarks in *Illiustratsiia* (see Chapter I).[64] The hypocrisy and the stupidity of the Russian press, and not just its anti-Jewish element, elicited an angry response from Landau. The liberal press, he said, claimed that it championed the cause of human rights. But when Jewish rights were at issue, "the Russian periodical press refuses to utter a word...."[65]

He furiously castigated the press which for years had referred to the Jews as exploiters: "Well, the pogroms began; the masses believed the word of the low, dishonest shouters in the newspaper, believed that it was necessary to deal with the "exploiters" by force, believed that no one but the Jews are the cause of all Russian misfortunes and evils...."[66] The tragedy was compounded by the fact that it was not only the "dark masses" that believed the purveyors of hate. After all, Landau hinted, it was not the masses that promulgated the restrictive laws for the Jews.

"Russian liberalism"—Landau put the words in quotes—was beneath contempt. He compared the Russian liberal intelligentsia to foreign liberals and found his countrymen sorely deficient.

We understand the liberal from France, England, Germany, and America: he does not lower himself to justify pogroms by "exploitation"; he does not inspire the *pogromshchiki* by shouts of exploitation; he is not silent about the limitation of rights only for Jewry...; moreover, he does not permit any unsubstantiated public insults against the Jewish nation.... "The Russian liberal" repeats over and over again one word, "exploitation." He is silent or even openly approves all that has happened—this is something truly monstrous![67]

THE JEWISH INTERCESSORS

The Jewish intelligentsia, for all its cleverness, courage and ability to articulate its views, could not influence the course of events. It could not intervene in the current crisis and solve the Jewish Question on terms beneficial to the Jews. This was a task, according to Jewish tradition, for the wealthiest and most prestigious elements within the Jewish community. In the case of Russia, this meant the St. Petersburg plutocracy and the professional people and intellectuals that were grouped around it. Tradition accorded these people the role of *shtadlanim*, intercessors with the authorities who would somehow make things right for the Jews. In every place and every time there was *shtadlanut* (intercession). In the modern period, the most famous *shtadlan* was the Rothschild family of Vienna. The record of such practice was not a bad one although the popular consciousness tended to forget the failures, remembering and exaggerating the successes. In the period 1881–1882, Russian Jews from all walks of life looked to the titans of Russian Jewry for assistance in getting the government to change its policies toward the Jews and in organizing and subsidizing a mass emigration movement from Russia. On both counts, Russian Jewry was to be sorely disappointed.

Part of the problem, of course, was that the Russian government as well as a large segment of the Russian population, was composed of people like Alexander III and Ignatiev—possessed of such visceral hostility toward the Jews, that no amount of intercession, no matter how skilled, could alter the fate of the Jews. The other aspect of the problem lay in the nature of the *shtadlanim* themselves. They were so different and so isolated and removed from the great mass of Russian Jews that the passions and desperate needs generated in the Pale could only find a weak echo in their hearts, minds, and mouths.

The differences between the two groups were enormous. The St. Petersburg Jews were wealthy, possessed privileges that their coreligionists could only dream of, and were Russified to the point that many not only refused to speak Yiddish, they did not even know the language. Their elegant, modish dress was very different from that in the Pale. Most important, the St. Petersburg Jews were not under the gun of persecution. There were no pogroms in the capital city and there was never any fear that one would occur there. What could these people have in common with the beaten, plundered, raped Jewish masses of the southern and western parts of the empire? The very intimate connections with the government which were prized by the Günzburgs, Poliakovs, and Brodskiis served to weaken forceful and effective intercession.[68] What could have been an asset to *shtadlanut* was really a liability, since many of these men seemed, throughout 1881 and 1882, to be afraid of jeopardizing their precious but fragile links which had taken decades to develop. Nothing would be done, no position would be advanced, that could in any way damage what had taken so long to create.

This is not to say that the St. Petersburg Jews were not concerned with the well-being of their people. Some of them, to be sure, were indifferent, but others gave incredibly large amounts of time and money to ameliorate the position of Russian Jewry. The outstanding *shtadlan*, the man whose name became linked synonymously with *shtadlanut* in Russia, was Horace Günzburg, son of the creator of the family fortune. Günzburg had been involved all of his life in Jewish affairs. In the reign of Alexander II he had tried constantly to expand the privileges and opportunities of the Jewish masses, and by subsidizing books and articles, had fought the growing anti-Semitism in the last years of the reign.

His biographer, S. L. Tsitron, relates that Günzburg, who had so passionately believed that emancipation was not long in coming, was caught by surprise by the pogroms and was severely shaken.[69] He soon recovered, and he took the lead in conducting the process of *shtadlanut* that carried over into the spring of 1882. It was Günzburg, for example, who led the delegation to the Tsar in Gatchina in early May of 1881, and it was Günzburg who began with the humble, and in the eyes of some contemporaries, humiliating manner that tended to mark the entire course of this *shtadlanut*. He had begun the Gatchina sessions by speaking of the "boundless gratitude [of the Jews] for the measures adopted to safeguard the Jewish population at this sad moment," but added: "One more imperial word and the disturbances will disappear."[70] Together with other members of the delegation, he attempted to take a firmer position in countering the Tsar's statement that hatred of the Jews resulted from their economic domination and exploitation of the Russian people.

Günzburg devoted himself exclusively to Jewish affairs after the pogroms. He placed subordinates in charge of his business interests and for some twelve months, from May 1881 to May 1882, he dedicated himself to the task of ameliorating the position of his people, or, at the very least, staving off even greater abuse of Jewish life, property, and rights. He sought information on the work of the *guberniia* commissions so as to prepare counterproposals, and he arranged subsequent meetings of Jewish notables to discuss current issues. One such meeting took place in September 1881 in St. Petersburg. Meeting in secret session, Günzburg and a small number of prominent Jews that he invited from the provinces discussed the problems of emigration and the struggle with the anti-Semitic press. They even met with Ignatiev, who comforted them by speaking of the benevolent intentions of the government. Either because they were lulled by Ignatiev's talk or because they suffered from an acute paralysis of will in the face of the enormous problems confronting Russian Jewry, the conference adjourned without having accomplished anything.[71] Good will and gentility, it was becoming clear, were not enough.

The growing and blatant hostility of Ignatiev and his associates, a new wave of pogroms in the early spring of 1882, and, most important, the almost hysterical cries from the Pale for assistance and guidance led to the convening of another conference, this one larger, more visible, and certainly more controversial than the one held in September. Once again it was Günzburg who took the initiative, and, with the approval of Ignatiev, twenty-five delegates from the provinces, including Dr. Mandelshtam from Kiev and Rabbi Yitschak Elhanan Spektor from Kovno, joined fifteen notables from the capital, including Günzburg himself and the railroad magnate Poliakov. The conference met from April 8 to 11, 1882, in the shadow of the most ferocious pogrom of all, the one that occurred in Balta on March 29, 1882.

It would be a mistake, a natural one in view of the prior behavior of the notables, and also in light of the protocols signed by the delegates at the end of the conference, to see the participants as being only timid men, frightened of angering the government and anxious only to preserve their privileged positions. This was true of some but not all. A close look at what was said demonstrates that most of the delegates were men of principle whose primary motivation was to somehow help their people. The material interests of the St. Petersburg representatives and their isolation from the Pale certainly were factors in the decisions made but nonetheless their concern for the well-being of Russian Jewry was genuine if somewhat tempered. Passions indeed reached such a peak that (as mentioned in Chapter II), one speaker, after recounting the horrible situation in which Russian Jewry now found itself, fainted and soon died.

The main but not the only issue of the conference was the question of emigration. It quickly became apparent that there could be nothing approaching unanimity. Dr. Mandelshtam spoke for those supporting the idea that assistance be granted to the emigration movement and that it be organized with the help of prominent Jews. "They tread underfoot our human dignity, they rob us, they assault the honor of our women and daughters, we are not slaves: Either human rights are granted us or we will go wherever our eyes may desire."[72] Mandelshtam had no illusions concerning the government's willingness to grant those "human rights." For him migration to Palestine was the only answer. Other delegates from the provinces advocating emigration claimed that the desire to emigrate was so great and the mood so desperate that there would be revolts by Jews if the conference refused to support emigration.

The bulk of the conference was opposed to emigration. One delegate feared that emigration would call forth further pogroms because, once it became known that the Jews had decided to leave, there would be an incentive to plunder their property. Others looked upon emigration as a form of protest and, therefore, as treason against the government. Still others, like Professor Bakst, continued to believe that the Jews would eventually be made fully equal to other Russians. "Who knows," said the professor, "perhaps the malevolent events that have befallen us constitute that narrow path along which we will go into the light of [possessing] the full rights of Russian citizens."[73] That there continued to exist in Russia considerable sympathy and support for the Jews—not a foolish idea in view of some of the statements made by the *guberniia* commissions and the occasional manifestations of support from ordinary people—and that eventually Russian society would come to its senses was felt by many of the delegates.

Samuel Poliakov, the financier, who fancied himself a confident of Ignatiev, related to the conference that the minister regarded efforts to stimulate emigration as "an incitement to sedition." Ignatiev allegedly told Poliakov that he opposed Jewish resettlement in most of Russia outside of the Pale but was sympathetic to the idea of Jews settling in central Asia and in parts of the Trans-Caspian region. In the light of Ignatiev's statements, Poliakov vehemently opposed emigration, proposing Jewish settlement instead in the areas indicated by the minister.[74] The proposal caused an uproar. Mandelshtam argued that once again the government was heaping ridicule on the Jews.[75] Even Professor Bakst, an indefatigable believer in a bright future for Jewry in Russia and an opponent of emigration, declared that such a proposal really signified "deportation" and was synonymous with classifying the Jews as criminals.[76]

In the end, the conference, which was composed of conservative, wealthy, and decent men but which did not include representatives from the really beleaguered elements in the Pale or the traumatized members of the Jewish intelligentsia, approved, after four days of intensive debate, a number of resolutions. First, it rejected completely the thought of organizing emigration. To facilitate and encourage emigration was considered by the conference as "subversive of the dignity of the Russian body politic and of the historic rights of the Jews to their present Fatherland."[77] Second, the conference pointed to the necessity of—it did not demand—eliminating all anti-Jewish legislation. Only in this way would the relationship between Jews and non-Jews be normalized so as to preclude hostility. Third, the conference agreed to make the government aware of the passive attitude of certain officials during the pogroms.

Fourth, the conference agreed to "petition" the government to find ways to compensate the Jews who had suffered from the pogroms "as a result of inadequate police protection." Finally, the conference, showing sensitivity to the charge of anti-Semites that there existed in Russia a malevolent Jewish conspiracy declared:

We, the undersigned, the representatives of various centers of Jewish settlement in Russia, rabbis, members of religious organizations and synagogue boards, consider it our sacred duty, calling to witness God omniscient, to declare publicly, in the presence of the whole of Russia, that there exists neither an open nor a secret Kahal administration among the Russian Jews; that Jewish life is entirely foreign to any organization of this kind and to any of the attributes ascribed to such an organization by evil minded persons.[78]

The spirit of Brafman continued to haunt Russian Jewry.

Decent and well-intentioned though the conference members may have been, their conduct was found wanting by many Jews in the Pale as well as by members of the Jewish intelligentsia. Where were the militant demands upon the government? Where were the stirring calls to action addressed to Jewish communities throughout Russia and abroad? Above all, it was clear that the thousands of Russian Jews who were on the move seeking to emigrate would receive absolutely nothing from those that proclaimed themselves the leaders of Russian Jewry.

The response from the Jewish intelligentsia and the Jewish press was not long in coming. *Razsvet* attacked the "Petersburg bosses" who were so afraid of assisting the emigration movement, the only way out for Russian Jewry. It hammered away at the "egoism" and indifference of the Jewish bourgeoisie which was prepared to sacrifice the interests of the suffering Jewish people for the sake of their patriotic image.[79] The bourgeoisie was committing a terrible crime by refusing to demand of the government that it legalize emigration. *Razsvet* argued that this, together with the reluctance of wealthy Jews to provide financial support for the emigrants, was causing them great hardship and might even make Jewish settlement in Palestine an impossibility.[80] From the Pale, *Razsvet* received articles from its correspondents relating that in many cities and towns the emigration circles were furious at the refusal of the conference to provide assistance. *Nedel'naia khronika Voskhoda*, which opposed emigration and therefore could not be critical on this issue nonetheless attacked the work of the conference. It castigated the obsequious behavior of the delegates, their refusal to mount a militant defense of the Jewish people. "What degree of demoralization and moral disparagement is it necessary to reach.... Instead of the sharpest and most decisive protest against the pogroms and all the reprisals which make the life of the Jewish population one that is worse than death, [there are] only ... petitions, instructions, and explanations."[81]

RADICAL RELIGIOUS RESPONSE

The conference was only one of a number of Jewish responses to the tragedy that had befallen the community. All of these responses—immigration to America or Palestine, the struggle in whatever form for civil rights in Russia, self-defense, even the lack of response, the indifference and inertia of some Jews—can be considered normal reactions. They were all traditional devices Jewish communities over the centuries had practiced in the face of adversity. In no way did the proponents of these alternatives envisage them as a break either with the Jewish people or with Judaism. But in the midst of the pogroms there did occur on two occasions episodes that deviated from the usual behavioral pattern. These were attempts at religious reforms so radical in nature that it is problematic whether they can be considered as falling within the bounds of Judaism, no matter how elastic that term may be.

The first episode occurred in the spring of 1881, around the time of the first pogroms. It is linked with Iakov Gordin, later famous in Eastern Europe and America as the founder of the Yiddish theater. At this time, however, Gordin was under the influence of both Russian Protestantism and Populism. Not long before the pogroms he had established the Spiritual-Biblical Brotherhood, which advocated a total break with the Talmud and rabbinical Judaism and the placing of Jewish socioeconomic life on an agricultural foundation. The Talmud was held to be the principal cause of hatred of the Jews, along with the fact that Jews stubbornly clung to their roles as petty traders and commercial agents.[82]

Shortly after the pogrom in Elizavetgrad a letter signed by a *bibleiitz*, a "Brother Biblist," but presumably written by Gordin, appeared in the journal *Iuzhnyi Krai*.[83] The writer placed responsibility for the pogroms on the Jews because of their greed, stubborness, pushiness, and generally obnoxious economic behavior. Now is the time, according to the writer, to root out the unfortunate aspects of Jewish life and to model Russian Jewry along the religious and economic lines proposed by the Spiritual-Biblical Brotherhood. The letter was republished in many Russian newspapers and was acclaimed by the anti-Semitic journal, *Kievlianin*. Among Jews, however, it generated great animosity and received virtually no support.[84]

A more sophisticated and radical "reform" surfaced in January, 1882 with the appearance of the group, New Israel, led by Iakov Priluker, a graduate of a government-run Jewish teacher's institute. Priluker, like so many of the graduates of such institutions, developed a passionate loathing for everything that smacked of traditional Judaism. In early 1882, at the age of twenty-one, he wrote an article in an Odessa newspaper announcing the foundation of a Jewish sect, New Israel, and proclaimed its fundamental tenets.[85]

The sect totally rejected the Talmud, as did the *bibleitzy*. The Talmud had brought harm and disgrace to the Jewish people, argued Priluker. The sect recognized as holy only the five books of Moses. The Sabbath was to be observed on Sunday, not Saturday, so as to enhance relations with the Christian population. Circumcision was to be eliminated since it was a pernicious and shameful vestige carried over from barbarous times. Many of the Hebrew prayers written in the medieval period were to be eliminated and new ones, also in Hebrew, were to be created. The dietary laws, *kashruth*, were abolished.

In addition to a new religious program, New Israel had a social agenda. Members considered as holy and binding all the civil and criminal laws of the Russian state and promised to participate in military service. They were forbidden to engage in usury and would give all of their children Russian names. The government was to be asked to give full civil rights to the members of the sect and also to permit mixed marriages. In order to be distinguished from the "Jew-Talmudist," New Israel members would, with the permission of the government, wear a special insignia on their clothing.

The appearance of the sect had no impact on orthodox Jewish circles, which apparently were oblivious of its existence. But it did cause a furor within the ranks of the Russian-Jewish intelligentsia. Priluker was denounced for playing into the hands of the anti-Semites, for seconding their accusations against the Jewish people. He was confirming, said his opponents, the charge that the Talmud was harmful, that Jews were exploiters and usurers, and that Jews were not prepared to serve in the military. By implication, all Jews except those in New Israel were to be held suspect and denied equal rights with other Russian citizens.[86]

Despite interest and support from the authorities—they subsidized the publication of his book—Priluker's ideas made virtually no inroads into Russian Jewry. He himself encountered great personal hostility. Harangued on the streets of Odessa, he was reluctant to show his face. He managed to keep his position as a teacher in a Jewish school only because of the intervention of government officials in Odessa, who compelled the leaders of the Jewish community to keep him on. Perceiving no future for himself or his movement Priluker eventually left Russia in 1891 for England. Before he left, he converted to Lutheranism, and in England became involved in missionary work. The historian Shaul Ginsburg claims that all along Priluker aimed to use New Israel and its program as a bridge over which Russian Jewry was to pass to Christianity.[87]

CONCLUSION

Thus ends the discussion of Jewish response to the pogroms. Flight, fear, resistance, indifference, protest, proto-Zionism, longing for America, and radical religious reform were the reactions of a community assaulted by violence and encountering hostility from the highest authorities. It is the misfortune of the historian that he is dependent, in reporting the past, on documents emanating from the more articulate, educated, and therefore more privileged elements of the group under investigation. The moods and aspirations of the inarticulate, silent masses often are ignored. The same is true of this study, since it is upon the educated and the affluent, exhibiting their feelings in a variety of forums, that so much attention has been lavished. But no one who has looked at the period can be oblivious to the action of the most active segment of Russian Jewry, the ordinary Jewish folk of the Pale. They were in motion; no inertia for them. They were moving to America or Palestine. Those going to Palestine have already been discussed. It is time to look at the much larger group which sought refuge in a land whose riches and promise of freedom exercised tremendous appeal to a people under siege. As Bilu and the handful of other settlers in Palestine during the years 1881–1882 began to create a modern Yishuv, so, too, did the Russian Jews who arrived in America begin the process of establishing a new center of Jewish life, upon which, as a consequence of the twists and turns of history, so much in the way of Jewish existence would depend.

VI

The Golden Land

AMERICA REACTS TO THE POGROMS

The object of affection for many Jews in Russia, the United States of America, had been communicating with the Russian Empire on matters involving Jews for some time. In fact, during the nineteenth century and with respect to Jews, it is fair to say that the most correspondence between the American government and any foreign government was that between it and Russia.

In the decade before the pogroms, the United States and Russia had been involved in a series of disputes relating to certain American Jews, nearly all of whom had been born in Russia and were returning as American citizens to their country of origin for business or family reasons. The American Jews of Russian background were subjected to the same discriminatory legislation as were Russian Jews. A number of returning naturalized Americans, for example, were expelled from St. Petersburg and Kharkov on the ground that these cities were off limits to all Jews except those of the First Merchants' Guild.

The initial response of the American State Department was to object to the actions of the Russian government merely on the grounds that all American citizens, regardless of religion, are equal and therefore must enjoy equal privileges both at home and abroad. The Secretary of State and other American diplomats refused to accept the Russian view that the religion of Americans had any bearing whatsoever on their rights in Russia.

Slowly, however, the American perspective began to expand. By the end of the 1870s and the beginning of the 1880s, just prior to the pogroms, American diplomats were beginning to speak on behalf not only of American Jews in Russia, but of Russian Jews themselves. As their new persecution in the pogroms became known to these American officials, it appeared that the surest guarantee of the rights of American

Jews residing in Russia was a general amelioration of the position of Russian Jewry.

American government involvement in the affairs of Russian Jews reached a peak in the second half of 1881, when the new Garfield administration, with James G. Blaine as Secretary of State, tried to bring about an improvement in their situation. Whether touched by the plight of the Russian Jews, as were a number of Americans who saw in their situation something comparable to that of the recently emancipated black slaves, or reacting to mounting public opinion in support of the Jews, Secretary of State Blaine made the strongest attempt to date in behalf of Russian Jewry. He went so far as to try to enlist the support of the British government, but Her Majesty's government chose to reject the Blaine approach and continued to view the question of Russian Jewry as an internal matter for the Russian Empire, as we have seen in Chapter III. This position was only to be expected, since the British Government had been reluctant to defend even the interests of Jews who were British citizens residing in Russia. Unlike the case of American Jews in Russia, it was with the permission of their own government that British Jews were put in the inferior class of most Jews in Tsarist Russia.

Chester A. Arthur's accession to the presidency at the death of President Garfield on September 19, 1881, from an assassin's bullet of the preceeding July, did not lead to an abrupt change in American policy. In his message to Congress on December 6, 1881, Arthur referred to Jewish suffering in Russia. On April 15, 1882, the new Secretary of State, Frederick T. Frelinghuysen, wrote to Wickham Hoffman, the Charge d'Affaires of the American Embassy in St. Petersburg, that the American people lamented the suffering of the Jews in Russia. The Secretary suggested that perhaps Hoffman should express to Russian officials, in a deferential way, that the American government hopes that the "Imperial government will find means to call the persecution of these unfortunate fellow beings to cease."[1]

By the end of 1882, however, the Arthur administration had cooled its ardor in behalf of persecuted and suffering Russian Jewry. Other concerns, perhaps a belief in the futility of any American effort and the need to maintain friendly relations with a formidable state, combined to eliminate any further official American concern for Russian Jewry. On December 9, 1882, President Arthur justified the new policy of his administration by informing Congress that he was confident that the time was not too far off when Russia would be able to insure tolerance for all religions within its borders.

The American government had grown tired of the Jewish Question; there were other more important issues. It was a pattern of behavior that would bedevil Jews and their supporters over the next hundred years as the position of European Jews, contrary to the optimism of the late nineteenth century, continued to deteriorate.

The normal practice of diplomacy is one of delicacy and deference. It is just the opposite when broad circles of society as well as elected officials are involved. Even before the pogroms, news of the Russian government's discrimination against Jews had provoked a number of Americans to speak out. The most notable and the one with the most influential audience was Samuel S. Cox, a Congressman from New York City. He informed the House of Representatives in May 1880: "The laws of Russia make a residence in that country for the Jews a prolonged agony, a life in death, a death in life."[2] Cox would, over the next few years, become the tribune of the Jews, as he time and again rose in their defense in Congress and advanced resolutions calling for American governmental intervention in behalf of Russian Jewry.

Beyond Congress, the American public began to respond to the pogroms when news of the horrors finally reached these shores. On February 1 and March 4, 1882, two large protest meetings, in New York City and Philadelphia, were convened. In New York former President Grant together with Senator Carl Schurz took the initiative, while in Philadelphia prominent citizens of that city, including the Mayor, organized the meeting. The New York meeting heard one speaker quote a letter written by Pope Innocent IV in 1237: "What a shame it is they should be more miserable under Christian Princes than their ancestors were under Pharaoh." The gathering in New York adopted a resolution "against the spirit of medieval persecution thus revived in Russia," and called upon the American government to make forceful representations to the Russian government on behalf of Russian Jewry.[3]

The Philadelphia meeting led to a stream of resolutions that found their way into both houses of Congress, as representatives from Pennsylvania and Philadelphia brought the outrage of their constituents to the attention of their colleagues. The result of this furor was the resolution proposed by James B. Belford of Central City, Colorado, which was passed by both houses. The resolution protested against the persecution of Russian Jewry and called upon the President of the United States to request the Tsar to protect his Jewish subjects from violence.

The Belford resolution did not calm the waters. News of the outrages inflicted on the Jewish citizens of Balta in the spring of 1882 stimulated further protest meetings in the United States. The American press carried articles dealing with the suffering of the pogrom victims. The public outcry reached such proportions that, once again, Congress was forced to respond. The initiator of further Congressional action was the same Samuel P. Cox who had on several earlier occasions alerted his colleagues to the suffering of Russian Jewry. His passion had been fueled by a trip taken to Jerusalem in 1881, where he met refugees from the pogroms. His long speech of July 13, 1882, is the clearest explication of the problem and the sharpest denunciation of the Russian authorities that had ever been made by an American public figure.

Cox held nothing back. He detailed the atrocities of the previous year, providing names, figures and maps. He stated that the Russian government was responsible for the violence perpetrated against the Jews:

Is it said that the Russian peasantry and not the government are responsible? I answer: If the peasantry of Russia are too ignorant or debased to understand the nature of this cruel persecution, they have warrant for their conduct in the customs and laws of Russia to which I have referred. These discriminate against the Jews. They have reference to their isolation, their separation from Russian protection, their expulsion from certain parts of the empire, and their religion. When a peasant observes such forceful movements and authoritative discrimination in a government against a race, it arouses his ignorance and inflames his fanatical zealotry. Adding this to the jealousy of the Jews as middle men and business men, and you may account for, but not justify, these horrors. The Hebraic-Russian question had been summed up in a few words: "Extermination of two and one-half millions of mankind because they are Jews!"[4]

Cox addressed himself directly to the question of whether the United States had the right to intervene on behalf of one group of subjects of that government. For Cox, the answer was most decidedly in the affirmative. Simple feelings of humanity, he claimed, demanded that the United States of America speak out: "We are recreant to every advanced idea of our age, if we do not utter our protest against the vindictive evangel of the Sclav against the Jew." He referred not only to the fact that Russia had repeatedly intervened in the affairs of the Ottoman Empire on behalf of beleaguered Christians—interventions which led to war—but he cited numerous precedents in the recent and far past of states' intervention with other states on behalf of persecuted religious minorities. He gave the example of Morocco, where Jews had been treated horribly; the European powers and the United States successfully protested against this maltreatment. Accordingly, Cox proposed a resolution calling upon the Arthur administration to use its influence with the Russian government to stop the persecution directed against the Jews, and to protect Russian Jews and American Jews in Russia against the recurrence of discrimination and violence. The resolution was eventually passed by the House of Representatives on February 23, 1882.

The protest movement was the forerunner of many similar episodes in the United States later in the nineteenth century, and in the twentieth century as well. Like nearly all of them, this one of the early 1880s failed to achieve its primary purpose. The Russian government did not end its persecution against the Jews, but in fact increased the burden of discriminatory legislation. It was virtually impossible, as many later would sadly learn, to persuade or compel a nation to alter its policies vis-à-vis a hated minority. Subsequent occasions would demonstrate that American action that went beyond Congressional resolutions, such as economic sanctions, would offer no significant succor to the oppressed group. In the 1880s, however, this was not yet clear, and the participants in the protest meetings in behalf of Russian Jewry and the sponsors of Congressional resolutions, were sincerely convinced that they could bring about substantial amelioration in the condition of Russian Jews.

Interestingly, the protest movement in behalf of Russian Jewry in the 1880s did not have a substantial Jewish participation in its leadership circles. Prominent American Jews, were, to be sure, concerned about the suffering of their coreligionists in Russia—Simon Wolfe and Adolphus Solomons had expressed their concern to Secretary of State Evarts in early 1880—but when it came to actual protest, the leaders of American Jewry were not in the forefront. Indeed, they were exceptionally cautious. In Philadelphia, for example, the Jewish member of the committee organizing the March protest meeting, Moses Dropsie, was adamant in his insistence that any resolution passed at the meeting should not criticize the Russian government but only the "unconscious masses." The meetings and the protest movement in the United States in general were primarily Gentile phenomena. While anti-Jewish sentiment, as will be seen, was making inroads into American society, the antipathy to religious bigotry that had characterized the Republic in its earliest days was still a strong force in American life.

THE LURE OF AMERICA

The protest movement in America was known to readers of the Jewish press in Russia. Together with articles from recent immigrants to the United States, it helped create a notion of America, a highly impressionistic view of Jewish life in the New World. Long before the pogroms, in fact, information in the form of books and articles about the United States had penetrated into the Russian Empire. The presence in the United States of thousands of Russian Jews who had come to the United States in the late 1860s and 1870s, as mentioned in Chapter I, added to the knowledge of American life possessed by East European Jews. That America was on the mind of some Russian Jews even before the pogroms was evidenced by the poignant remarks addressed by a group of Russian Jews to American Jewry in early 1880. After recounting the cruel suffering of Jews in Russia, the Russian Jews pledged:

Come, brothers of Israel in America, come to our help. Give us the means to migrate to your shores. Let us touch with our feet the sacred soil of Washington, and with our freedom we then become newly created for the struggle of life. We do not fear work. We ask you thus to land us on your free territory and send us to your Western lands, and we will answer for the rest.[5]

After the onset of the pogroms, particularly those in the early spring of 1882, when hopes for the abatement of violence turned out to be misplaced, a veritable emigration fever aiming for America developed.

It permeated the Pale of Settlement, even in the north, where there were no pogroms. Abraham Cahan, the future editor of the *Forward* in New York, who emigrated in 1882 from Vilna, relates that those Jews whose economic position made it possible were selling everything and joining groups that were traveling to America.[6] Another immigrant, Bernard Weinstein, wrote that in Odessa in 1882 young people were dreaming about America and many were preparing to leave. For them, "America was the place where one uses the shovel to bring in the gold and where all men, Jews and Christians are equal."[7] A group of Jews from Elizavetgrad, the site of the first pogrom, sent a letter in October 1881 to the Alliance Israélite Universelle in Paris begging for assistance in going to America, which, they said, "is the most civilized region and offers the most guarantees of individual freedoms, freedom of conscience, and security of all property . . . and endows every one of their inhabitants with both civil and political rights."[8]

The far-flung correspondents of the Jewish press were continually reporting to their papers that the passion for America was growing daily. From Kovno, Lithuania, a correspondent wrote that every day more and more families were immigrating to America and that the desire to emigrate was particularly strong among the young. Similar news was reported from correspondents in Berdichev, Vilna, Warsaw, and other cities. In Kiev, according to one correspondent of *Ha-Melits* writing in late October 1881, Jews were selling their possessions at any price in order to acquire the financial means for emigration.[9] Everywhere there was talk of emigration. In the spring of 1882 right after Passover, crowds of Jews began moving to the Russian frontier.

Rumor, too, played a role. Everywhere in the Pale there were people who believed that the Jewish committees, which had been established in other countries to assist the emigrants who had made their way to Brody just over the Russian border in Austria-Hungary, desired the mass emigration of Russian Jewry. It was believed that the committees would provide money not only for travel but also for settlement in America for every emigrant.[10] This was far from correct, as will be shown below, but belief in the rumor was nearly universal among Russian Jews. Letters, allegedly signed by Moses Montefiore, the famous British philanthropist, and Isadore Loeb, head of the Alliance, and promising support for emigration circulated in the Pale.[11] The Jewish press, too, served as a source of the rumors. In the summer of 1881, *Ha-Melits* published a long letter and a circular, both printed under the letterhead of the Alliance, stating that Russian Jews should not attempt to go into the Russian interior nor to Palestine, nor in fact to any country other than America. Future immigrants to the United States were urged to take their families with them and were promised stipends for the children. As if this were not enough, the letter and the circular went on to state that everything was being prepared in America for the immigrants and that the Alliance had purchased fields and gardens for them. Six weeks later *Ha-Melits* published a denial from Isadore Loeb that such documents had ever been written by the Alliance and a warning that one should be wary of rumors and spurious letters. Loeb added emphatically and unambiguously that the Alliance would provide assistance only to good artisans, and only for a limited number even of them. As for the claim that the Alliance had purchased plots of land for the immigrants, Loeb said this was a figment of a writer's imagination.[12]

The appearance of forged letters and circulars led a number of contemporaries to believe that an organized effort to spur immigration to America was at work. The guilty parties, it was believed, were the transoceanic shipping companies, particularly those of Belgium and Germany, which were locked in fierce competition to capture the Atlantic market. It was common knowledge that the companies were seeking East European Jews as passengers. One shipping agent had German and Yiddish handbills printed that promised cheap fares and "all kinds of advantages" for prospective customers.[13] This huckstering, combined with the cheap fares—eighty marks, about twenty dollars, from Hamburg to New York—were a factor in the emigration movement. The various relief committees suggested that representatives of the shipping companies had let their competitive zeal get the better of them and had planted the false reports in the Jewish press.

FLEEING ABROAD

Whatever the stimulus, Jewish emigrants began to stream across the Russian border into neighboring countries. Some managed to do it easily, paying bribes or crossing the border at those points where there was negligent surveillance. Others had to pay smugglers to lead them through well-patrolled areas; these people, years later, would speak of the fear that stalked them at the time. For all of the emigrants, leaving was not an easy process. Not that it was Mother Russia pulling at their heartstrings, since the vast majority of people were leaving because of the pogroms and other violence, or because of the spread of anti-Jewish sentiment, or because they had no further hope for their future in backward, authoritarian Russia. Many an émigré would agree with the young George Price, who wrote in his diary on May 14, 1882, "It is impossible and unthinkable that a Jew should regret leaving Russia. Be thou cursed forever, my wicked homeland, because you remind me of the Inquisition."[14] What tugged at their emotions were the people they left behind. Memoirs are replete with scenes of husbands tearfully parting from wives and children, and fathers and mothers, promising to see them soon, but really not knowing if that would ever be. The last minute pleas of those to be left behind, urging the young men not to leave, fill the literature.

Given the paucity of data, it is impossible to describe the emigration of 1881–1882 with the same exactitude as studies that cover later periods of Jewish flight from Eastern Europe. Therefore, impressionistic contemporaneous accounts will have to suffice; although imprecise, they do reveal some interesting characteristics of emigration in the period 1881–1882. First, as would be true also of later East European Jewish emigration, the refugees of the pogrom years included large numbers of women and children. It was truly a family emigration. The Jewish emigrants came from all regions of Russia and engaged in all sorts of occupations; many were still students. It was a diverse group, in terms of experiences and attitudes.

George Brandes, the Danish writer, in 1882 interviewed Russian Jews at the Berlin railroad station on their way to America; he described the young *am olamkes* with their ideological passion for socialism, who had despaired of a future in Russia because of the anti-Semitism there, but who had had no direct experience of the pogroms.[15] They were filled with optimism concerning prospects in America. But there were others at the railroad station, families who had lost sons, daughters and husbands to the *pogromshchiki*, and women and girls who had been raped. The saddest case for Brandes was the young woman whose husband had left earlier for America and had sent two tickets for his wife and child to join him. But the child had been killed in a pogrom, and the wife looked forward to the meeting in America with foreboding. Among all the emigrants there were mixed emotions—joy on leaving Russia, yet fear of what lay ahead in the new country. What typified nearly all of them, regardless of their experience and occupation in Russia, was their alarming poverty. Brandes, who saw many other people from Eastern Europe in addition to Jews, wrote that of all the groups, including Polish peasants, none compared to the Jews from Russia in terms of poverty and squalor. The low level of Russian economic life, the pogroms, anti-Semitism, robbery, and the extortion experienced by many of the emigrants had combined to impoverish the vast majority of those who fled.

There was no one route taken by those who left Russia in the years 1881–1882. Many from Lithuania, White Russia, and Russian Poland, like Alexander Harkavy, the future Yiddish lexicographer, traveled from Vilna to the border, where they were smuggled into East Prussia; from there they went by train to Hamburg, and then by ship to London, Liverpool, or America.[16] For those refugees fleeing from South Russia, the pogrom region, the city of Brody just over the border in Austro-Hungarian Galicia became their gathering place. To Brody streamed thousands upon thousands of Jewish refugees. They flooded the city, hoping for aid from the various Jewish assistance committees formed outside of Russia in the aftermath of the pogroms. For all those who passed through Brody, the experience was traumatic, leaving an indelible imprint on the emigrant mind.

George Price's diary entry for May 10, 1882, provides an appropriate introduction to the discussion of "The Brody Experience": "We arrived in Brody yesterday. What pandemonium! Fifteen thousand Jews are stranded here awaiting their turn."[17] Price exaggerated somewhat as far as the numbers were concerned; at most, the figure never exceeded twelve thousand refugees in Brody at any one time. But he can be pardoned for this slight mistake, because to anyone who happened to be in Brody, it appeared that the city had been hit by an avalanche of people. On May 11, 1882, one day after Price arrived, thirteen hundred people came into Brody, nine hundred by train and four hundred on foot.

The Jews in Brody were given over to chaos and absolute confusion, as Price noted. Since the city did not have adequate accommodations, Jews slept in private homes, in stables, in unused parts of factories and on the streets. Due to overcrowding, the heat, and the abysmal sanitary conditions, the odor was terrible. In the stables and factories the emigrants crowded together on the floor, hungry and thirsty. Most of them were so poor that even on the hottest days in June the sellers of soft drinks did a bad business because there were so few people who could afford them. A very large number were able to eat only as money and provisions were provided them by the various assistance committees.

The Russian Jews were not the only poor Jews in Brody. Galicia was not a garden spot, and the bulk of its large Jewish community lived a marginal existence. Death from starvation was not a common phenomenon among Galician Jewry, but it did happen. Abraham Cahan wrote about spending his first night in Brody with a Jewish family whose home turned out to be the only room that remained of a ruined brick structure. In this "apartment" lived a man, his wife, and a twenty-year-old niece. One of the men who traveled with Cahan related that the woman had offered the niece to him for a few cents. "She is a poor orphan and wants to earn a few pennies," she had pleaded.[18]

The most harrowing aspect of the Brody experience was acquiring registration cards and train tickets for the trip across Central Europe to the ports of Hamburg and Bremen. The card was a prerequisite for the ticket, but having the one did not guarantee the other, and it most certainly did not assure getting the tickets speedily. Many emigrants remained in Brody for two months or more. Price noted that the Russian proverb, "Punctual like a German," did not hold in Brody.

The fact of the matter was that the representatives of the various Jewish assistance committees were unable or unwilling to expedite the registration and ticketing process. Their inexperience in dealing with what must have seemed mass hordes of their Russian coreligionists led to delays. Another reason, to be discussed later, was the bitter controversy among the assistance organizations concerning the ultimate destination of the Jewish emigrants in Brody. The heated give and take of the negotiation process among the organizations led to interruptions in the emigrant flow out of the city.

Whatever the reason for the delays, they stunned the emigrants, extracting from some of them a terrible price. More than a few families broke under the strain, as husbands, despairing of the situation and humiliated at being unable to provide for their families, simply abandoned them. In this, Brody was a harbinger of the American experience.

The real chamber of horrors was the textile factory where the registration cards and train tickets were given out. Price describes how thousands of refugees in no comprehensible order struggled for their cards and tickets.

When one observes it from a close range, one cannot grasp the situation. He is stunned by the multitude and the noise and shouts of the tens of thousands of people. When one sees the picture from a distance, it looks as if the walls are plastered with ants moving one on top of another. Upon close observation one is chilled by what he sees. Here a Jew clad in rags and perspiring, who seems to have been here many hours managed . . . to get to the middle. He tries to figure out a way to get to the window as quickly as possible. He does a somersault, hoping to hurtle over the heads of several people and thus advance his position. This causes chaos. He is beaten, his clothes are rent; finally, still alive, he nears the window, only to be pushed back by a strong-armed man who has tried to clear a space. He falls, and drags others with him. Immediately the space is occupied by others. In such an attempt, one is trampled by the mob. The mob pays no attention and goes on fighting and mauling each other in order to get closer to the windows.[19]

In such a situation, Price, who was fortunate in possessing some money of his own, came to the conclusion that, "the Russian way would work." He slipped some money into the hands of one of the Austrian soldiers who were striking at the mob with clubs; the soldier, gun extended, escorted him to the window where tickets were being dispersed. The Price family was soon on its way to Hamburg, each one provided with a loaf of bread and two eggs for the first part of the trip that was to take them to America.

The journey to the European ports and to London was a pleasant interlude for many of the emigrants. Once out of Brody, their situation improved dramatically. They were considered exotic by those they met, and many of them were actually treated to music, toasts, and cheers. At each large train station, representatives of the Jewish relief organizations came on board and supplied the travelers with bread, milk, coffee, cigars, cheese, meats, and other delicacies. In Berlin and Hamburg, many of the emigrants were given delicious dinners and treated as important personalities. George Price was overwhelmed by the experience.[20]

The unexpected pleasures of the trip across Europe served the Russian Jews well. It not only helped them recover from the Brody experience, it fortified them emotionally and physically for the next hurdle on their way to America, the very difficult, often terrible sea voyage. Nearly every account of the time on ship relates a tale of horror and incredible discomfort. Nausea, seasickness, and vomiting were part of the common suffering, as were the crashing of glass and the screaming of children. George Price was so sick he was unable to eat for six days. Harris Rubin, who traveled from Vilna to London by himself without going through Brody and who encountered in London, at the hands of the London assistance committee, a miniature version of the Brody experience, had to watch carefully from his lower birth so as to avoid the vomit of those who were stacked one on top of the other above him.[21]

Even worse than the pain and discomfort was the fear. When storms struck the ship, the emigrants, virtually none of whom had ever been on a ship, became hysterical. People huddled and prayed. On Rubin's ship, the fear was so great that not only did the passengers recite psalms, as was the custom for Orthodox Jews confronting sickness and danger, but they promised that if saved from the storm they would not forget the Torah when they reached profligate America; and all of the traditional observances would be honored. When the storm was over and the people were at last hungry, they were unable to eat: It was Passover, and since the only food on the ship was *chometz* (forbidden food for Passover), the people could not eat in view of the promises they had just made.

An incident occurred on Rubin's ship that serves as a prologue to the Russian Jewish experience in America. Upon boarding the vessel, the refugees were introduced by members of the London committee to a man who was referred to as a *mashgiach*, a supervisor of the Jewish dietary laws, whose job it was to see that all food complied with the dietary laws and who would also see to religious services on board. In a short time, however, it became clear that the *mashgiach* was an ignoramus. The meat was clearly not kosher and when the *mashgiach* at a Sabbath service lit candles, a violation of the traditional Sabbath ban on lighting fires, the Jews went wild. Only the intervention of the ship's captain saved the *mashgiach* from physical assault. For Rubin and his fellow passengers the real culprits were the "German Brethren," the London and American Jews of German descent who had taken charge of the emigration movement and who had so much contempt and so little feeling for the emigrants that they had chosen such a man to accompany them to America. Whatever the real cause for the choice of the *mashgiach*, it foreshadowed subsequent encounters between Russian

Jews and the American Jewish community leadership, which was largely of German origin.

Their arrival in New York harbor meant that the European part of the emigrants' experience was over. For many, if not most, it had been a brutal and enervating experience. There were some, however, who weathered the European and Atlantic storms relatively easily. The *am olamkes*, young men and women of the idealistic agricultural organization discussed in Chapter V, seemed to surmount without great anguish the difficulties in Central Europe and the trip across the ocean. Young, unattached, and filled with ideological zeal, they maintained their high spirit and overcame every obstacle.

Abraham Cahan claims that even in Brody the *am olamkes* found time to meet, and in some cases marry, the attractive Jewish girls of Galicia.[22] Cahan was not alone in being struck with the Jewish beauties of Brody and Lemburg (Lvov). George Price in one of his few references to pleasant aspects of existence in Brody makes mention of the good looking young ladies. It seemed to be the only compensation Brody offered.[23]

Alexander Harkavy, another *am olamka*, wrote of the sense of superiority felt by members of his Am Olam group. They considered themselves above the other Jewish passengers on the ship going to America. The other Jews were going to America because it would be more comfortable there, but the people of Am Olam were going to America to prove to the world that the Jews could work the land. On board ship their imaginations ran wild speculating about the community institutions they would build, even the books that should be put in the library. Nothing that happened on ship could dampen their spirits. "In spite of seasickness, storms, and tempest which had visited us on our journey we were happy and big-hearted. All the days of our Atlantic voyage were filled with joys."[24]

Whether ordinary Jews or *am olamkes*, the thousands of immigrants had managed to survive Europe and the transatlantic journey. They were on the verge of entering a country of which they knew almost nothing. Furthermore, they were oblivious to the one group with whom, at least initially, they would have the greatest interaction—American Jewry. The latter knew equally little about their Russian coreligionists. The relationship between "new Jews" and "old Jews" is the stuff of which so much American Jewish history after 1881–1882 was made.

THE EXISTING AMERICAN JEWISH COMMUNITY

American Jews in the period just prior to the pogroms numbered approximately 280,000 people.[25] The community was dispersed all over the continent but with relatively large concentrations in New York City, Philadelphia, Cincinnati, and San Francisco. There were also numerous smaller communities in the South. The Germanic element predominated among American Jews both in numbers and culture. By 1880 the German Jews who had arrived in the United States as part of the great German immigration wave after 1840 had absorbed the native born community, composed of a mixture of *sephardim* (Jewish descendants of the immigrants from the Iberian peninsula) and Jews from other parts of Central Europe, such as Posen, Silesia, and Bohemia. The leading rabbis were of German extraction and many Jews subscribed to or wrote for German-language periodicals and journals. A number of Jewish organizations recorded their minutes in German. Some Jews, in fact, were more identified with the German ethnic group than they were with any American Jewish community. Most, however, had a triple loyalty. They agreed with the view expressed by Rabbi Bernard Felsenthal of Chicago who declared:

Racially, I am a Jew, for I have been born among the Jewish nation. Politically, I am an American, as patriotic, as enthusiastic, as devoted an American citizen as it is possible to be. But spiritually I am a German, for my inner life has been profoundly influenced by Schiller, Goethe, Kant, and other intellectual giants of Germany.[26]

In economic terms, the American Jewish community on the eve of the mass immigration of Russian and East European Jews can be said to have been fairly well off. German Jewish immigrants had entered a myriad of occupations. Tailoring, shoemaking, dealing in secondhand clothes and dry goods, all occupations brought over from Europe and all connected with the garment industry, became the livelihood in America for many of the immigrants. Even before the much larger immigration of the 1881–1914 period brought hordes of tailors, seamstresses, and other clothing workers to America, Jews in this country had begun to play a major role in the production and selling of all types of clothing.

The most common means of work, however, was peddling. At a time when there were very few retail stores outside of the large cities, there was a place for audacious men who could bring the manufactured products of the city to the outlying areas. The existence of a sophisticated railroad system allowed the peddlers to take a giant step into what would otherwise have been an almost inaccessible interior. Peddling as an immigrant occupation was also facilitated by the fact that it operated on credit and therefore demanded very little capital. With the passage of time large numbers of immigrant German Jewish peddlers had prospered to the point that they had moved up to the next rung on the economic ladder, acquisition of a retail store. In many a small town throughout the country, the only retail outlets that existed were those owned by Jews.

By the 1860s and 1870s there existed in the larger American cities a class of affluent Jews. These families had started in relatively humble occupations such as peddling and tailoring, or in a few cases meat-packing; by skill, hard work, and luck they had accumulated extremely large sums of capital. The wealthiest among them moved from merchandizing into investment banking or into retail selling on a larger scale than had ever been the case before for Jews in America.

The city that became the magnet for these patrician Jews was New York. Its rapid growth in population and its simultaneous rise to financial preeminence led many wealthy Jews from all over the country to establish offices in the city and later to make it their primary residence. The Lehmans, Strauses, and Seligmans, along with other prosperous Jews, gravitated to New York City and became the leaders of the city's Jewish community. Not as wealthy but still prosperous were large numbers of Jewish retailers, wholesalers, and manufacturers, the great bulk of them attached to the garment industry. As early as 1859 a New York Merchants Guide listed 141 wholesale firms with Jewish names, nearly all of which were involved in the garment industry. By 1880 the New York garment trade was largely in the hands of Jews of German extraction.

A knowledge of Jewish demography and economic structure in the United States is not sufficient to understand the real nature of American Jewish life around 1880. It is necessary to probe attitudes, religious and secular, to acquire both a feel for the sense of the community, and to understand the sources of conflict and tension that would soon divide the existing American Jewish community from the immigrants that were to land in such large numbers on American shores. If there was any ideological feature that distinguished the majority of American Jews, it was adherence to Reform Judaism. Beginning in Germany, the Reform movement came to the United States and quickly spread throughout the country. The absence of a powerful Orthodox community, the arrival of a number of gifted German Reform rabbis and the desire of the German Jewish immigrants to acculturate as rapidly as possible contributed to the fact that Reform Judaism had much greater success in the United States than in its place of origin.

Reform Judaism of the American variety was utterly different from the Judaism of Eastern Europe. The briefness of the service, the emphasis on decorum, the use of a choir and organ, prayer in English with a minimum of Hebrew and certainly no Yiddish whatsoever in any part of the service, were only the most visible aspects of Reform Judaism. The ideological assumptions were worlds apart. Although the Pittsburgh Platform was not adopted until 1885, large numbers of American Jews had subscribed to its basic principles already for some time. The Jews were no longer a nation but a religious community, Reform Judaism proclaimed. There was no expectation of a return to Palestine. Judaism was a progressive religion which must always strive to be in accord with reason and science. Therefore, much of the Mosaic and rabbinical legislation, including that of diet (*kashruth*) and dress, were declared null and void since they originated in a more primitive period and were not consistent with the modern and progressive outlook of contemporary civilization. No wonder then, that so many American Jews looked upon the new immigrant Jews from Eastern Europe as superstitious religious fanatics.

A feeling of contempt, or, if that word is too strong, at least of dislike for East European Jews on the part of Jews already in America had surfaced decades before 1881. Both the B'nai B'rith and the Young Men's Hebrew Association did not welcome members whose origins were in Eastern Europe. Religious differences were only part of the problem. The dress and the language of Russian Jews who arrived in the 1860s and 1870s were irksome to American Jews, who looked down on their Russian coreligionists as wild men from Asia. Feeding this contempt for East European Jewry was the pride that all Americans of German descent, Jews and Gentiles, felt in the achievements of the new Germany. The creation of the Second Reich in 1871, the removal of all disabilities placed upon German Jews, the economic boom in Germany in the 1870s, all contributed to a belief in the superiority of German civilization to every other in Europe, particularly to anything and anyone of East European derivation. Eastern Europe was the continent's cowshed and the people inhabiting it were looked upon as inferior breeds.

Underneath all this contempt and dislike, however, was another sentiment—fear. American Jews—respectable, hard-working, affluent, assimilated—were growing nervous. There was more than a little unease in American Jewry as Jews became fearful of losing at least part of their hard-won gains. American Jews of German descent might, in public forums, speak pridefully of the new Germany, but they were not oblivious to the fact that it was precisely in Germanic Europe that the new secular anti-Semitism based on economic and racial theories was finding its most vocal support. Fear that the anti-Semitism of Europe would cross the ocean played a role in the formation of American Jewish attitudes toward the very different and apparently backward Jews from Russia who could conceivably prejudice Americans against all Jews.

Evidence that anti-Jewish sentiment was becoming a factor, albeit not a decisive one, in American Jewish life is provided by two famous incidents occurring in the 1870s. In 1877, the Jewish financier, Joseph Seligman, was refused accommodations at the Grand Union Hotel in Saratoga Springs. Seligman was told that the hotel's manager, Henry Hilton, had given instructions that "no Israelites should be permitted in the future to stop at this hotel."[27] In July 1879, less than two years before the outbreak of the pogroms, a similar incident took place in the Manhattan Beach area of Brooklyn, a well-known resort area.[28] Austin Corbin, the President of the Manhattan Beach Company, had publicly opposed the admission of Jews to the beach and the hotel. Jews, according to Corbin, were pretentious, contemptible, ill-behaved, rapacious, detestable, and vulgar. Hilton and Corbin were not alone. Jews were being barred from private resorts, social clubs, and schools. Privileged and affluent Americans, the old elite of American society, were reacting to the new rich, many of whom were Jewish, who had come on the scene in the industrial boom that followed the Civil War. These were not exclusions that affected the overwhelming majority of American Jews. Nonetheless, wide publicity surrounded many of the discriminatory incidents and served to heighten the sense of nervousness felt by many American Jews.

The American Jewish attitudes already described should not mislead the observer of American Jewry in the third quarter of the nineteenth century. American Jews were still Jews and they could still feel more than a tinge of sympathy for their coreligionists suffering in less hospitable lands. In the 1840s, American Jews had participated in a large-scale protest movement in support of the Jews who stood accused in the notorious Blood Libel case in Damascus; several had been charged with the murder of a Christian monk for the alleged purpose of using his blood for the baking of the matzoh, the unleavened bread for Passover. For the first time American Jews had acted forcefully in an organized fashion. Public meetings were convened in which non-Jews participated, and the American government was called upon to intervene. A repetition of this public action occurred in the 1850s over the Mortara Affair, the incident in which a Jewish infant in Bologna was baptized by his nurse without the knowledge of his parents and was later abducted by church authorities to be raised as a Catholic. American Jews, it seems, for all of their passion to become American, could still respond to the plight of Jews in far-off places.

Such a mixture of attitudes led to a somewhat ambivalent response on the part of American Jews toward the problems posed by Jewish immigration in the late 1860s and 1870s. At that time, famine and cholera in Lithuania and parts of Russian Poland had triggered a migration of thousands of Jews. In the rest of Europe, various Jewish assistance committees—it was a precursor of the response to the 1881–1882 pogroms—were created for the purpose of helping the immigration of the Russian Jews to other European countries and the United States, primarily the latter.

Problems arose, however, when the Board of Delegates of American Israelites, the foremost American Jewish organization of the time, expressed opposition to a sizeable immigration of Russian Jews and gave as its reason the belief that a large influx of Jews might endanger the Jewish position in America. The Board subsequently did go ahead and raise money, some seven thousand dollars, "to be expended on the spot for the relief of the necessitous," but it continued to oppose large-scale immigration. The Board's attitude was endorsed not only by its press organ, the *Jewish Messenger*, but even by the Philadelphia branch of the Alliance Israélite Universelle, which had taken upon itself much of the cost involved in finding new homes for the immigrants.[29]

The position of the Board and the Philadelphia section of the Alliance did not reflect the attitudes of all American Jews, however. From the very first, in 1869, American Jewish voices were raised in support of the immigration of large numbers of Jews. Benjamin Franklin Peixotto, a Jew of Sephardic origin who had served as an American diplomat in Romania and was, therefore, familiar with the persecution of East European Jewry, was a strong supporter of immigration. So was the prominent American Jew, Simon Wolfe, who labored indefatigably to reconcile American Jews with the immigrant. In distant California, the small number of Russian Jews who had settled there as early as the 1840s established a relief society for immigrants, a step that received support from the *Jewish Times* of New York in early October 1869.[30]

Nonetheless, strong opposition to all but the smallest number of immigrants continued throughout the 1870s. The *American Israelite* and the *Hebrew Leader*, a weekly, became forums for this view. In an article of April 15, 1870, entitled "The Approaching Arrival of Russian Jews," the *Hebrew Leader* expressed the view that immigration of Russian Jews to America would not help the former but only worsen their position due to the difficulties of adapting to American life.[31] One might not be wrong in believing that concern for the well-being of American Jews rather than sympathy for the Russian Jews was the real motive behind the article.

The prolonged opposition, coupled with the unequivocal attitude of the Board of Delegates that it would cooperate with the European assistance committees only if the latter agreed to ship groups of not more than one hundred able-bodied persons, led one of the important Jewish assistance committees, the one based in Koenigsberg in East Prussia, to adhere rigorously to the principle of selection. Out of five thousand families that registered with it from July 1870 to July 1871, only three hundred were shipped to the United States.

Selections notwithstanding, the immigrants continued to come, sometimes with the assistance of the committees, at other times without it. Precise figures for arrival of Russian Jewish immigrants in the United States are impossible to obtain, but a figure of fifteen to twenty thousand for the decade 1871–1880 seems reasonable.[32] By 1880, therefore, American Jewry had received a small but important infusion of Jews from the Russian Empire, and their presence was already being felt, particularly in New York City. More important, in Europe and America, an institutional infrastructure had been created to deal with the problems of emigration and immigration. This structure, on both sides of the ocean, would be severely tested in the year and a half following the pogroms.

CONFLICT AMONG ASSISTANCE ORGANIZATIONS

The institutional framework was first put to the test in the summer of 1881, as the immigrant population in Brody began to swell. Filled with pity, European Jewry began to respond; in addition to the already existing committees, new ones sprung up all over Central and Western Europe. They began to send men to Brody to ascertain the magnitude of the problem. The largest, wealthiest, and most prestigious of these organizations, the Alliance Israélite Universelle, the only one possessing an international character, delegated Charles Netter to organize the work of assistance in Brody. By the autumn of 1881, Netter and the Alliance were coordinating a host of European committees whose representatives were providing clothing, food, train passage and ship tickets for the emigrants.

Initially, the Alliance together with the other organizations opposed the idea of immigration either to Palestine or to America, and above all to Western Europe. If they had had their way, the European Jewish organizations would have sent the emigrants back to a more tolerant Russia, one prepared to allow Jews into the empire's interior. Obviously, this was not to be, since the Russian government remained inflexible and intolerant; and the emigrants had absolutely no desire to return to Russia in any case. Some threatened to starve themselves and their families if they were forcibly repatriated.

Gradually, the Alliance began to shift ground. America was rich, free, and possessed enormous quantities of arable land. In the early autumn of 1881, S. H. Goldshmidt of the Alliance informed the leaders of American Jewry of the European plan to facilitate the migration of the emigrants to the United States. The Americans were assured that only young and mostly unattached people would be sent. They were also told that the Alliance and the other European Jewish organizations would transfer substantial sums of money to the American Jewish community for the purpose of defraying the costs of the resettlement. Goldshmidt made it clear that one of the reasons for the choice of America was the European belief that anti-Semitism was not an important element in American society. "Envy and jealousy which lie at the bottom of persecution in Germany and elsewhere in Europe, are not likely to exist for many years to come against the Jews in America."[33] European concern over growing anti-Semitism on the Continent was to be an important factor in subsequent policy decisions.

It soon became clear that the policies of the Europeans could not be implemented in the fashion detailed by Goldshmidt and endorsed by the European assistance committees. It was just not possible to sustain a selective immigration. The refugees piling into Brody expected, even demanded assistance for immigration to America; what was even worse from the perspective of the assistance committees was that the emigrants were adamant that there be no separation of families. Fathers refused to be separated from wives and children, and sons from parents and dependent siblings. The result was that the Alliance and the London Mansion House Committee began to sponsor a large-scale immigration across the Atlantic.

This situation was bound to present problems, given the already luke-warm attitudes of American Jewry toward Jewish immigration. The Union of American Hebrew Congregations, for example, the umbrella orga-nization of the Reform movement, in August of 1881 called upon Amer-ican Jews to welcome the exiles. However, the Union stated that the immigration must be a selective one. Only immigrants who would have no difficulty finding work should be allowed to come.[34] The Russian Emigrant Relief Fund, which was established in New York City after news of the pogroms arrived, also appealed to American Jews to grant financial support to emigrants who chose to come to America, "the haven and refuge for the oppressed of all nations." But significantly, the fund assured American Jews that only skilled workmen would be sent to the United States.[35]

More unequivocal support came from a number of Jewish periodicals, one of which, the *American Hebrew*, showed no reluctance to mildly castigate the American Jewish community for its modest response to the sufferers of the pogroms:

That the fulness of the misery of the Russian Jews has not been appreciated in America is apparent from the response to the appeals for aid England, France, Germany and Austria have, with large-hearted benevolence, and with righteous recognition of the need, contributed according to their means to aid the sufferers. The American Jewish community, untrue to its best traditions, has not yet done its duty. It is urgently necessary to put forth our endeavors to aid these exiles from their homes which have been cruelly devastated; it is our duty to give material aid to them, enabling them to become industrious citizens. Many are seeking shelter and homes on our shores; they have the bones and sinew that are needed to build a peaceable, thrifty citizen; they have been trained to a life of labor, as well as to a sphere of thoughts and morals; all that they need is the first hand of encouragement that shall set them on their feet in their environments.[36]

On the other side, the *Jewish Messenger* published a number of articles in 1881 against the mass immigration of Russian Jews to the United States. One such article proposed that American Jewish missionaries be sent to Russia for the purpose of civilizing the backward brethren. Then, if the worst possible scenario—mass immigration—did, in fact, take place, the American Jewish community would be spared Russification.[37] The periodical shifted its position in the summer of 1881 and became more sympathetic toward the refugees, calling upon American Jews to be generous in support of those who had already arrived. Nevertheless, it adhered, like virtually everyone else, to the selection principle.[38]

A more vocal critic of immigration was the prominent Cincinnati rabbi and former "learned Jew" in Russia, Dr. Max Lilienthal, who had over the years drastically changed his position. When he arrived in the United States in 1846 he had appealed, on the basis of first-hand knowledge of the conditions of Russian Jewry, for that group to come to America. By 1881, however, Lilienthal had become a fervent advocate of Russian Jewish migration to Palestine. In this vein, he corresponded with prominent European Jews and wrote articles for the American Jewish press. In Palestine, he claimed, land was either free or could be purchased cheaply, and many Russian Jews would wish to go there. Moreover, in Palestine Russian Jews could become farmers and, once and for all, demonstrate that the anti-Semites were wrong: Jews are able to do productive labor and work the land.[39]

The less than enthusiastic sentiment in behalf of immigration, coupled with what seemed to be a massive flow of immigrants in 1881 and 1882 who had defied the selection principle, provoked an angry response from those American Jewish organizations involved in the question of immigration. In October 1881, a cable was sent from New York to the Alliance in Paris. Its message was terse: "Send no more immigrants. Committee [The Russian Relief Fund] must return incapables."[40] In the same month, the Russian Relief Fund sent a long and bitter letter responding to one sent by Goldshmidt earlier. It laid out the Americans' opposition to the policies of the Alliance, and advanced the American view on what had to be done. It also, incidentally, provides insights into some of the problems faced by the new immigrants.

The letter began with a flat denial that America was the panacea for the woes of Russian Jews. Only a small number could be settled here. The Alliance was taken to task for going back on its word that only strong, abled-bodied people, willing to work, and possessing knowledge of handicrafts would be sent. One-third of the immigrants, the letter claimed, had none of the requisite qualifications. Most of the immigrants were clerks or tradesmen who knew nothing about crafts. All they wanted to do was peddle; yet "we are overrun with peddlers already who have become a source of much annoyance to us."[41] The immigrants, even those who said they had farming experience, were unable to do hard labor and quit their jobs after one or two days. This was in contrast, the letter claimed, to immigrants of other faiths who were almost always either skilled mechanics or able-bodied laborers capable of subsisting on little and of working on the canals and railroads.

The second half of the letter admonished the Alliance to honor its word and send over only the able-bodied. It was necessary that the immigrants be provided with "clean substantial clothing adequate for our rigorous climate," that no more than 50 people per week be sent and, for the time being, not more than 150 per month. In sum, the New Yorkers wanted a tight selective process to be implemented: "Do not send any married couples nor any men who leave their wives at home, as the latter class frequently soon get homesick and cause us trouble; above all let us have mechanics or actual farmers or laborers, and of course, only those entitled to our special assistance on account of being exiles from their Russian homes."[42] The Alliance was also urged to make it clear to the immigrants in Brody that "a rigid adherence to the rites of Judaism will in many cases be entirely impossible."

At the very end of the letter there appeared a brief statement that perhaps underlay much of the equivocal American Jewish response to the immigration. The Alliance was urged not to forget that the Jewish position in America was not very secure, that American Jews could not afford to run the risk of incurring the ill will of their compatriots. Implicit in the letter was the belief that the American people might tire of seeing so many unadaptable and consequently burdensome Jews and would hold American Jews responsible for bringing them over. There was also the fear that the unfavorable image of the Russian Jews would soon reflect on all American Jews and that some of the Gentiles would make no distinction. American as well as European Jewish responses to immigration were conditioned by the specter of anti-Semitism.

Nothing changed with the disappearance of the Russian Relief Fund and its replacement by the Hebrew Emigrant Aid Society, which was founded in late 1881 and soon became the leading American relief organization dealing both with the European organizations and the immigrants themselves when they arrived in New York. In letter after letter to Europe and in the repeated words of its spokesmen, the message was always the same: Send few emigrants, and make certain these are skilled workers able to make a living. Moritz Ellinger, a representative of HEAS, laid it out succinctly and simply: "America is not a poorhouse, and we would not be made an asylum for the paupers of Europe. If the European Jews ask what is to be done with the sick and the old we should reply that this is your business, not ours. We take care of our own sick and aged."[43]

In fairness to HEAS and the Russian Relief Fund, it is necessary to note that the New Yorkers were feeling considerable pressure from precisely those places where it was sending the new arrivals. From the earliest days in 1881 it was decided that broadly dispersing the immigrants would be in their best interests. Then they would not be crowded into foul-smelling tenements and ghettos in New York City. The problem was that the cities on the receiving end were not ecstatic about accepting the Russian Jews. A letter from Milwaukee to HEAS aptly summarizes the sentiments of assistance organizations in Cleveland, Providence, Baltimore, Rochester, and Philadelphia, all of which sent notification to HEAS that they would not receive any more of the immigrants. The letter from Louis B. Schram of Milwaukee dated June 30, 1882, states: "If you send many more Russians to Milwaukee, whether it be to this society or 'To Whom It May Concern,' they will be shipped back to you without permitting them to leave the depot."[44] In June 1882, the Boston branch of the Hebrew Emigrant Aid Society did just that. When 415 Russian Jews sent by the Mansion House Fund arrived in Boston, they were promptly shipped back to New York.[45]

This animosity toward the immigrants cannot be totally explained by the fear that their presence would generate a more vehement anti-Semitism. There was, as will be seen in the next section, a personal loathing for the immigrants. For many American Jews the appearance of the immigrants only served to confirm their belief that these were indeed "wild Asiatics," uncouth and uncivilized savages. The immigrants' difficulties in adjusting to hard physical labor led many American Jews, most of whom themselves did not engage in such labor, to view the immigrants as lazy and shiftless. A further stain on the image of the immigrants were their religious practices. American Jews, especially the prominent ones engaged in resettlement work, were accustomed to Reform Judaism, and the immigrant's passion for *kashruth* and strict Sabbath observance appeared to be a superstitious vestige of antiquity.

Since America was the desired destination of the immigration stream, the opposition of the American Jewish assistance organizations inevitably had significant impact on the entire movement. If in the winter of 1881 and 1882 there was considerable tension between the Jewish groups in America and Europe over the type and number of immigrants to be received in the United States, with all sorts of threats made by both sides, the situation became clarified by the summer of 1882. Edward Lauterbach and other representatives of HEAS attended an international meeting of relief organizations held in Vienna on August 2, 3, and 4, 1882, one of several that year; they stated unequivocally in the name of HEAS that the organization would receive no more immigrants except in a few exceptional cases.[46] The gates were closed, as far as the American Jewish relief organizations were concerned, and European Jewry had to deal with this fact.

The action of HEAS was softened by the fact that the pogroms had stopped by the summer of 1882, and Tolstoi's firm rule as Minister of the Interior implied safer times ahead for Russian Jewry, at least physically. By the late summer and early autumn of 1882 the stream of emigrants began to slow down appreciably. It would soon pick up again under the influence of the "cold pogrom," new discriminatory legislation aimed at the Jews. But what was of pressing importance now was a final place of settlement for the thousands of Jews that were still in Brody as of September 1882.

With America seemingly closed to the emigrants, and Palestine not acceptable to the relief organizations, there were only two viable options:

repatriation to Russia or migration from Brody to other European countries. It soon became clear that the latter option was impossible. Prefiguring events of fifty to sixty years later, the Jewish organizations in the period 1881–1882 operated according to the principle that resettlement of the Jews was desirable as long as it was not in one's own country.

N. S. Joseph of the London Mansion House Fund, which had assisted in sending close to eight thousand Russian Jews to America in the years 1881–1882, provides a good example of this point of view. He wrote that England had accepted enough refugees. He and others feared they would become a permanent burden on British Jewry. Repatriation, urged Joseph, is the most practical, satisfactory, and "humane" course to pursue.[47]

Even more vehement opposition to resettlement came from the Viennese Jews active in relief work. Joseph Wertheimer, leader of the Vienna branch of the Alliance, maintained that Austria-Hungry could not accept any more immigrants because Jews in the Hapsburg Empire had enough trouble with growing anti-Semitism. He asked whether it was worthwhile to endanger the 1.5 million Jews of the empire for the sake of a few hundred immigrant families in Brody.[48]

Various assistance committees in Germany also refused resettlement. The Berlin organization was prepared to accept fifty or sixty children, and to send additional money to the Americans if they would change their minds. The distinguished writer and educator, Heinrich Graetz, wrote from Breslau that attempts to form a joint Jewish-Christian committee under the sponsorship of the Alliance to aid the Russian immigrants had to be cancelled because prospective members were convinced that it would soon be characterized by the anti-Semites as an international Jewish conspiracy.[49] The same situation existed in Frankfort-am-Main. Jewish organizations in Budapest, Brussels, Geneva, Amsterdam, and Rome gave similar answers, as did Jews from Alsace-Lorraine, recently annexed to Germany. Here, too, it was pointed out, anti-Semitism had increased and no immigrants could be accepted.

Only Paris was prepared to accept more than a few additional refugees from Brody, but the figure had to be limited to five hundred. In France, as elsewhere, Jews were concerned about the response of their Gentile compatriots. To be sure, such a great personality as Victor Hugo had rallied to the cause of Russian Jewry, but there were also dissenting opinions. Socialist and other newspapers spoke about an "invasion of Paris by Russian Jews." A number of Parisian workers expressed fear that immigrant Jews would take away jobs from Frenchmen. There was also considerable tension from the fact that when houses were purchased for the immigrants a number of French workers had been forced to move. In the end, French assistance committees, including the Alliance, were like all the others, supporting resettlement anywhere but within their own country.[50]

Everyone, it seems, was caught up in the fear of anti-Semitism. Such fear says much concerning the nature of newly emancipated European Jewry. Wealthy, assimilated, contributing mightily to the countries of which they were citizens, European Jews still feared that what had been given could very easily be taken away. It was part of what later generations would refer to as a Diaspora mentality. But not all fears are the result of paranioa. Without proceeding to a protracted discussion of European anti-Semitism in the final quarter of the nineteenth century, there can be no denial of the fact that, optimistic nineteenth-century liberal opinion notwithstanding, anti-Semitism turned out not to be a vestige of the Middle Ages. Fueled by the great depression of 1873, anti-Semitic spokesmen began to espouse their cause all over Europe, particularly, but not exclusively, in Germany and the Hapsburg Empire. It ought not to be forgotten that the pogroms were coincidental with the appearance of such luminaries of the anti-Semitic impulse as Treitschke, Stoecker, and Wilhelm Marr. In 1881 Karl Duehring had published *Die Judenfrage als Rasen-Sitten und Kulturfrage*, a vicious anti-Semitic work. In the same year the first international congress of anti-Semites was convened in Leipzig, and in 1883 Theodor Fritsch was to publish his *Anti-Semiten Katechismus*, a decalogue for racists. Small wonder that European Jews were nervous.

Whether this nervousness in the face of anti-Semitism justifies what was done at the end of 1882 is a matter for speculation. There can be no doubt, however, that the second half of 1882 witnessed behavior on the part of all of the Jewish organizations that does not speak well of Jewish solidarity or peoplehood. At the August conference in Vienna it was decided to repatriate those refugees remaining in Brody. With an efficiency and speed not seen during the large-scale emigration, the Jewish organizations proceeded, with the assistance of Hapsburg authorities who were equally eager to get rid of the emigrants, to implement this decision. They emptied Brody of refugees by sending most of them back to Russia. Repatriation finally had its day. By January 1883, there were few if any of the 5,275 refugees that had been in Brody in the late autumn of 1882; most of them had been returned to Russia.

The unfortunate fate of the thousands of repatriated Jews in Brody did not, of course, mark the end of the emigration movement. It only served as an end to the Brody chapter in the history of that movement. By early 1883, the stream of emigrants from Russia was beginning to flow again, this time bypassing not only Brody but the assistance organizations themselves. It was an independent and also more massive movement. The repatriation of the Brody refugees also should not blind the observer to the fact that although thousands were sent back to the despised homeland, many thousands more actually did succeed in finally leaving Russia, and most of them did, in fact, eventually reach America. It is to their fate in America that the discussion must turn.

GERMANS AND RUSSIANS

From everything that has been said, it can be inferred that relations in America between American Jews, largely German in culture, and the Russian Jewish immigrants would not be harmonious. Without exaggeration, it can be said that the gulf between the groups was so vast that for some time to come it was virtually unbridgeable. Israel Friedlander, a noted commentator on Jewish affairs writing in the early twentieth century, was accurate in describing the relationship as it existed in the early 1880s: For native American Jews—wealthy, assimilated, and adherents of Reform Judaism—"America was the Zion and Washington was the Jerusalem of American Israel."[51] The Russian Jews, said Friedlander, were very different in a myriad of ways. They were orthodox and their Orthodoxy was not the neo-Orthodoxy of Samson Raphael Hirsch and his attempts to reconcile traditional Judaism with modernity. More than a small dose of Palestinophilism existed among large numbers of the new immigrants, even though they had chosen America rather than the ancient homeland. Above all, said Friedlander, there were differences in economic and social position that created difficulties between the two groups. The German Jews were now American natives; the Russian Jews were new arrivals. The German Jews were rich, the immigrant Russian Jews were poor. The German Jews dispensed charity, the Russian Jews were on the receiving end. The German Jews often were the employers, and the Russian Jews were low paid employees working under terribly difficult conditions.

On both sides there were additional complications. American Jews, as already noted, were convinced, even before the immigration, that Russian Jews were an inferior breed whose coming to this country might lead to the Russification of the American Jewish community and its eventual descent into backwardness and barbarism. On the immigrant side, difficulties were bound to arise as a result of the expectations held by many of the newcomers. Some of them really did believe that the streets were paved with gold; of those that did not share this belief, the great majority no doubt were convinced that in America earning not only a living but a comfortable one would be an easy task. This was particularly true of those immigrants who dreamed of working the land either as part of groups such as Am Olam or as individuals. As will be seen, whether it be agricultural work or urban enterprise, the problem of earning a living was to be a monumental one for the immigrants. This further complicated and embittered their relations with the American Jewish community from whom they had expected so much.

One final element was the fact that the various relief organizations did not have sums of money at their disposal commensurate with the numbers of immigrants and their needs. There was less than $200,000 for the nearly ten thousand immigrants served in one fashion or another by HEAS in New York and by its branches throughout the country. There was also the problem of cash flow: Since 60 percent of the budget came from overseas, HEAS was dependent on a regular and expeditious transfer of funds from abroad. Yet some of the European groups, particularly the Mansion House Fund in London, delayed sending money because of their bitter debate with HEAS over the question of who should control the dispersion of the Russian Jews in the United States. The result of the shortage of money was that HEAS was forced to be very frugal with the institutions and enterprises that dealt directly with the immigrants, another source of bitterness for the Russian Jews arriving in America.[52]

In view of what has just been said it may seem surprising that the initial, spontaneous response of ordinary American Jews to the immigrants was quite positive. *Nedel'naia khronika Voskhoda*, in early January 1882, and *Ha-Melits*, in October 1881, carried articles and letters from immigrants who spoke about the friendly treatment they received in New York.[53] Philadelphia was especially warm to the Russian immigrants, receiving them "with open arms." The first transport to Philadelphia which arrived from England on February 23, 1882, was met by crowds of Christians and Jews who created a holiday-like atmosphere for the occasion. One immigrant to Philadelphia from the first ship wrote his wife that "they care for us here as if we were children."[54] Food and clothing were provided; "You would not recognize us," the same immigrant told his wife.

Within a short time, however, the mood began to change and hostility toward the immigrants mounted. The statements of relief committees in various cities demanding that no additional immigrants be sent to them testifies to the changed outlook. The written reports issued by the committees and their correspondence confirm the change. "They are alien to our civilization," became a common theme in this literature. It seemed that almost no one was immune to these sentiments. The young Jacob Schiff, subsequently one of the great benefactors of East European Jewry, was beginning his career as a social figure; he wrote to Baron Maurice de Hirsch that the leaders of American Jewry are "called by Divine Providence to stand guard" and defend American Jewry against the onslaught from Eastern Europe.[55]

One of the harshest attacks against the immigrants came from the German Jewish periodical, *Tseitgeist*, which circulated in Chicago and Milwaukee and was read by prominent Jews of German extraction. The editor, Adolf Moses, raised the question of Russian Jewish immigrants in the May 25, 1882, issue in his article, "Messen wir die russische Einwanderung nicht mit einem falschen Massstab?" (Are We Measuring the Russian Immigration with a False Standard?). Moses wrote that American Jews certainly must help the immigrants but must also free themselves from all illusions concerning them: "The Russian Jews are just like the unfortunate Russian people to whom they belong. . . . They are half barbarian. . . . The Russians Jews through hundreds of years of terrible pressure, through living side by side with an ignorant, enslaved, rightless barbarian people have become wild [themselves]."[56] The immigrants, wrote Moses, have a slave psychology and lack the courage of free men. "The dirt of a repulsive barbarianism adheres to them also." Even the best of the immigrants, the Russian Jewish aristocracy, cannot be considered European but only Russian, with all that this word connotes. "Their ways are not our ways." If the Russian Jews could have stayed for some time in Germany, then they would now be different. Our obligation is clear, argued Moses; it is to help "the better elements among them." These will soon be able to adapt to American society. In time their grandchildren, in conjunction with ours, will further develop the spiritual life of American Jewry. Moses, and presumably other American Jews, were not devoid of a sense of graciousness. There was a place in America for good Russian Jews, for the educated elite of the immigration. The fate of the others, the lower and middle level, or, in other words, the great majority of immigrants, was not a matter of concern, unless, as some American Jews believed, it was necesary to send them back whence they had come.

NEW YORK

Most new immigrants disembarked at New York City's Castle Garden, located at the lower end of Manhattan. It was the place that received nearly all immigrants arriving in New York and would do so until other facilities were prepared on Ellis Island. It was the place where most immigrants had their first encounter with American officials—and if they were Jewish, with the primary Jewish assistance organization, the Hebrew Emigrant Aid Society. In both respects, according to the memoirs, the meetings were not felicitous. The Yiddish pun, *"a regular keslgarten"* (a *kesl* is a cauldron), signifying a place of large crowds and great tumult and filth, testifies to the lasting imprint that this first encounter with America had upon immigrant Jews.

In the words of George Price, Castle Garden was a *gehenna* (hell). At least part of this sentiment derived from the disappointment experienced by the new immigrants, some of whom remembered being wined and dined after they had left Brody. There were few comforts in Castle Garden. Instead, the transfer from the ship to land "was nothing more than going from the frying pan into the flame."[57] Thousands upon thousands of people just sat around waiting to be processed. The facilities, built in an earlier time, did not suffice for the immigrant waves that descended on the city in the 1880s. Price recalled that thousands of people were forced to sleep in the open courtyard for up to a week. The rain and the screams of women and children made it appear to Price and to a multitude of others as if they had landed in Hades. Even Brody had not been as bad as this. To Price and to others, this treatment was not accidental. The Americans, he maintained, believed that Europeans were unaccustomed to even small luxuries and thus the most minor conveniences could be dispensed with.

After leaving Castle Garden, the Jewish immigrant may have had another contact with HEAS. It might be that the immigrant would be sent by the organization to one of the refugee centers it had established in Greenpoint in Brooklyn or on Ward's Island in Manhattan's East River. As will be demonstrated below, these were not institutions bursting with harmony and goodwill. In the case of Price and others, the first contact with HEAS came immediately after leaving Castle Garden, as they proceeded to the nearby offices of HEAS, located at 15 State Street. Here it was Brody and Castle Garden all over again. Thousands of people, all new immigrants, without lodging or jobs, pressed in upon 15 State Street in order to get succor from "the committee." But it was almost impossible to gain access to the offices of HEAS. Its doors were guarded by policemen who were not reluctant to use their clubs. Price decided to do without HEAS and strike out on his own. These first encounters did not bode well for the future.

The "society" or the "committee," as HEAS was often referred to by the immigrants, was forced to deal with the large numbers of Russian Jews who could not find suitable accommodations and were unable to get work, the thousands who crowded around 15 State Street. HEAS decided that as a temporary emergency measure it would have to provide places of refuge for the immigrants as well as labor bureaus to assist them in finding work. Eventually employment agencies were set up at 35 East Broadway, not far from Castle Garden, where a labor bureau was also established. The *New York World* reported that in Castle Garden "two or three members of a special committee, consisting of 18 Hebrew merchants," were "constantly in attendance examining applicants . . . so that the ability of each one" would become known to the Superintendent of Immigration.[58] Large places of refuge such as Greenpoint and Ward's Island were created, the latter built with funds provided by the Emigration Commission, a federal institution, by HEAS itself, and by Jacob Schiff, who contributed $10,000. In addition, a restaurant and home was established at 27 Greenwich Street. Many immigrants received lodging and apartments for which HEAS paid the rent. Soup kitchens were also provided by HEAS.

In nearly all of these institutions, relations between the immigrants and those in charge of them were, to say the least, not very good. The newspaper *Ha-Magid* published an article by a former student from Odessa who wrote that in one of the refuge houses established by the committee the supervisor beat and embarrassed male and female immigrants. The writer also complained that the supervisor separated husbands from wives and parents from children. The immigrants were so angry, the article continues, that a meeting was convened and a message was sent to HEAS demanding that it create decent and respectable occupations for the immigrants and not allow them to become peddlers. HEAS should either return them to Russia or send them to Palestine where they could become agricultural laborers.[59]

In another incident, reported in *Ha-Melits*, a supervisor in one of the refuge centers was beaten by immigrants because he wanted to divide their families. Eight immigrants were arrested and placed in prison.[60] It should not be thought that fault lay only with the supervisors, most of whom were of German descent. Harkavy relates that his stay in Greenpoint was punctuated with hostility between the supervisor and the immigrants, most of whom were young men. Harkavy concedes that "we did not act honorably."[61] The supervisor was a religious, old German Jew who was fanatical in his insistence that the immigrants observe the rules governing procedures in Greenpoint. Harkavy relates that the immigrants would provoke the supervisor by screaming and dancing late at night when the elderly gentleman was already asleep. Not even visits from HEAS members who came from Manhattan to pacify the group had the desired effect. When HEAS placed Harkavy and his friends in a large room on Division Street in Manhattan, the young men "paid no attention to cleaning, which we considered unnecessary." The elders of HEAS most certainly were not comfortable with that state of affairs.

The worst incident of this type was the infamous "revolt" that occurred on Ward's Island, "the Schiff refuge," on October 14, 1882.[62] According to Emma Lazarus, who had investigated conditions on the island, and George Price, the incident was inevitable. The supervisor of the island, who preferred to be called Father, but was referred to by the immigrants as the Tsar, treated his charges with contempt. The situation was made worse by the abominable food, which included spoiled meat, wormy soup, and indecent coffee. Price was convinced that the supervisor and his staff were pocketing HEAS money instead of providing for the immigrants. The sleeping arrangements were an overstatement of German orderliness: The 500 immigrants in each building slept on 500 cots arranged in four long rows of 125 each. According to Price, the overall impression that life on Ward's Island made on the immigrants was a terrible one. They came to the belief that they were living in exile, in prison, and were being treated like common criminals. The high expectations of America were being trampled in the dust.

The frequent arrival on the island of representatives from HEAS did not ameliorate the situation, for they, said Price, treated the immigrants with the same contempt as did the supervisor. Conditions on the island always seemed to deteriorate after the HEAS people paid a visit. Price believed that this was the supervisor's way of avenging himself on the immigrants for leveling complaints against him. In sum, the island was a powder keg waiting to explode over the slightest provocation.

The spark igniting the affair occurred on October 13, when, according to Price, the supervisor's assistant slapped a sick woman who had begged him for medicine. The assistant then drew a revolver to ward off the woman and her friends. On the following day a delegation of immigrants met with the supervisor concerning the incident and were given a rude reception. By this time, Ward's Island was seething. At dinner on the 14th, an immigrant who was not served dessert loudly complained and cursed the waiters. A fight soon broke out and the waiters together with the supervisor and his staff were thrown out of the dining room.

According to Price, quiet would have returned had the supervisor not called in the police. In any event, when the police arrived and tried to arrest the immigrant who had begun the fight in the dining room, pandemonium ensued. Stones were thrown at the police who, in turn, beat the crowds of immigrants with their nightsticks. Ward's Island had turned into a battlefield and the casualties were numerous; fortunately there were no fatalities. Property damage, however, was extensive as mobs of immigrants stoned the buildings housing the supervisor and his staff and destroyed not only the windows and doors but furnishings as well. In all, fifty immigrants were hurt, together with a number of policemen and island staff people. Six of the immigrants were arrested. It was the nadir of immigrant-HEAS relations.

The incident became public very quickly and did nothing to brighten the image of the immigrant. That the immigrants had dared to take up weapons against the police, the duly constituted authorities, shocked American Jews probably more than it did their Gentile compatriots. The *American Hebrew* went so far as to compare the uprising with the Paris Commune.[63] One of the few voices defending the immigrants was that of Emma Lazarus, whose open letter published in the *American Hebrew* pointed to the terrible conditions on Ward's Island.[64] HEAS understandably did not dwell on the incident and in its official report for the year 1882 does not refer to it in any detail. It somewhat contemptuously described the people causing the incident as coming from the dregs of the emigration movement ("... rekrutierte sich aus der Hefe der Emigration, ... aus Subjecte, deren Vergangenheit keine nahere Untersuchung vertrug").[65]

Contempt and "revolt" notwithstanding, it would be a distortion of history to deny the positive role played by HEAS. Thousands of immigrants were, after all is said and done, supported by HEAS. Perhaps support is too ambiguous a word. The immigrants were clothed, fed, and given shelter. They were also quite often provided with jobs. To be sure, the manner in which HEAS dealt with the Russian Jews was sorely deficient. Even if Price, Harkavy, and all of the other memoirists greatly exaggerated matters, it should be clear to a much later observer that the haughty and contemptuous attitude of American Jews in New York and elsewhere who took charge of immigrant affairs was cruel and led to unnecessary difficulties for everyone. Nonetheless, HEAS and its branches did provide basic support for the immigrants.

There were even times, in the summer of 1882, when HEAS exhibited a tender and humane face. This was due to the presence in the organization of the famous literary figure, Michael Heilprin, himself a Polish Jew. Heilprin had not been attached earlier to the Jewish community or its institutions. He did not even belong to a temple or synagogue. But he was conscious of the Russian Jews as persecuted human beings, and reacted strongly and sympathetically to their plight. He became secretary of HEAS in the summer of 1882 and did everything humanly possible to make it more sensitive to immigrant needs. He is the one figure about whom the memoirs are unanimous. To the immigrants he was a saint, a warm and sympathetic man who exhausted himself in their behalf. This, too, must be factored in to any evaluation of the role of HEAS, and compels the observer to soften judgment upon that organization.[66]

THE SEARCH FOR WORK

Apart from dealing with their American coreligionists, the immigrants faced another more difficult and fundamental problem, that of *parnossa* (making a living). Without capital and contacts, unable to speak the language of the land, and unfamiliar with American habits and customs, the hordes of former merchants, artisans, and students who struggled through Castle Garden had a difficult time staying afloat in American society. They were "greenhorns" desperate to do anything to survive, and as a result were frequently exploited by Jew and Gentile alike.

The immigrants entered into a variety of occupations. They labored in factories, producing cigars, shirts and other clothing, and worked at anything having to do with the garment industry. Some were self-employed tailors working in cramped apartments under contract to small manufacturers. Quite often their first employers were members of HEAS who, combining business with charity, would take workers straight from Castle Garden into their homes or small factories. Whatever work the immigrants did, whether in the home or in the factory, one thing was sure: the conditions were likely to be horrible. Even those American Jews who were contemptuous of the immigrants and insensitive to their problems made occasional reference to the hardships faced by immigrant laborers. One of them wrote in late 1881 about the life of immigrant tailors who worked in their apartments. He described how they sat up half the night in their poorly ventilated rooms desperately trying to eke out a living. Combined with their poor diets, this work led to deteriorated health, and they often developed pulmonary diseases.[67] The sweatshop was yet to be born, but the pernicious effects of work in the garment industry as it began its period of growth were already being felt.

On occasion the immigrants' desperate desire for work led them into tragic situations. In June and July of 1882, a large dock workers' strike took place in New York. In order to break the strike, employers sent agents to Castle Garden to hire immigrants, including Jews, as replacements. The immigrants, oblivious to the strike and longing for work, went down to the docks where they were met by the clubs, stones, and violence of the strikers. A delegation of members of Am Olam, the agricultural socialist organization, sought to persuade the Jews among the strikebreakers not to act as scabs, a term that the *am olamkes* had quickly picked up but that was unknown to the strikebreaking immigrants, who had not understood it when hurled at them by the strikers. Bernard Weinstein, who, as a recently arrived immigrant participated in the episode, wrote that the Jewish strikebreakers wrestled with their consciences and held meetings in Castle Garden and Battery Park in an effort to decide what to do.[68] Finally, many of them resolved not to work, and, in fact, participated in the large street demonstration held by the strikers, a step which, together with their own meetings, may be considered the first working-class action in which Jewish immigrants participated.

For many Jewish immigrants who arrived in 1881–1882, their first venture into the American economy came in the form of peddling, which by now had become a traditional Jewish occupation. German Jews, as noted, had often become peddlers in the 1840s and 1850s, and the small number of Lithuanian and Polish Jews settling in America in the late sixties and seventies also peddled. The city of Chicago had a fair share of Jewish peddlers by the mid 1870s. With the arrival of those fleeing the pogroms in the early 1880s, peddling once again attracted large numbers of Jewish immigrants—too many in fact, for in the larger cities, particularly New York, hordes of Jewish peddlers competed with each other, and the chances of making a decent living were greatly reduced. Ironically, peddling in large American cities began to take on the character of Jewish economic life in the Pale of Settlement; too many Jews in a myriad of occupations competing against each other and devouring one another.

In America all sorts of individuals gravitated toward peddling. There were former merchants, brokers, yeshiva students, Hebrew school teachers, and some members of the intelligentsia as well. Repelled by the prospect of physical labor, or simply physically unable to engage in such heavy work, these people were attracted to peddling. The fact that one could become a peddler with very little capital—one writer says that only a dollar was needed and that the rest of the merchandise could be bought on credit—was another incentive to become a peddler.[69]

The memoirs of the early 1880s and of later periods as well speak of a peddling hierarchy. At the bottom rung, occupied by the majority, was the door-to-door peddler. He went from apartment to apartment in the tenements offering such trifles as garters, socks, toys, and sweets.

It was also not devoid of danger. Often hoodlums attacked the house-to-house peddler. If the peddler dared to enter non-Jewish neighborhoods, he was often the target of ruffians.

The rural analogue to the house-to-house peddler was the country peddler. The advantage of the latter was primarily that people on the farms and in small towns and villages were generally more appreciative and receptive. The great disadvantage was, of course, the long periods spent away from one's family. A higher rung on the peddling ladder was the custom-peddler, who had regular customers who bought substantial quantities of goods from him, usually on installment. The custom-peddler is a familiar if caricatured figure in the memoir literature. Dressed foppishly with a big cigar in his mouth, he was one of the first of the immigrants to shed his "greenhorn" status and become an immigrant success story.

At the highest levels were pushcart peddling and storekeeping, the last being the ultimate payoff that the occupation offered. For the pushcart peddler there still remained a certain danger. Hoodlums harassed him and he had to worry about the local police, who badgered him to obtain a license. This could be difficult to procure for one reason or another, the principal one being an inability to come up with the required fee. For all types of peddlers more than hard work was necessary. Everyone worked hard; it was personality that seemed to be the decisive factor. Modesty and shyness were not virtues, nor was pride or an obsessive concern with legality. Many a successful peddler began his career by *schnorring* (begging food, lodging, and merchandise) and by selling goods that were of defective quality. One also had to be flexible on profit margins. It was a hard life and elicited behavior which corresponded to the milieu. The peddler always had an excuse ready if he was caught being dishonest. If he did not have one, that was all right too. "There are enough peasants in America," was a peddler's aphorism. If one of the farmers became angry, there was always another one down the road. Honest or dishonest, however, it was a very tough way to make a living. It took Harris Rubin three years dragging himself around the country to accumulate the $64 necessary to bring his family to America.

Not every immigrant labored in the city or peddled in the countryside. Rubin, who while in Russia had dreamed of working the land, tried his hand as an agricultural laborer before moving into peddling. If peddling was difficult, farm work for Rubin and others such as Alexander Harkavy, was absolutely unbearable. It turned out that dreams were not enough. Knowledge and physical stamina were equally if not more important. Rubin writes sadly of his inept attempts at milking cows, or the ache in every part of his body after a day's work on the farm, especially during the harvesting. In addition, his lack of familiarity with English, together with the sad awareness that he had torn himself away from his Jewish roots, from religion and *landsleit* (friends from the old country) tormented Rubin. He collected his wages, after becoming very ill, and returned to New York.[70]

Alexander Harkavy, an *am olamka* who became tired of waiting in Manhattan for his group to settle on its own plot of land, decided to seek farm work by himself. Like Rubin he too suffered from the sixteen hour days and the hard physical labor. He writes about the somewhat comical problems confronting the Jew who wished to observe *kashruth*. At the railroad station, where Harkavy met his employer, he was promptly taken to lunch at the station cafeteria. Not desiring to eat any pork, Harkavy, exercising his almost nonexistent English, pointed to the word on the menu that he believed was for an egg. When the waiter returned, it was with eggnog. Once on the farm, cows ran away from him and kicked over the buckets of milk he had labored so hard to fill. Harkavy soon found his strength ebbing and the work becoming loathsome. The beautiful vision of farm life that had so excited him in New York and in Russia, and which had sustained him for two weeks on the farm in Pawling, New York, soon evaporated. He left the farm a month after he arrived; because he did not have much money—the farmer only paid him half his twelve-dollar monthly salary—he walked the whole eighty miles to New York City. It was a journey marked by the appearance of one of the plagues mentioned in the Passover *Haggadah*. While lying on the ground exhausted from continuous walking, Harkavy was "jumped by frogs."[71]

JEWISH AGRICULTURAL SETTLEMENTS

The yearning for the land exhibited by Harkavy and Rubin was not limited to mere handfuls of individuals. In Russia, as we have seen, there were people who believed that the solution to the Jewish Question lay in the formation of a Jewish agricultural class. Among those coming to the United States, the foremost proponents of Jewish agriculture were the members of the various Am Olam groups that sprang up in the Pale of Settlement in 1881 and 1882. In addition to these, there were numbers of people who had no definite ideological perspective but who wanted for themselves and their families a life of farming in the United States.

Across the Atlantic there were also people who saw great benefits to be derived from placing large numbers of immigrant Jews on the land. Mass agrarian colonization would eliminate the congestion and ghettos in the cities. It would demonstrate to American Gentiles that Jews were capable of hard physical labor. The *American Israelite* was the leading supporter of Jewish agriculture in the Jewish press; it called upon the American Jewish community to provide the necessary funds.[72] At the same time, a group of New York rabbis championed the cause, attracted by the possibility that once and for all the calumny that Jews were not fit for honest toil could be repudiated. The movement also benefitted from the fact that perhaps the most prestigious rabbi of the time, Isaac Mayer Wise, was an ardent supporter of agricultural settlement.[73]

The moving spirit in the drive to settle the Jews on the land was the already mentioned Michael Heilprin. It was he who, in March 1882, established the Montefiore Agricultural Society, which was to later prove so beneficial to the infant colonies, and it was Heilprin who made repeated and urgent appeals to American Jewry to contribute funds. Above all, Heilprin succeeded in convincing the leaders of HEAS to contribute financial support to the movement. It was not an easy task, given both the pessimism of the American Jewish elite about the prospects for Jewish agriculture and their biases against the immigrants. Heilprin would write of his efforts: "We had also to contend with anti-Russian prejudice, an outgrowth of ignorance and self-overestimation, kindred to anti-Semitism."[74]

Due to the efforts of Heilprin and others, the first Jewish agricultural settlements appeared in 1882. They were composed, as could be expected, of essentially two groups; the ideologues of Am Olam and of groups closely linked with them, and individuals and families who had set their hearts and minds upon farming. It is interesting to note that most of the *am olamkes* never reached the agricultural settlements. The groups coming from Kiev, Balta, and part of the group from Vilna dissolved upon meeting the realities of immigrant life in New York City. Most of the members of these groups, like Harkavy, tried their hand at work for private farmers, or drifted into other occupations. Abraham Cahan describes how some of the *am olamkes*, unable to reach the goal of establishing agricultural socialism, remained for some time attached to socialism and practiced it by living in urban communes on the Lower East Side where all earnings were contributed to a common fund.[75]

By early 1883 the following agricultural settlements had been created: Sicily Island (Louisiana); Bethlehem Yehuda (South Dakota); Crémieux (Dakota Territory); New Odessa (Oregon); Cotopaxi (Colorado); Painted Woods (Dakota Territory); Beersheba Colony (Kansas); Alliance Colony (New Jersey); Carmel (New Jersey); and Rosenhaym (New Jersey). Since they involved no more than several hundred Jews, and because most of their histories postdate 1882, it would be out of place to provide a detailed analysis of this interesting experiment in Jewish agricultural living.

It would, however, be proper to make some general remarks, the first of which is that, with the exception of several colonies established in southern New Jersey, they were unhappy failures.

The reasons for failure did not include lack of hard work. All sources, even those most hostile to the Jewish farmers, concede that they worked exceedingly hard. In some cases, the objective conditions proved insurmountable for the settlers. In New Sicily, in Louisiana, it was the terrible heat and the flooding waters of the Mississippi. At New Odessa, in Oregon, and in other areas in the north it was the terrible winters. There was also demoralization from the fact that a number of the colonies were started by family men who had left their wives and children in the city. Their spirits were undermined because many of the farmers were urban people who missed the hustle and bustle and the intellectual vitality of large cities. For the religious among them, there was the additional problem of being deprived of the friendship and services that could only be provided by the religious institutions of a large Jewish community.

Among the more subjective reasons contributing to failure was the frequent quarreling. In the various colonies, debates over political issues divided members; in at least one case, New Odessa, this was an important factor in the dissolution of the enterprise. According to Cahan, New Odessa had another source of conflict: "The sex problem caused considerable difficulty. There were many cases of jealousy ... and all sorts of amorous intrigues, both open and secret."[76] The natural diminution of idealism also affected some *am olamkes* as they grew older. Many of them became unwilling to put up with hardship once their ideological impulses had drained away.

Perhaps the most important reason for failure, however, lay in the fact that very often the colonies were situated poorly, far from markets or from water for irrigation. The colonies in New Jersey were not in this position, which contributed to their success. So too did the fact that they were able to hang on long enough until such organizations as the Baron de Hirsch Fund were prepared to allocate the sums of money necessary for survival and prosperity. Throughout the 1880s, all of the Jewish farm colonies suffered from insufficient funds.

There were a number of reasons for this. The HEAS people and prominent American Jews never overcame their skepticism concerning Jewish agricultural prospects. In their heart of hearts, these wealthy men of the cities believed that the clock could not be turned back. They were also pressed by the needs of immigrants crowding into the cities. There was not enough money for them; how could money be expended on such utopian schemes as Jewish farms? There was also the problem of ideology. Several prominent Jewish visitors to the settlements were appalled at the social and sexual freedom and the absence of religion in the settlements. For staid and bourgeois Jews whose Reform Judaism meant membership in the new "temples," such irreligiosity was too abhorrent; this did not facilitate the raising of funds in behalf of the farms. The cries of the farmers for additional funds to bail them out of difficult circumstances went unheeded.

Finally, the farmers themselves were deficient in their skills and plans. The men of HEAS may have been right. Intellectuals and urban-dwellers may not constitute the best farmer material. So few of the men and women who went to the settlements really knew anything about farming. Harris Rubin, Alexander Harkavy, and, it will be remembered, the men and women of Bilu in Palestine, also did not hold to the land. The American agricultural settlements of 1882 should be placed in this category. It would take new ideology, new experience, new conditions, and new failures before large-scale Jewish agriculture would become viable in the form of the Jewish *kolkhoz* in the U.S.S.R. and the *kibbutz* and *moshav* in Israel. The best epitaph to American Jewish agriculture in 1882 may be the words of one of the participants in the Sicily Island colony: He summed it all up in the following words: "Work—mostly useless—hope, despair, love, song, poetry, happiness and misery—life as we lived it there in Louisiana."[77]

CONCLUSION

The agricultural experience echoed the life of the immigrants in the urban areas where living conditions were hard and failure was a constant threat. The number of immigrants who starved in the cities, and the number of families broken by the harshness of life there will never be known. There is also no precise count of those who left because they were urged to do so by the Jewish organizations, or simply because they threw up their hands at their miserable life and decided to return to the old country. There is one estimate that three thousand or 29 percent of those who came in 1882, returned to Europe.[78] For them and for so many who stayed, it was a "pox on Columbus." The Jewish press in Russia, particularly those periodicals supporting immigration to Palestine, dwelled at length on the perils confronting Jewish immigrants in America. *Yiddishkeit* will die and anti-Semitism will appear, they argued. A warning was issued by the Hebrew press in Russia that all of those who helped the immigration to America would have to eventually "answer before the Master of the Universe."[79]

But there was another side to life in the *goldene medine* (golden land). Some may have left, and many who did not were bruised, some permanently, but many, many thousands stayed and would recover from the initial trauma. They were eking out a living and clawing their way upward. The country was free and the natives were hospitable. To be sure, the sentiments expressed in the *New York Herald* editorial on September 27, 1869, welcoming Romanian Jews with the words: "They make good peaceful prosperous citizens. We have no reason to object to a large Jewish immigration," were beginning to dim.[80]

Here and there caustic comments were made concerning the massive influx of Jews and there were calls for government regulation of immigration. The satirical magazine, *Puck*, caused considerable stir when in November 1881 it published a cartoon that depicted Jews in an unfavorable way. They were fat, had long noses, and wore top hats. The Jewish press in America reacted strongly to the cartoon and compared the editor of *Puck* to the German anti-Semites, Stoecker and Henrici.[81] But the critics of *Puck* had acted too quickly They had neglected to note that the commentary accompanying the cartoon had been highly favorable to the Jewish immigrants. The Jews, said *Puck*, will make good citizens and were held up as a model for the rough and tumble Irish. Stung by the critical remarks of the Jewish press, *Puck* struck back with a harsh call for Jewish assimilation. The Jews deserved satire, claimed *Puck*, because they clung to antiquarian and foolish ways. They must become complete Americans, mixing and marrying with the rest of the population. The *Puck* affair had gotten out of hand, but the crucial thing was that *Puck* never suggested that the Jews not be allowed to come to America. Moreover, its call for the shedding of the old ways and for rapid assimilation was the same program that was advanced by many American Jews, who differed only in that they drew the line on intermarriage.

Whatever the complaints about the Jews, whatever the problems that confronted them, the gates remained open, and there was a sense of freedom in America that even the most oblivious immigrants could feel. With all of their *tsores* (hardships), the immigrants knew that America was different. It was a land without slaves, barons, counts, and *pogromshchiki*. One of the immigrants of 1882 put it aptly when he told Abraham Cahan: "In the old country I used to bow my head and my neck. Here, I hold my head high and my neck the same."[82] The year that had begun in crisis was ending with hope.

Epilogue

The assault against Russian Jewry in the 1881–1882 period must be placed in the context of the general upsurge of anti-Semitism that occurred in many parts of Europe in the final quarter of the nineteenth century. The causes of this phenomenon are too complex to be examined here in detail, but some general statements are in order. The emergence of a vigorous industrial capitalism had a deleterious impact on certain segments of the European populations, who demonstrated great antipathy toward the most visible and vulnerable beneficiaries of the new political and socioeconomic order: the Jews. There had been competition between Jews and non-Jews, particularly in urban areas, for many decades, even centuries, but it was now sharpened by the massive influx of rural dwellers into the cities, itself a consequence of the capitalist transformation of the economy. The depression of 1873, the worst in the nineteenth century and one which had pan-European dimensions, gave to this competition a ferocity and sense of desperation that had not been evident in better times. Perhaps most important was the ubiquitous belief that the Jews were aliens. For a variety of reasons many Europeans subscribed to the tenet that the Jews did not belong in their societies and exerted a pernicious influence on their national economies, social and political morality, cultural life, and general well-being.

The chief difference between anti-Semitism in Russia and in other parts of Europe is not to be found in the themes expressed by the haters of the Jews. To be sure, Russian anti-Semites seemed to dwell more on the alleged Kahal and the Talmud, along with the baneful economic and political activities of the Jews, while anti-Semites in Western and Central Europe, without ignoring these themes, added a racial component to their arsenal of invectives. The most important contrast was in the manner through which the anti-Semitic impulse became manifest. Only in

Russia did anti-Semitism lead to large-scale violence, to rape, death, and attacks on Jewish property.

The low level of education in Russia, a long tradition of religious hostility toward the Jews, economic competition in urban areas against a background of endemic poverty, and a history of peasant revolt contributed to the outbreak of violence. The existence of a large and seemingly alien Jewish community, far larger and less assimilated than those in Central and Western Europe, tended to give credence to all sorts of fears about the Jews, including that of their inundating and dominating the country. The absence of a strong liberal tradition in Russian government and society also played a role in stimulating the use of physical force, as did the fact that the army and police, crucial bastions of order in society, shared the widespread anti-Jewish sentiment. Of equal if not greater importance is the point stressed repeatedly by Jews and their supporters during the pogroms. In Western and Central Europe, they argued, the Jews were emancipated; before the law they were equal to other citizens of the state; in Russia the Jews were legal pariahs. They were not granted the same rights and privileges as full Russian citizens, and were targets of specifically discriminatory regulations. In fact, for many citizens of the Russian Empire, the Jews were completely outside the law. The temptation to resort to violence was therefore very strong, and could be triggered in times of heightened tension, as in the period after the assassination of Alexander II.

One result of the pogroms was that many European Jews became convinced that the great threat to European Jewry came from the east, from the Russian Empire. They were not oblivious to anti-Semitism in the rest of Europe but were convinced that only in Russia was physical survival problematic. Zionism and emigration they saw as the means of salvation for Russian and East European Jews, not for the more fortunate Jews of such advanced and progressive nations as Germany, Austria, France, and Hungary.

Yet in Russia, violent attacks against Jewish life diminished considerably after the appointment of Tolstoi as Minister of the Interior in May 1882, and virtually disappeared by late 1884. The passing of the pogroms, however, did not signify an amelioration of the position of Russian Jewry. Starting with the May Laws of 1882, there followed in the aftermath of the pogroms what could be called the "cold pogrom," a veritable tidal wave of laws and decrees that placed an enormous burden on Russian Jewry.

The mere implementation of the May Laws would by itself have caused grievous damage to the rapidly expanding Jewish population of the Pale of Settlement. Corrupt police and local officials manipulated the "Temporary Rules" to bleed the Jews unmercifully, interpreting the regulations in such a way as to make life unbearable for many of them. What was even worse, local officials often went beyond the regulations and allowed what the Committee of Ministers had specifically prohibited: Peasant assemblies voted for the expulsion from their villages of Jews who had long lived there. In many cases actual expulsions took place.

In addition to the harsh and corrupt implementation of the May Laws, there were other decrees that generated great dismay among Russian Jews. Perhaps the most disturbing was the law establishing a *numerus clausus* for gymnasiums and institutions of higher learning. According to this law, promulgated in 1886, no more than 10 percent of the students in such schools in the Pale of Settlement could be Jews. Outside of the Pale the figure was 5 percent, and in the cities of St. Petersburg and Moscow the number was 3 percent.

In terms of sheer drama and sorrow, the expulsion of large numbers of Jews from Moscow in 1891 surpassed anything else perpetrated by the Tsarist government. This step, taken by the authorities in an effort to purge the city of what appeared to them as a noxious and pernicious group, wreaked havoc upon the Jews of Moscow and caused consternation among foreigners, particularly in England and the United States. One of the classic accounts of Russian Jewry in this period, *The New Exodus* by Harold Frederic, was the product of these events and depicts them poignantly.

The discriminatory legislation, the steady growth of the Jewish population penned up in the Pale, and the continued backwardness of Russia generally at the turn of the century all contributed to the further impoverishment of the Jewish community. A delegation of visiting Americans that toured the Pale in the first years of the twentieth century was appalled at the poverty, the unemployment, and the ubiquitous squalor that was so much a part of Jewish life. Large numbers of Jews, the delegation learned, subsisted only by virtue of the charity they received from Russian Jewish relief agencies and Jewish assistance organizations in the United States.

The accession to the throne of a new Tsar, Nicholas II, in 1894, and the coming of a new century did nothing to change the lot of Russian Jewry. Nicholas II, faithful to wife, family, and Russian Orthodoxy, was a catastrophe both for Russia and for the Jews. The Tsar's indecisiveness, lack of intelligence, and intense dislike for Jews, among other unfortunate personal characteristics, are too well known to be elaborated upon here. But it is necessary to remember that it was in this reign of the last Romanov that anti-Semitism in word and deed reached monumental proportions.

Pogroms, the most infamous of which occurred in Kishinev in the spring of 1903, were, in terms of violence and property loss, far worse than those of 1881–1882. In contrast to the earlier pogroms, the twentieth-century variety seems to have had substantial government support.

The years prior to the outbreak of World War I also saw the publication of the *Protocols of the Elders of Zion*, the most ferocious and effective piece of anti-Semitic literature of the modern period and one that most probably originated deep in the bowels of the Okhrana, the Tsarist secret police. Finally, one year before the outbreak of war, an avalanche of anti-Semitic abuse descended upon Russian Jewry as the inevitable concomitant of the Russian analogue to the Dreyfus Affair, the Beilis trial. It was a measure of the backwardness of Russia and the ignorance of its ruler, that in the twentieth century, a Jew, Mendel Beilis, could be accused of committing a ritual murder. The decent and courageous stance taken by prominent Russians who rallied to the defense of Beilis and the Jews, and the defendant's ultimate acquittal, could not obscure the fact that anti-Semitism was rampant in the country and reached into the highest offices of state.

It was becoming clear to larger and larger numbers of Russian Jews that the situation, always precarious, was now untenable. Of course, a small number of Jews continued to believe in a bright future in Russia not only for Jews but for all Russians. For this group of Jews the panacea was a revolution; hundreds, even thousands of young Jewish men and women entered the ranks of the different revolutionary parties, where they exercised an influence far greater than in the 1860s, 1870s, and 1880s. There were also Jews who eschewed the revolutionary movement but believed in some version of evolutionary change in Russia, and therefore joined the liberal and progressive movements represented by such organizations as the Constitutional Democratic Party. Most Russian Jews, not politically active, remained where they were, held back by inertia, a sense of resignation about the present, and mild hope for the future.

These hopes were not to be disappointed, at least not in the short run. First the Provisional Government and then the new Soviet government presented the Jews with opportunities they had never before experienced. By the end of the 1930s, however, and most certainly in the "black years" of Soviet Jewry between 1945 and 1953, Stalinist oppression would once again place Jews in a difficult position, one that with modification continues for them right up to the present time. In this period of its history Soviet Jewry has confronted a situation unprecedented in Russian Jewish history. Even in the worst days of Tsarist Russia, in the midst of the pogrom violence of 1881–1882, Russian Jews could defend themselves in the press and before the courts. Non-Jewish sympathizers could offer assistance, and Jews, with some difficulty, found it possible to emigrate. Authoritarian Russia had its limits. That has not been the case with the totalitarian creation of the twentieth century, the Soviet Union. Like other targets of Soviet wrath, the Jews have found themselves totally isolated and without any power to defend their interests. This is the current tragedy and dilemma of Soviet Jewry.

But there were already millions of Jews who were convinced before the Revolution that there was no future for them in Russia. The emigration of thousands, begun in 1881 and 1882, turned into tens and hundreds of thousands. In the period 1881–1914, almost two million Jews left the Russian Empire, and about three-quarters of these came to the United States. The remaining half million scattered to Western and Central Europe, Argentina, and, most important for the future of the Jewish people, to Palestine. Jews were on the march and Jewish history was not to be the same again.

America was different, the immigrants said, and so it was. In America there was a long tradition of religious freedom, as well as religious and ethnic pluralism. The nation, as the newcomers would discover, was rich and possessed large areas of arable land. It was also in its period of industrial takeoff. In the United States there would not take place the same terrible competition for land, jobs, and university places that helped generate European anti-Semitism. There were no major threatening revolutionary movements here that might attract large numbers of young Jews who, instead, were rapidly moving into American society and therefore did not elicit so much of an anti-Semitic response from conservative elements. "Beat the Jews," the phrase that resounded so ominously in the Russian Pale not only in the years 1881–1882 but in the twentieth century as well, had no parallel in America. A nation of such different racial, religious, and ethnic groupings presented so many targets of opprobrium that each one took its turn being the recipient of popular hatred. There would be no national obsession with the Jews. The result was that East European Jews, scorned on the Continent, entered a hospitable land which offered great opportunities for peaceful settlement and the acquisition of a certain degree of wealth.

If the nation was rich and accommodating, it was also true that Russian Jews brought with them the cultural baggage and aspirations that would serve them well in the New World. By and large they were more literate than other immigrant groups. Their passion for learning and education, a distinguishing characteristic of Jewish life for over two millennia, was very conducive to advancement in a dynamic and increasingly sophisticated economy. In comparison with other immigrant groups, a greater number of Jews came from urban or semiurbanized areas. They flocked into the larger American cities and towns, adapting better there than did other immigrants from more rural backgrounds. The Russian Jews also came with their families, testimony to the fact that they had come to stay. Jewish men may have left their wives and children in the old country, but only with the expectation that they would be brought over as soon as circumstances permitted. The idea of working in America in order to accumulate money for the purchase of land back home was alien to the Jewish immigrants. Since they came to stay, they were prepared to invest the time and money that other more temporary immigrants were often reluctant to make. The presence of families also provided a refuge to which the Jewish immigrants could cling and from which they would draw sustenance and strength as they confronted the difficulties of adapting to a strange and sometimes harsh society.

Russian Jews had one other advantage over most other immigrants arriving in the United States between 1881 and 1914. They were assisted by an already existing group of fairly affluent and influential American Jews, those of largely German extraction. As indicated in the last chapter, the relationship between "native" Jews and the immigrants provided much of the tension, drama, and comedy of the Jewish immigrant experience. Yet for all of the difficulties between the two groups, it cannot be denied that the assistance provided by the established Jewish community was extremely important for the subsequent successes achieved by Russian and East European Jews.

After the early 1880s, when these tensions were highest, the American Jews of German origin awakened to a sense of responsibility for their coreligionists. It was they who fought the good fight to keep the door to America open and for so long successfully opposed the promulgation of laws restricting immigration. It was young American Jewish attorneys, mostly born in the United States, who went to Castle Garden and later Ellis Island to ensure fair treatment for the Jewish immigrants at the hands of immigration officials. From the 1890s on, the Educational Alliance on the Lower East Side, established by the *yahudim*, the wealthy uptown Jews of German extraction, provided lessons in English and civics for hundreds of thousands of East European Jewish immigrants.

By the first decade of the twentieth century, Jews were moving rapidly ahead into the American mainstream. A Jewish middle class was in the process of formation. This is not to say that there were no casualties along the way. The literature of the 1890s and the first decade of the twentieth century indicates that there was starvation, crime, prostitution and abandonment. The letters to the editor of the *Forward* speak poignantly of the personal problems confronting the Russian Jewish immigrants. And, anti-Semitism, mild by European standards, nevertheless persisted up to the Second World War. Before World War I there was talk in some circles of American society of the "mongrelization of the white race." Complaints were heard about the great influx of "inferior" elements from Eastern and Southern Europe. In New York City officials noted that Jewish immigration was making the city dirtier and more crime ridden.

In the interwar period, anti-Semitism grew significantly. The presidents of Harvard and Columbia Universities and of Williams College spoke publicly of the need to establish Jewish college-entrance quotas. It was also a time—perhaps the only time in the history of the Republic— that men of influence, prestige, and, in at least one case, enormous wealth, endorsed the anti-Semitic impulse. Henry Ford and Father Coughlin hammered at the theme of Jewish treachery, Jewish capitalism, and Jewish socialism. Charles Lindbergh challenged the loyalty of American Jews and warned that they were moving the nation in the direction of war.

Nonetheless, the rapid advance of American Jews continued. The Jews were rapidly becoming the American middle class par excellence. What was remarkable, given this achievement, was that the golden age of American Jewry was still to come. It arrived in the aftermath of World War II. After Auschwitz, anti-Semitism became thoroughly unfashionable in American society, and quota systems and other forms of anti-Semitism were no longer acceptable to large numbers of Americans. Beginning in the late 1940s, the barriers against Jews, never very high in America, came tumbling down. The almost total elimination of anti-Semitism, the nearly universal Jewish support for the new Jewish State of Israel, and most significant for its internal structure, the occupational professionalization of American Jews would all be concomitants of this happy period. Compared to their position in the United States, the Jewish grandeur even of Moorish Spain seems insignificant. The immigrants of 1881–1882 were absolutely right. Life was good in America. It was so good and so attractive, in fact, that one hundred years after the pogroms, the descendants of the Russian Jewish immigrants would be very much concerned that the American Jewish community could not withstand the blandishments of Gentile America. In America, as some writers during the pogrom wave had predicted, assimilation, and not anti-Semitism, became the great problem confronting what had by now become the largest, wealthiest and most secure Jewish community that had ever existed.

Russian Jews in much smaller numbers continued to flee to Palestine. The hundreds of 1881–1882 were followed by the thousands that came in the 1890s and in the period before World War I. These Russian Jews made the Yishuv a concrete and irrevocable reality. Their presence also made sure that the future Jewish state would receive their indelible imprint. Informality of dress, equality for women, a belief in socialist ideas and the creation of the first labor parties, the foundation of the Ha-shomer (The Watchman), a Jewish self-defense group, and the settling of the first *kibbutzim* (collective farms) were all achievements of the Second Aliyah (1904–1914), most of whose participants came from the Russian Empire. David Ben-Gurion, Moshe Sharret, Beryl Katznelson, Shmuel Dayan, A. D. Gordon, Yitschak Ben Zvi and his wife Rachel, and many other founders and defenders of Israel came to Palestine at this time: The history of Palestinian Jewry and of the State of Israel is inextricably bound up with them. These Russian Jews voted with their feet in the most literal sense for Zionism and Palestine.

In sum, what had taken place in the pogroms of 1881–1882 and the ensuing flight of Jewish emigrants was the beginning of a dramatic shift in the center of gravity of Jewish life. Life in the old East European centers was becoming too difficult for the Jews; oppression was pressing in upon Russian and East European Jewry. What began with the pogroms would be finished by the Nazis. Those Soviet Jews who survived would confront harsh constraints on their religious, cultural, and national life, and eventually a Soviet *numerus clausus*. America and Palestine became the new centers of Jewish life. Once again, under duress, Jews were demonstrating an important feature of their history. Having played out their role in one part of the world, they were resurrecting themselves in other more hospitable environments.

In the last two decades of the twentieth century the large and dynamic Jewish communities of Israel and the United States, both heavily influenced by Russian Jewry, have become the new centers of Jewish existence. The mutually beneficial and sometimes difficult relationship between these two communities constitutes one of the most important aspects of Jewish life in the latest stage of Jewish history.

Notes

CHAPTER I: THE GREAT REFORMS

1. Michael Stanislawski, *Tsar Nicholas I and the Jews* (Philadelphia: Jewish Publication Society of America, 1983), p. 36.

2. Simon M. Dubnow [Dubnov], *History of the Jews in Russia and Poland*, trans. I. Friedlaender, 2 vols. (Philadelphia: Jewish Publication Society of America, 1916. Reprint. New York: Ktav, 1975), II, pp. 24–25.

3. The problem of Uvarov is a complicated one. The conventional view has it that Uvarov did, indeed, desire to utilize the new schools for the purpose of conversion. Stanislawski (Tsar Nicholas I. . ., pp. 59–69), argues that this was not the case, that Uvarov was in his own way a defender of the Jews and a passionate adherent of their enlightenment. Stanislawski makes a good case, but I am inclined to stay with the conventional viewpoint. For Max Lilienthal's relationship to Uvarov and his work, see Stanislawski, pp. 69–96.

4. On the Haskalah, see Isaac E. Barzilay, "The Ideology of the Berlin Haskalah," *Proceedings of the American Academy for Jewish Research*, XXV (1956), pp. 1–37; Jacob Katz, *Out of the Ghetto* (Cambridge, Mass.: Harvard University Press, 1973); *Tradition and Crisis* (New York: Schocken, 1971); and Jacob Raisin, *The Haskalah Movement in Russia* (Philadelphia: Jewish Publication Society of America, 1913). For Levinsohn, the premier figure in the early Russian Haskalah see Joseph Klausner, *Historyah shel hasifrut ha ivrit hahadashah*, 2nd ed., 6 vols. (Jerusalem: Achiassaf, 1951), III, pp. 33–115; and Zinberg, "Levinzon i ego vremia," *Evreiskaia Starina*, III (1911), pp. 504–541.

5. On Lithuanian Jewry, see *Lite*, ed. M. Sudarsky, U. Katzenelenbogen, and Y. Kissim (New York: Jewish Lithuanian Cultural Association, 1950). For Odessa in general and the Odessa Jewish community in particular, see V. J. Puryear, "Odessa: Its Rise in International Importance," *Pacific Historical Review*, III (June 1934), pp. 185–202; D. Kogan, "Pervye desiatiletiia evreiskoi obshchiny v Odesse i pogrom 1821 goda," *Evreiskaia Starina*, III (1911), pp. 260–275: O. M. Lerner, *Evrei v novorossiskom krae; istoricheskie ocherki* (Odessa: Levinson, 1901);

and Steve J. Zipperstein, "Jewish Enlightenment in Odessa," *Jewish Social Studies*, XLIV (Winter 1982), pp. 19–36.

6. J. Maze, *Zikronot*, 4 vols. (Tel Aviv: Hotsa'at Yalkut, 1936), I, pp. 73–74.

7. For a summation of the laws see Louis Greenberg, *The Jews in Russia* (New Haven: Yale University Press, 1944), I, pp. 75–76. For a more detailed look, see I. Orshanskii, *Russkoe zakondatel'stvo o evreiakh* (St. Petersburg: Landau, 1877); and Lev Levanda, *Polny khronologicheskii sbornik zakonov i polozhenii kasaiushchikhsiia evreiev* (St. Petersburg: Trubnikov, 1874). The most authoritative source is the *Polnoe Sobranie Zakonov Rossiskoi Imperii, Sobranie vtoroe*, the official collection of all Russian laws.

8. *Russkii Vestnik*, 17 (1858), pp. 132–135, cited in John D. Klier, "The Illiustratsiia Affair of 1858: Polemics on the Jewish Question in the Russian Press," *Nationalities Papers*, V, no. 2, p. 129. The ulterior motives of some of the defenders of the Jews, as well as the comical aspects of the episode, are revealed in Klier's article.

9. *Russkii Invalid* (1858), p. 39. Cited in Greenberg, *The Jews...*, I, p. 78.

10. For a detailed discussion of the views of the Russian Jewish press as well as those of Yiddish and Hebrew publications in the 1860s, 1870s and very early 1880s, see the following articles by I. Sosis in the journal *Evreiskaia Starina* published in St. Petersburg: "Obshchestvennaia nastroenia epokhi velikh reform," VII (1914), pp. 21–41, 182–197, 341–369; "Natsional'ny vopros v literature 60-kh godov," VIII (1915), pp. 38–56; "Period obruseniia," VIII (1915), pp. 129–146; "Na rubezh dvukh epokh," VIII (1915), pp. 324–337; and "Period Krizisa," IX (1916), pp. 46–60, 194–209. See also I. Sosis, *Di Geshichte von di yidishe gezelshaftleche shtremungen in rusland in XIX y.hy.* (Minsk: Meluche, 1929), pp. 80–99.

11. For a discussion of the Jewish press in Odessa, see Alexander Orbach, *New Voices of Russian Jewry: A Study of the Russian Jewish Press of Odessa in the Era of the Great Reforms, 1860–1871* (Leiden: E. J. Brill, 1980).

12. Paul R. Mendes-Flohr and Jehuda Reinharz, *The Jew in the Modern World* (New York: Oxford, 1980), p. 322.

13. Ibid., pp. 312–313.

14. Orbach, *New Voices...*, p. 34.

15. L. O. Levanda, "Goriachee Vremia," *Evreiskaia Biblioteka*, ed. A. E. Landau (St. Petersburg: A.E.L., 1872), p. 87.

16. I. Orshanskii, *Evrei v Rossii* (St. Petersburg: O. I. Bakst, 1877), p. 75.

17. The source for the numbers is Orbach, *New Voices...*, p. 183.

18. For Lilienblum the best source is his collected works, *Kol kitve Moshe Leib Lilienblum* (Krakow and Odessa: Y. Tseitlin, 1910–1913). See also Irving Gersh, "Moshe Leib Lilienblum: An Intellectual Biography" (Ph.D. diss., Brandeis University, 1967).

19. See the introduction by Milton Hindus in Isaac Joel Linetski, *The Polish Lad*, trans. Moshe Spiegel (Philadelphia: Jewish Publication Society of America, 1975), p. 12.

20. Ibid., p. 31.

21. Ibid., p. 32.

22. For a literary analysis of Mapu, see David Patterson, *Abraham Mapu: the Creator of the Modern Hebrew Novel* (London: East and West Library, 1964).

23. Dubnow, *History...*, II, p. 234. For Smolenskin, see *Kol sifre Perez Smo-*

lenskin (Wilna: M. Katzenelenbogn, 1901). See also Charles Freundlich, *Peretz Smolenskin: His Life and Thought* (New York: Yeshiva University, 1961).

24. Greenberg, *The Jewish...*, I, p. 144. A recent discussion of Ben Yehudah's role in modern Jewish history is found in *Eliezer Ben Yehudah: A Symposium* (Oxford: Oxford Center for Post Graduate Studies in Hebrew, 1981).

25. Markus Kagan, "K istorii natsionalnogo samosoznaniia," *Perezhitoe*, III (1912), p. 143.

26. Dubnow, *History...*, II, p. 213.

27. Ben-Ami, "Odesskii pogrom 1881 goda i pervaia samooborona," *Evreiskii Mir*, V (1909), p. 19.

28. Greenberg, *The Jews...*, I, p. 180.

29. N. I. Sidorov, "Statisticheskie svedeniya o propagandistakh 70kh godov v obrabotke III Otdeleniia," *Kotorga i ssylka*, I (1928), pp. 31, 38–39, 47, 55. A good discussion of Jewish revolutionaries in the reign of Alexander II is found in E. Tcherikower, "Yidn revolutsionern in Rusland in di 60-er un 70-er yohrn," *YIVO Historishe Shriftn*, III (1939), pp. 60–172.

30. For Lieberman, see Jonathan Frankel, *Prophecy and Politics: Socialism, Nationalism and the Russian Jews* (London: Cambridge University Press, 1981), pp. 28–48.

31. *Sbornik materialov ob ekonomicheskom polozhenii evreiev v Rossii* (St. Petersburg: Izdanie evreiskago kolonizatsionnago obshchestva, 1904), I, p. 198.

32. The books by Ginsburg, written in Yiddish, provide a perspective on Jewish life in nineteenth-century Russia not often found in books published in other languages. The material used in the preparation of this essay is found in S. Ginsburg, *Amolike Petersburg* (New York: Tashid, 1944) and *Mishumodim in Tsarishn Russland* (New York: Cyco, 1946). The man described by Ginsburg was the father of the writer Abraham Uri Kovner.

33. *Sbornik...*, I, p. xxi.

34. Greenberg, *The Jews...*, I, p. 160.

35. Orshanskii, *Evrei v Rossii*, p. 141.

36. A. Subbotin, *Evreiskaia Biblioteka*, x, pp. 76–77. For a discussion of Jewish poverty in the 1880s, see the report of the Pahlen Commission, *Obshchaia Zapiska vysshei kommisii dlia peresmotria deistvuiushchikh o evreiakh v imperii zakonov* (1883–1888), pp. 153–160. The report (p. 153) states that half of the Jews in the cities and towns cannot pay their taxes.

37. *Sbornik...*, II, p. 224.

38. *Sbornik...*, I, p. 189.

39. On the small number of artisans able to go into the Russian interior, and the difficulties faced by all Jewish artisans trying to get out of the Pale, see I. M. Rubinow, *The Economic Condition of the Jews in Russia* (Washington, D.C.: U.S. Labor Bureau, 1907), pp. 521–522.

40. Ibid., p. 500.

41. *Sbornik...*, I, pp. xx, xxiii.

42. *Ha-Magid*, July 22, 1866. Cited in E. Tcherikower, "Di tsarishe politik un di yidishe emigratsiia," *Geshichte fun der Yidisher Arbeiter-Bavaygung in di Fareinikte Shtaten*, ed. E. Tcherikower (New York: YIVO, 1943), p. 95.

43. Ibid., pp. 95–96.

44. Ibid., p. 96.

45. On the Jewish plutocracy, see S. L. Tsitron, *Shtadlanim* (Warsaw: Ahisfr, n.d.), pp. 334–376. There is also a good discussion in Tcherikower, "Yidn revolutsionern...," pp. 85–93.

46. E. Tcherikover, "Yidn revolutsionern...," p. 116.

47. Ibid., p. 78.

48. Dubnow, *History...*, II, pp. 214–215. A very detailed discussion of the society is found in E. Tcherikower, *Istoriia Obshchestva dlia rasprostraneniia prosveshcheniia mezhdu evreiami v Rossii* (St. Petersburg: 1913).

49. Ibid., pp. 215–216.

CHAPTER II: "THE SOUTHERN STORMS"

1. *Nedel'naia khronika Voskhoda*, 18 (May 1, 1882), p. 471 reports that many Jews, for religious reasons, would not allow autopsies to be performed on their murdered relatives. Since the government would list as victims of the pogroms only those who had been autopsied, official figures of dead Jews were probably understated. In all likelihood, the number of rapes ascertained by government officials is also probably not reflective of reality since many women were unlikely to have admitted being raped or to have undergone medical examinations to certify the attacks. See *Nedel'naia khronika Voskhoda*, 3 (January 15, 1882), p. 52.

2. *Razsvet* (St. Petersburg), 19 (May 8, 1881), pp. 741–742. For an equally vivid account of a pogrom, see the *Jewish Chronicle* (London), January 6, 1882, p. 6. The *Chronicle*, with its correspondents and network of sources in Russia, provides much important information on the pogroms.

3. Such an incident occurred in Balta during the great pogrom of March 28–30, 1882. See the account of the trial of the rapist in *Razsvet*, 27 (July 4, 1882), pp. 1042–1044. The accused, Ivan Sidorov, made the customary defense of rapists from the beginning of man. He claimed that the girl had agreed to sexual relations with him. The defense was rejected by the court.

4. *Nedel'naia khronika Voskhoda*, 3 (January 15, 1882); 16 (April 15, 1882); 21 (May 22, 1882); pp. 61, 402, 573, respectively.

5. Ibid., 18 (May 5, 1882), p. 470.

6. Ibid., 5 (January 29, 1882), p. 105; and 15 (April 9, 1882), p. 386.

7. Ibid., 20 (May 15, 1882), p. 549. A random, apparently unprovoked murder of a Jewish family by soldiers is reported in *Nedel'naia khronika Voskhoda*, 13 (March 26, 1882), p. 326.

8. Ibid., 6 (February 5, 1882), pp. 132–133; and 20 (May 15, 1882), p. 549. Pressures on Jewish students must have been unusually great, since *Nedel'naia khronika Voskhoda*, 7 (February 12, 1882), p. 154, notes the suicides of two Jewish students in Zhitomir who failed the examinations to become pharmacists.

9. Ibid., 12 (March 19, 1882), p. 298; and 141 (April 2, 1882), p. 357.

10. Ibid., 13 (March 26, 1882), p. 324.

11. For the beginning of the *ochistka*, see *Russkii Evrei*, 47 (November 18, 1881), p. 1852.

12. *Nedel'naia khronika Voskhoda*, 13 (March 26, 1882), p. 315.

13. Ibid., 25 (June 19, 1882), p. 681; and *Russkii Evrei*, 51 (December 16, 1881), p. 2011.

14. *Nedel'naia khronika Voskhoda*, 12 (March 19, 1882), p. 298.

15. Ibid., 14 (April 2, 1882); 15 (April 9, 1882); 16 (April 15, 1882); 19 (May 8, 1882); pp. 346, 388, 421, 426, 511 respectively. See also *Russkii Evrei*, 28 (July 8, 1881), p. 1092. According to *Kievlianin*, a rabidly anti-Semitic paper, Jews in Kiev who were subject to deportation were living in barges on the Dniepr. See *Russkii Evrei*, 30 (July 22, 1881), p. 1171.

16. *Russkii Evrei*, 30 (July 22, 1881), pp. 1171–1172. This report appeared in *Kievlianin* and was mentioned in *Russkii Evrei*, which did not comment on it.

17. Ibid., 47 (November 18, 1881), p. 1852.

18. *Nedel'naia khronika Voskhoda*, 5 (April 9, 1882), p. 386. As early as the summer of 1881, many a *zemstvo* was calling for restrictions on Jews' buying and renting land, living in the villages, and selling liquor. See *Russkii Evrei*, 27 (July 2, 1881), pp. 1050–1051.

19. *Nedel'naia khronika Voskhoda*, 14 (April 2, 1882), p. 352.

20. *Russkii Evrei*, 48 (November 25, 1881), p. 1891.

21. *Nedel'naia khronika Voskhoda*, 15 (April 9, 1882), p. 385.

22. For the devastating impact that fires had in the cities of Kovno, Suvalki, Zhitomir, and Minsk, see *Nedel'naia khronika Voskhoda*, 21 (May 22, 1882), pp. 572–573; and *Razsvet*, 10 (March 5, 1882), pp. 385–386. The first series of fires had occurred in the summer of 1881. See *Russkii Evrei*, 27 (July 2, 1881), pp. 1050–1051.

23. *Nedel'naia khronika Voskhoda*, 19 (May 8, 1882), p. 508.

24. Ibid., p. 509, for examples.

25. Ibid., 12 (March 19, 1882); 16 (April 15, 1882); 17 (April 23, 1882); 19 (May 8, 1882); and 20 (May 15, 1882); pp. 296, 421, 453, 508, 509, 510, 548 respectively. See also *Razsvet*, 10 (March 5, 1882), pp. 385–386.

26. *Nedel'naia khronika Voskhoda*, 19 (May 8, 1882), p. 511.

27. Ibid., 8 (February 19, 1882), p. 190.

28. Ibid., 1 (March 12, 1882), p. 270.

29. Ibid., 20 (May 15, 1882), p. 544.

30. Ibid., 21 (May 22, 1882), p. 681.

31. *Russkii Evrei*, 30 (July 22, 1881), p. 1169.

32. *Razsvet*, 3 (January 15, 1882), p. 101.

33. Ibid., 32 (August 11, 1882), p. 1225.

34. *Nedel'naia khronika Voskhoda*, 16 (April 15, 1882), pp. 420–421.

35. I. Michael Aronson, "Geographical and Socioeconomic Factors in the 1882 Anti-Jewish Pogroms in Russia," The *Russian Review*, 39 (Janaury 1980), pp. 23–26. The *Jewish Chronicle* (June 17, 1881), p. 12, reported that two railroad officials were implicated in fomenting pogroms.

36. See *Nedel'naia khronika Voskhoda*, 22 (May 29, 1882), p. 596; and anon. [S. Dubnow], "Anti-evreiskoe dvizhenie v Rossii v 1881 i 1882g.," *Evreiskaia Starina*, I (1909), p. 92. Dubnow wrote this piece for the Pahlen Commission, which met between 1883 and 1888 to discuss the Jewish Question. See also G. Ia. Krasnyi-Admoni, ed., *Materialy dlia istorii antievreiskikh pogromov v Rossii* (Petrograd: Gosudarstvennoe izdatel'stvo, 1923), II, pp. 206–208, 232. The bulk of this volume is the report presented to the Tsar in the summer of 1881 by Prince P. I. Kutaisov, who had been sent by the government to the areas affected by the pogroms to discover their causes. The sources cited reflect his conclusions.

37. The evidence from contemporary sources is overwhelming on the leading

role of the *meshchanstvo*. See *Russkii Evrei*, 17 (April 24, 1881), p. 648; 18 (May 1, 1881), p. 687; 19 (May 11, 1881), p. 734; 20 (May 14, 1881), p. 778; *Razsvet*, 1 (January 1, 1882), p. 14; 3 (January 15, 1882), p. 97; 19 (May 11,1882), pp. 701–702; and *Nedel'naia khronika Voskhoda*, 2 (January 8, 1882), p.40; 3 (January 15, 1882), p. 63; 15 (April 9, 1882), p. 375; 17 (April 23, 1882), p. 438; 18 (May 1, 1882), p. 472; 19 (May 8, 1882), p. 509; 21 (May 22, 1882), p. 573; and 25 (June 19, 1882), pp. 690–691. See also Kutaisov in Krasnyi-Admoni, *Materialy...*, pp. 276–279, 354. For a discussion of *meshchanstvo* attitudes toward Jews in Elizavetgrad, see p. 276. The appendix in Krasnyi-Admoni, *Materialy...*, pp. 529–541, giving the occupations of *pogromshchiki* arrested in 1881, demonstrates the important place of the *meshchanstvo* in the pogroms all across Russia. See also *British Documents on Foreign Affairs: Reports and Papers from the Foreign Office Confidential Print*, ed. Dominic Lieven, Part I, Series A: *Russia, 1859–1914*, 2, *Russia, 1881–1905* (Frederick, Md.: University Publications of America, 1982), Document 24, p. 39, for the view of a British observer. Two fine secondary sources which shed light on the dominant role of the *meshchanstvo* are Aronson, "Geographical...", p. 22; and A. Linden, "Prototyp des pogroms in den achtizer Jahren, in Vol. 1 of *Die Judenpogrome in Russland* (Köln: Judischer Verlag, 1910), p. 46.

38. On peasant benevolence toward Jews, see Krasnyi-Admoni, *Materialy...*, pp. 106, 124; and *Obshchaia Zapiska vysshei kommisii...*, pp. 69, 95. See also *British Documents...*, Document 32, p. 47; and Linden, "Prototyp...," p. 46. There were occasions when peasant actions against the Jews were especially vicious, as in the case of the Balta pogrom. See *Nedel'naia khronika Voskhoda*, 15 (April 9, 1882), p. 379; and *Obshchaia Zapiska...*, p. 95.

39. S. Dubnow, "Iz istorii vos'midesiatikh godov," *Evreiskaia Starina*, VIII (1915), p. 270.

40. [Dubnow], "Anti-evreiskoe dvizhenie...," p. 92.

41. N. M. Gelber, "Di Rusishe Pogromen in di 80er yoren in sheyn fun es traykhisher diplomatisher korespondents," *Historishe Shriftn*, II (1937), p. 478. British diplomats also made note of the inaction of the military and the police. See *British Documents...*, Documents 10, p. 7; 29, p. 44.

42. Aronson, *Geographical...*, pp. 19–20.

43. On the police and the military see *Nedel'naia khronika Voskhoda*, 1 (January 1, 1882), p. 10; 13 (March 26, 1882), p. 326; 16 (April 15, 1882), pp. 402, 411, 413; 18 (May 1, 1882), pp. 469, 471; *Razsvet*, 30 (July 25, 1882), pp. 1055–1056; and Krasnyi-Admoni, *Materialy...*, pp. 22, 41–42, 98, 106, 204, 206–208, 214–215, 227, 245, 263, 266, 276, 354, 433. Kutaisov was adamant in his criticism of local police, government, and military officials who did not act to stop pogroms. He was convinced that effective action could have prevented the disorders.

44. *Russkii Evrei*, 20 (May 12, 1881), p. 765.

45. V. D. Novitskii, *Iz Vospominanii Zhandarma* (Leningrad: Pribor, 1929), p. 182.

46. On the belief in a *ukaz*, see *Russkii Evrei* 20, 21, 26 (1881), pp. 774–775, 852, 1009, respectively; *Nedel'naia khronika Voskhoda*, 5, 7, 18, 19, 20, 22, 25 (1882), pp. 108, 157, 487, 498, 545, 598, 681–682, respectively. No. 19 (July 25, 1882), p. 498 quotes the liberal newspaper *Golos* (The Voice) on the persistent rumors of

a *ukaz*. See also Krasnyi-Admoni, *Materialy*..., pp. 9, 15, 36, 56, 80, 90, 106, 158, 170, 215, 241, 245, 251, 276; and *British Documents*..., Document 25, p. 39.

47. Kutaisov reported on the widespread popular sentiment that the Jews were responsible for the death of the Tsar. See Krasnyi-Admoni, *Materialy*..., pp. 90, 254, 395, 418, 481, 483.

48. Ibid., p. xiii.

49. On the presence of well-dressed young men who instigated pogroms, see [P. Sonin], "Vospominaniia o iuzhnorusskikh pogromakh 1881 godu," *Evreiskaia Starina*, II (1909), pp. 211–212; Dubnow, *History*..., II, pp. 247–248; Krasnyi-Admoni, *Materialy*..., pp. 358–364, 395, 412–413, 459–460; and *British Documents*..., Documents 10, p. 7; 20, p. 26.

50. Stephen Lukashevich, "The Holy Brotherhood: 1881–1883," *American Slavic and East European Review*, XVIII (December 1959), pp. 495, 497.

51. The articles by V. M. Smel'skii, under the title "Sviashchennaia Druzhina," are found in the journal *Golos Minuvshago na chuzoi storone*, Nos. 1,2,3,4,5–6 (1916), pp. 222–243, 135–162, 155–176, 95–110, 86–105, respectively.

52. A fine biography of Brafman is found in Ginsburg, *Mishumodim*..., pp. 65–79.

53. *Kahal* is the transliterated form for the Russian *kagal*.

54. For the impact of the law of 1844 on Jewish communities in the Pale of Settlement, see Stanislawski, *Tsar Nicholas I*..., pp. 123–133.

55. Ginsburg, *Mishumodim*..., p. 75.

56. Stephen Lukashevich, *Ivan Aksakov 1823–1886: A Study in Russian Thought and Politics* (Cambridge: Harvard University Press, 1965), p. 101.

57. A. E. Kaufman, "Evrei v russko-turetskoi voine 1877 goda," *Evreiskaia Starina*, VIII (1915), p. 62. Suvorin's anti-Jewish attitudes are discussed in Effie Ambler, *The Career of Aleksei S. Suvorin: Russian Journalism 1861–1881* (Detroit: Wayne State University Press, 1972).

58. V. Lvov-Rogachevsky, *A History of Russian Jewish Literature*, ed. and trans. Arthur Levin (Ann Arbor: Ardis, 1975), p. 90.

59. Dostoyevsky's intense dislike for Jews appears most explicitly in his *Dnevnik Pisatelia* (The Dairy of a Writer), particularly in the essay, "Evreiskii Vopros" (The Jewish Question). See F. M. Dostoyevsky, *Polnoe sobranie sochinenii v tridtsatii tomakh, tom dvadtsat piatyi, dnevnik pisatelia za 1877 god Ianvar-Avgust* (Leningrad: Izdatel'stvo Nauka, 1983), pp. 74–92. On Dostoyevsky and the Jews, see Leonid Grossman, *Confession of a Jew*, trans. Ranne Moab (New York: Arno, 1975), pp. 53–103, 132–151; and David I. Goldstein, *Dostoyevsky and the Jews* (Austin: University of Texas Press, 1981).

60. Orshanskii, *Evrei v Rossii*, pp. 71–72.

61. Dubnow, *History*..., II, p. 196.

62. Hans Rogger, "Government, Jews, Peasants, and Land in Post-Emancipation Russia," *Cahiers du monde russe et soviétique*, 17 (January-March 1976), pp. 16–17.

63. Kaufman, "Evrei v russko-turetskoi voine...," *Evreiskaia Starina*, VIII (1915), p. 177.

64. Ibid., p. 165.

65. Ibid., p. 178.

66. For Liutostanskii and his work, see *Evreiskaia Entsiklopediia*, ed. L. Kats-

nelson (St. Petersburg: Obshchestvo dlia nauchnikh evreiskikh izdanii, 1906–1913), VII, pp. 447–448.

67. I. Zinberg, *Istoriia evreiskoi pechati v sviazi c obshchestvennymi techeniiom* (St. Petersburg: Fleitman, 1915), p. 248.

68. *The Times* (London), March 16, 1880, p. 4.

69. Krasnyi-Admoni, *Materialy...*, p. xii.

70. Ibid.

71. Ibid.

72. Ibid., p. xi.

73. Ibid., p. xiv.

74. Ibid., p. xvi.

75. For the assortment of charges against the Jews, see Krasnyi-Admoni, *Materialy...*, pp. 166–167, 242, 321–322, 325, 328–336, 340, 344, 360–364, 373–376, 395, 405, 442, 445–446, 493, 500, 503, 505, 507, 525.

76. For a discussion of newspaper commentary after the assassination of Tsar Alexander II, see Dubnow, "Iz istorii...," pp. 269–270, and Krasnyi-Admoni, *Materialy* ..., pp. xxix-xxx, 12, 13, 276. The participation of Gelfman in the assassination and the proximity of Easter are cited by all historians as contributing to the outbreak of the pogroms. The *Jewish Chronicle*, May 6, 1881, p. 6, suggests some other immediate causes. Sources in Russia told the paper that the fact that mid-April was the time of the quarter-day, the day rents were paid by peasants and urban dwellers, contributed to the unrest. The occurrence of the holiday of Purim just before the assassination of Alexander II, according to these same sources, added to anti-Jewish sentiment because some people actually believed that the outbursts of Jewish revelry that customarily attend this holiday were signs of Jewish rejoicing over the imminent death of the sovereign.

77. Krasnyi-Admoni, *Materialy...*, pp. 226–227.

CHAPTER III: GOVERNMENT AND SOCIETY RESPOND TO THE POGROMS

1. *Russkii Evrei*, 20 (May 12, 1881), p. 765.

2. Dubnow, "Iz istorii...," p. 1.

3. See Chapter II and Hans Rogger, "Government, Jews, Peasants and Land...," pp. 5–25.

4. Robert F. Byrnes, *Pobedonostov: His Life and Thought* (Bloomington: Indiana University Press, 1968), p. 153. See also pp. 153–312, for a discussion of the relationship between the two men.

5. Ibid., p. 155.

6. Ibid., p. 204.

7. For the views of Alexander III on the Jews, see R. M. Kantor, "Aleksandr III o evreiskikh pogromakh 1881–83 g.g.," *Evreiskaia Letopis*, I (1923), p. 156.

8. V. P. Meshcherskii, *Moi vospominaniia* (St. Petersburg: Kniaz V.P. Meshcherskii, 1887–1912) II, p. 29.

9. Peter A. Zaionchkovsky, *The Russian Autocracy in Crisis, 1878–1882*, trans. Gary Hamburg (Gulf Breeze, Fla.: Academic International Press, 1979), p. 214.

10. For Kutaisov's views of the revolutionary movement and the pogroms, see Krasnyi-Admoni, *Materialy...*, pp. 218–219, 278, 385, 445–446, 447.

11. Ibid., pp. 205, 275–276, 278, 393, 418, 445–446. Kutaisov was also convinced (pp. 248–269, 370, 405) that Jews exaggerated their losses, were cowards, composed the threatening letters themselves, and deliberately disseminated anti-Jewish proclamations. He believed that these last two steps were taken by the Jews to guarantee their protection by the police and the military.

12. Iu. Gessen, "Graf N. P. Ignatiev i 'Vremennyia pravila' o evreiakh 3 Maia 1882 goda," *Pravo*, 30 (1908), p. 1632.

13. Ibid., pp. 1632–1633.

14. The Mandelshtam comments are found in M. Mandelshtam, "Ignatievskaia komissia v Kieve 1881g.," *Perezhitoe*, IV (1913), pp. 44–64.

15. For an analysis of the workings of the *guberniia* commissions, see I. M. Aronson, "Russian Bureaucratic Attitudes toward Jews 1881–1894" (Ph.D. diss., Northwestern University, 1973). See also his "The Attitudes of Russian Officials in the 1880s toward Jewish Assimilation and Emigration," *Slavic Review*, 34, No. 2 (March 1975), pp. 1–18.

16. For the Gotovtsev committee and its proposals, see Gessen, "Graf N. P. Ignatiev...," pp. 1634–1638; and Hans Rogger, "Russian Ministers and the Jewish Question 1881–1917," *California Slavic Studies*, VIII (1975), pp. 19–20.

17. Zaionchkovsky, *The Russian Autocracy in Crisis*, p. 264.

18. For reports of lenient treatment accorded to the *pogromshchiki*, see *Russkii Evrei*, 22 (May 28, 1881), p. 852; and *Nedel'naia khronika Voskhoda*, 7 (February 12, 1882), p. 155; 16 (April 15, 1882), p. 405; 18 (May 1, 1882), p. 485; 22 (May 29, 1882), p. 594. It was only in the late spring and early summer of 1882, after the Balta pogrom and Ignatiev's removal from the Ministry of the Interior, that the courts began to hand down stiff sentences.

19. For Ignatiev's statement in 1881, see *Razsvet*, 4 (January 22, 1882), p. 125. A government prosecutor in Kiev, Strelnikov, had said that the western frontier was open for the Jews as early as May 1881. See *Russkii Evrei*, 22 (May 28, 1881), p. 852.

20. *Razsvet*, 4 (January 22, 1882), p. 125.

21. Byrnes, *Pobedonostov...*, p. 207.

22. *Nedel'naia khronika Voskhoda*, 6 (February 5, 1882), pp. 129–130.

23. *Russkii Evrei*, 32 (August 12, 1882), p. 1238.

24. For the *guberniia* commissions and emigration, see I. Michael Aronson, "The Attitudes of Russian Officials...," *Slavic Review*, 34, No. 1 (March 1975), pp. 8–13.

25. Ibid., p. 13. Tolstoi's circular is also mentioned in *British Documents...*, Document 57, p. 64.

26. See the *Jewish Chronicle*, October 7, 1881, p. 7.

27. See the article republished in *Nedel'naia khronika Voskhoda*, 6 (February 5, 1882), p. 134.

28. Tcherikower, "Naya materialn vegen di pogromen in rusland onheyb di 80er yohren," *Historishe Shriftn*, II (1937), pp. 459–461.

29. The articles in *The Times* were republished in the form of a short pamphlet entitled *Persecution of the Jews in Russia 1881* (London: Spottiswoode, 1882).

30. Ibid., p. 21.

31. *Supplement to the Jewish Chronicle*, February 3, 1882, pp. 2–3. The campaign to mobilize public opinion in England in behalf of Russian Jewry actually began in the autumn of 1881 when a series of letters calling for such a step appeared in the *Jewish Chronicle*. The most articulate and forceful was the one signed by a writer taking the pseudonym Jurisconsultus, on November 4th. Supporters of Russian Jewry in England did not have it all their own way in the press. A Russian woman living in England, Madame Ragozin, sought to defend the Russian government and at the same time condemned Russian Jews for exploiting the peasants. See the *Jewish Chronicle*, March 31, 1882, p. 5; and April 7, p. 8.

32. Ibid., p. 3.

33. *Nedel'naia khronika Voskhoda*, 7 (February 12, 1882), pp. 163–164.

34. Ibid., 6 (February 5, 1882), pp. 123–124.

35. Ibid., 7 (February 12, 1882), p. 164.

36. For the French reaction to the pogroms, see Zosa Szajkowski, "The European Attitude to East European Jewish Immigration (1881–1883)," *Publications of the American Jewish Historical Society*, XLI (December 1951), pp. 147–153. See also *Nedel'naia khronika Voskhoda*, 6 (February 5, 1882), pp. 136–138.

37. *Pis'ma K. P. Pobedonostsova k Aleksandru III*, 2 vols. (Moscow: 1925), I, p. 344; and Byrnes, *Pobedonostov...*, pp. 207–208.

38. For Katkov's career, see Martin Katz, *Mikhail N. Katkov: A Political Biography 1881–1887* (The Hague: Mouton, 1966).

39. The Russian Jewish press, particularly *Russkii Evrei* and *Nedel'naia khronika Voskhoda*, closely monitored the Russian press in 1881 and 1882. In the first, the relevant section was *Za Nedel'iu* (For the Week) and in the latter it was *Otgoloski Pechati* (Echoes of the Press). Both sections were relatively long, running on the average between two and four detailed pages. For the letter in *Moskovskiia Vedomosti*, see *Russkii Evrei*, 24 (June 10, 1881), p. 932.

40. *Nedel'naia khronika Voskhoda*, 17 (April 23, 1882), p. 440.

41. On the danger to Russia and the harmful economic consequences from the pogroms, see ibid., 15 (April 9, 1882), p. 381, and 16 (April 15, 1882), p. 422.

42. Ibid., 15 (April 9, 1882), p. 381. For Katkov's view of the use of old legislation to harass the Jews, see 16 (April 15, 1882), p. 416.

43. Ibid., 15 (April 9, 1882), p. 381.

44. On Katkov's relationship with the Tsar and Pobedonostov see Katz, *Mikhail Katkov...*, pp. 165–184. In the eyes of some Jews, Katkov was a great hero. When he died in July 1887, the Hebrew prayer for the dead, *El mole rachmim*, was said for him by representatives of the Jewish community in St. Petersburg. *Nedel'naia khronika Voskhoda*, 30 (July 31, 1887), p. 761.

45. I. G. Oksman, "Otlik moskovskikh promyshlennikov na anti-evreiskie besporiadki," *Krasnyi Arkhiv*, XIV, no. 1 (1926), pp. 258–260.

46. The petition is in *Nedel'naia khronika Voskhoda*, 20 (May 15, 1882), pp. 541–542.

47. N. M. Gelber, "Di Rusishe Pogromen...," *Historishe Shriftn*, II (1937), pp. 482.

48. *Dnevnik E.A. Perettsa 1880–1883 gg.* (Moscow and Leningrad: Gosudarstvennoe Izdatel'stvo, 1927), pp. 130–131. See also Peter A. Zaionchkovsky, *The*

Russian Autocracy..., pp. 264–265; and Iu. Gessen, "Graf N. P. Ignatiev...,"
pp. 1678–1682.

49. Gessen, "Graf N. P. Ignatiev...," p. 1679.

50. Zaionchkovsky, *The Russian Autocracy...*, p. 265.

51. *Dnevnik Perettsa...*, pp. 131–132.

52. Zaionchkovsky, *The Russian Autocracy...*, p. 265.

53. *Nedel'naia khronika Voskhoda*, 20 (May 15, 1882), p. 534.

54. An early case of strict enforcement of the law came in the summer of 1882 when a Jew was barred from returning to his village after spending a day elsewhere. See *Razsvet*, 32 (August 11, 1882), pp. 1230–1231. The ways in which the May Laws were enforced over the years are discussed in Iu. Gessen, "Vremenniia pravila 3 Maia 1882 goda," *Evreiskaia Entsiklopediia*, III, pp. 816–822.

55. H. Frederic, *The New Exodus: A Study of Israel in Russia* (New York: Arno Press, 1970), p. 130.

56. G. B. Sliozberg, *Dela minuvshikh dnei: zapiski russkago evreia* (Paris: Izdanie komiteta po chestvovaniiu 70-ti letnago iubileia, 1933), I, p. 254. This is an excellent personal account of late nineteenth and early twentieth-century Russia by a very perceptive observer.

57. Zaionchkovsky, *The Russian Autocracy...*, p. 266.

58. *Nedel'naia khronika Voskhoda*, 20 (May 15, 1882), p. 535.

59. A Zemsky Sobor, literally a "landed assembly" representing different groups in Russian society, had met on several occasions hundreds of years before. Its convocation in the 1880s was opposed by such influential conservatives as Pobedonostov and Katkov. They and others argued that a Zemsky Sobor would limit the power of the Tsar and, worse, would be utilized by the revolutionaries for their own nefarious purposes. See Zaionchkovsky, *The Russian Autocracy...*, pp. 277–303.

60. The circular is quoted and discussed in *Razsvet*, 25 (June 20, 1882), pp. 938–947; and *Nedel'naia khronika Voskhoda*, 25 (June 19, 1982), pp. 665–667, 670–674.

61. Dubnow, "Iz istorii...," p. 275.

62. Dubnow, *History...*, II, p. 325; Greenberg, *The Jews in Russia*, II, pp. 57–58; and Sliozberg, *Dela...*, I, p. 107. See also Chapter V.

63. *Nedel'naia khronika Voskhoda*, 16 (April 15, 1882), p. 418. For *Rus* and the Jews, see *Russkii Evrei*, 23 (June 4, 1881), 40 (September 30, 1881), 42 (October 18, 1881), 45 (November 4, 1881), 48 (November 25, 1881), pp. 892, 1571–1572, 1651–1652, 1772, 1893, respectively. See also *Razsvet*, 5 (February 1, 1882), p. 177; and 10 (March 5, 1882), p. 374.

64. *Russkii Evrei*, 45 (November 4, 1881), p. 1772.

65. *Razsvet*, 5 (February 1, 1882), p. 177.

66. For *Novoe Vremia*, see *Russkii Evrei*, 19 (May 11, 1881); 22 (May 28, 1881); 30 (July 22, 1881); 34 (August 19, 1881); 41 (October 9, 1881); 43 (October 21, 1881); 44 (October 28, 1881); 48 (November 25, 1881); 49 (December 2, 1881); pp. 740–741, 849, 1130–1135 and 1169, 1332 and 1335, 1609, 1688, 1729, 1892–1893, 1930, respectively.

67. *Razsvet*, 19 (May 11, 1882), p. 709.

68. For *Kievlianin* and the Jews, see *Russkii Evrei*, 24 (June 10, 1881); 26 (June 25, 1881); 33 (August 12, 1881); 40 (September 30, 1881); pp. 932, 1008–1009,

1292, 1574 respectively; and *Razsvet*, 19 (May 11, 1882), p. 709. The three publications cited in the text do not exhaust the list of periodicals consistently
exhibiting a strong anti-Jewish tendency. In St. Petersburg, *Nedelia* (The Week)
was very hostile, and in the provinces, *Novorossiskii Telegraf* (The New Russia
Telegraph), published in Odessa, attacked the Jews with almost the virulence
of *Kievlianin*. For *Nedelia*, see *Russkii Evrei*, 46 (November 11, 1881), p. 1809;
Nedel'naia khronika Voskhoda, 18 (May 1, 1882), p. 470; and 19 (May 8, 1882), pp.
497–499. For *Novorossiskii Telegraf*, see *Russkii Evrei*, 46 (November 11, 1881), p.
1809; and 51 (December 16, 1881), p. 2009. See also *Razsvet*, 19 (May 11, 1882),
p. 709; and 32 (August 11, 1882), p. 1224. Kutaisov, in Krasnyi-Admoni, *Materialy...*, pp. 226–227, 229–230, also reported on the inflammatory nature of
editorials in *Novorossiskii Telegraf*.

69. *Razsvet*, 19 (May 11, 1882), p. 709.

70. *Russkii Evrei*, 24 (June 10, 1881), p. 932.

71. *Nedel'naia khronika Voskhoda*, 5 (January 28, 1882), p. 101.

72. *Russkii Evrei*, 25 (June 17, 1881), pp. 970–971.

73. Ibid., 44 (October 28, 1881), p. 1731.

74. S. Iuzhakov, "Evreiskii vopros v Rossii," *Otechestvennyia Zapiski*, 5 (May
1882), pp. 1–35.

75. Ben-Ami, "Odesskii pogrom...," p. 25.

76. *Russkii Evrei*, 17 (April 24, 1881), p. 656; and 18 (May 1, 1881), pp. 695–
696.

77. For *Moskovskii Telegraf*, see *Russkii Evrei*, 18 (May 1, 1881), p. 95.

78. Ibid., 18 (May 1, 1881), p. 695; 31 (July 29, 1881), pp. 1214–1215; and 34
(August 19, 1881), p. 1333.

79. *Nedel'naia khronika Voskhoda*, 7 (February 12, 1882), pp. 147–148.

80. Ibid., p. 152.

81. *Razsvet*, 10 (March 5, 1882), p. 373.

82. *Nedel'naia khronika Voskhoda*, 13 (March 26, 1882), pp. 316–317.

83. Ibid., p. 318.

84. *Nedel'naia khronika Voskhoda*, 14 (April 2, 1882), p. 343.

85. *Nedel'naia khronika Voskhoda*, 15 (April 9, 1882), p. 377.

86. For *Golos* on the Balta pogrom, see *Nedel'naia khronika Voskhoda*, 15 (April
9, 1881), passim; 16 (April 15, 1882), p. 411; 18 (May 1, 1882), p. 471; and 19
(May 8, 1882), p. 504.

87. *Nedel'naia khronika Voskhoda*, 18 (May 1, 1882), p. 477; and 19 (May 8, 1882),
p. 504.

88. Ibid., 16 (April 15, 1882), p. 417.

89. For *Zemstvo*, see ibid., p. 421, and for *Russkii Kurier*, see ibid., 19 (May 8,
1882), p. 505.

90. For *Novosti*, see ibid., 25 (June 19, 1882), p. 671. *Golos* also opposed the
May Laws because they impeded the assimilation of Jews into Russian society.
A correspondent of *Golos* had attended a Rothschild wedding in Paris and was
struck by how handsome and well turned out the Jews were. There were even
some Jews in military uniform. The moral of the story, according to *Golos*, was
that if Jews were to be assimilated and productive, they must be given full rights.
See *Nedel'naia khronika Voskhoda*, 22 (May 29, 1882), pp. 590–591.

91. For *Novosti*, *Golos*, and *Strana* see ibid., 25 (June 19, 1882), p. 671.

92. *Razsvet*, 27 (July 4, 1882), p. 1033.
93. Ibid.
94. *Razsvet*, 19 (May 9, 1882), pp. 707–708. There were cases where ordinary Christians did provide assistance even in the midst of pogroms. Kutaisov, in Krasnyi-Admoni, *Materialy...*, pp. 439–450, noted that German settlers on one occasion defended Jewish farmers from *pogromshchiki*. He also encountered a Christian businessman who strenuously defended the Jews against the charges made by other business people in his own town. *Nedel'naia khronika Voskhoda*, 17 (April 23, 1882), p. 439, and 18 (May 1, 1892) p. 472, reported that during the Balta pogrom some Christians saved Jews from attack. Among those helping Jews were clergymen of the Russian Orthodox Church. For examples of clerical opposition to the pogroms see *Russkii Evrei*, 22 (May 28, 1881); 23 (June 7, 1881); 31 (July 24, 1881); 32 (August 5, 1881); pp. 852, 890, 1206–1209, and 1249–1250, respectively. See also *Nedel'naia khronika Voskhoda*, 25 (June 19, 1882), p. 673, which claims that thirty-two Russian Orthodox clerics helped Jews during the 1881 pogroms. This contrasts with Kutaisov, in Krasnyi-Admoni, *Materialy...*, p. 409, who claims that local clergymen very often did not even assist the government in stopping pogroms. For instances of clerical hostility toward the Jews, see *Russkii Evrei*, 32 (August 5, 1881), p. 1249; and *Nedel'naia khronika Voskhoda*, 25 (June 19, 1882), p. 682. The greatest outpouring of support for Jews in the aftermath of a pogrom seems to have occurred in Warsaw in December 1881 and January 1882. See *Russkii Evrei*, 52 (December 23, 1881), p. 2056, for a report of Poles contributing thousands of rubles to assist Jews in Warsaw. *Nedel'naia khronika Voskhoda*, 1 (January 1, 1882), p. 15; and 3 (January 15, 1882), pp. 55, 63, reports Polish Catholic priests trying to calm the crowds during the pogrom there and of Polish assistance to Jews afterwards.
95. N. V. Shelgunov, "Vnutrennia obozrenie," *Delo*, 6 (June 1881) pp. 61–79. The famous philosopher, V. S. Soloviev, who wrote in the 1880s and 1890s many favorable articles about the Jews, did not address the pogroms in the years 1881–1882. He did, however, deliver a lecture on February 13, 1882, at the university in St. Petersburg which caused a stir in the capital. Soloviev spoke about the contributions of the Jews to civilization and expressed his sympathy to those Jews who had recently become the victims of the unruly passions of the Russian people. He accused unnamed journalists of stirring up the people to attack the Jews. See *Razsvet* 9 (February 13, 1882), pp. 335–337.
96. *Razsvet*, 19 (May 9, 1882), pp. 735–736. Mordovtsev also wrote a series of satirical feuilletons attacking Russian anti-Semitism. See his "Pisma mistera Plumpuddinga po evreiskomu voprosu," which appeared in *Razsvet*, 3 (January 15, 1882), pp. 114–118; 5 (February 1, 1882), pp. 194–198; 7 (February 12, 1882), pp. 276–279; and 10 (March 5, 1882), pp. 394–398.
97. *Otechestvennyia Zapiski*, 8 (August 1882), pp. 253–254.
98. Ibid., p. 258. For an abridged version of "Powerful Samson," see the translation by Krystyna Cekalska, *The Real Poland*, ed. Alfred Bloch (New York: Continuum, 1982), pp. 143–155. Orzeszkowa wrote a short pamphlet sympathetic to the Jews during the pogrom wave, republished in *Russkii Evrei* in article form. See *Russkii Evrei* 26 (June 30, 1882), pp. 982–986; 27 (July 7, 1882), pp. 1023–1027; 28 (July 14, 1882), pp. 1062–1064; 29 (July 21, 1882), pp. 1101–1104; 31 (August 4, 1882), pp. 1181–1186; 32 (August 11, 1882), pp. 1222–1225; 34

(August 25, 1882), pp. 1261–1264; 37 (Sept. 15, 1882), pp. 1394–1397. Orzeszkowa strongly condemned the pogroms and called upon Jews to integrate themselves into the countries in which they were living. She demanded that Jews renounce any type of Jewish nationalism.

99. Turgenev's correspondence reveals that he was highly critical of the pogroms and sympathetic to the Jews. However, he was reluctant to participate in the debate over the Jewish Question. He was, he claimed, a literary man, not a publicist. Turgenev was convinced that he would have little impact or, even worse, would be accused of having been bribed by the Jews. What was necessary, he felt, was a strong declaration against the pogroms by the Tsar. By early 1882, as a result of appeals from Jewish friends, Turgenev was prepared to write a short article condemning the pogroms and displaying his support for the Jews. But as one of his letters makes clear, the pain from his illness, cancer of the spine, was so great that he could not write. See I. S. Turgenev, *Pisma, tom trinadtsatyi, kniga pervaia, 1880–1882* (Leningrad: Izatel'stvo Nauka, 1968), pp. 100, 205, 219, 268, 457–458, 516, 521, 543.

CHAPTER IV: THE BRIDGE TO REVOLUTION

1. Abraham Yarmolinsky, *Road to Revolution* (New York: Collier, 1962), p. 296. Tcherikower, "Yidn revolutsionern...," p. 172, claims that by the late 1870s, Jewish revolutionaries were very much aware of anti-Jewish sentiment in the revolutionary movement, especially among Ukrainians. Y. Maor, *Ha-tenu'ah ha-tsiyonit be Rusyah* (Jerusalem: Hasifria Hatsionit, 1973), p. 35, states that in the 1870s the revolutionaries already viewed the Jews as exploiters of the workers and peasants.

2. Vasily Iakovlev Bogucharskii, *Literatura partii Narodnoi Voli* (Moscow: 1907), p. 197.

3. The full text of the proclamation is in S. Valk, "G.G. Romanenko," *Katorga i ssylka*, 48 (1928), pp. 50–52. Valk finds that Romanenko was the author of the document and that it reflected his intense anti-Semitic feelings. Lev Deych (Deutsch), "Vo imya nelitsepriyatnoy istiny," *Vestnik literatury*, 6, no.18 (1920), p.12, confirms Romanenko's authorship and his anti-Semitism. Tcherikover, "Yidn revolutsionern...," p. 101, also maintains that Romanenko was the author, as does Abraham Liesin, "Epizodn," *YIVO Historishe Shriftn*, III (1939), p. 199. For further discussion of these general issues, see Shmuel Ettinger, *Toldot am Yisrael mi-mahpekhot 1848 ad le-hakamat medinat Yisrael* (Jerusalem: Dvir, 1966), pp. 88–89. Maor, *Ha-tenu'ah...*, p. 37; M. Mishkinsky, "Al Hadeot Ha-kdumot shel ha-sotsialistim hamahapkhanim shelanu neged ha-yehudim," *He-Avar*, 21 (1975), pp. 20–34, and "Tenuat ha-poalim ha-yehudit beRusyah ve-ha-tenu'ah ha-sotsialistit ha-Polanit," *Asufot* 1, no. 14 (1970), pp. 81–132.

4. Lev Deych, "Vo imya...," p. 12; V. Ia. Bogucharskii, *Iz istorii politicheskoi borby* (Moscow: Russkaia Mysl, 1912), p. 222; and G. Ia. Krasnyi-Admoni, "Literatura podpolia i pogromy," *Vestnik literatury*, no. 3 (16), 1920, pp. 11–12.

5. Valk, in "G. G. Romanenko," p. 52, claims wide distribution and republication in Elizavetgrad. Krasnyi-Admoni, "Literatura...," pp. 11–12, also claims that the proclamation was well distributed. Bogucharskii, *Iz istorii...*, p. 222, and Deych, "Vo imya....," p. 12, claim that very few of the proclamations were

distributed. Liesin, "Epizodn," p. 199, writes of the Executive Committee's dissatisfaction with the proclamation and states that some members were able to stop its dissemination.

6. Bogucharskii, *Literatura partii...*, p. 215.

7. Ibid., p. 219.

8. Ibid., p. 311.

9. Ibid., p. 313.

10. The quotation is found in V. S. Voytinsky et al., *Iz arkhiva P. B. Akselroda* (Berlin: Russkii revoliutsionnyi arkhiv, 1924), pp. 213–216; and Krasnyi-Admoni, *Materialy...*, p. 225.

11. Quoted in Bogucharskii, *Iz istorii...*, p. 230.

12. Voytinsky, *Iz arkhiva...*, p. 215. Liesin, "Epizodn," p. 200, indicates that Jewish printers who worked for *Chernyi Peredel* in Minsk refused to print an article attacking Jews.

13. Lev Deych, *Rol' evreev v russkom revoliutsionnom dvizhenii*, 2 vols. (Berlin: Grani, 1923), I, pp. 237–239, 249.

14. Ibid., p. 8.

15. Ibid., pp. 8–9.

16. Voytinsky, *Iz arkhiva...*, p. 217. For Akselrod's changing attitudes on Jewish affairs, see Abraham Ascher, "Pavel Axelrod: A Conflict Between Jewish Loyalty and Revolutionary Dedication," *The Russian Review*, 24, no. 3 (1965), pp. 249–265. An excellent presentation of Akselrod's career is found in Abraham Ascher, *Pavel Axelrod and the Development of Menshevism* (Cambridge, Mass.: Harvard University Press, 1972).

17. P. B. Akselrod, "Pogromen un di revoliutsionere bavaygung mit 43 yohr tsurik: Vi di yidishe soytsyalistn hobn dan farshtanen zeyere oyfgabn," *Di Tsukunft*, XXIX (1924), p. 555; and Deych, *Rol'...*, pp. 251–252.

18. Voytinsky, *Iz arkhiva...*, p. 222.

19. Ibid., p. 223.

20. Ibid., p. 224.

21. Ibid., p. 225.

22. Ibid., pp. 225–226.

23. Ibid., pp. 226–228. Akselrod believed that a fairly long period of time would have to pass before a merger of the Jews and the indigenous population could occur. The Jews were on a higher cultural plane than the rest of the populace and therefore could not be expected to merge. In the meantime, Akselrod implied that Jewish socialists should defend the interests of the Jewish poor.

24. Ibid., pp. 29–30. Lavrov and other revolutionaries were much impressed by an article, "Krestianin o sovremennikh sobitiakh," which appeared in the journal *Otechestvennye zapiski* in March 1882. The article gave the impression that the peasants were filled with animosity toward the Jews.

25. Ibid., p. 31.

26. Ibid., p. 217.

27. Ibid.

28. This appeal and postscript is found in M. Dragomanov, *Sobranie politicheskikh sochinenii M. P. Dragomanova*, 2 vols. (Paris: Osvobozhdenie, 1905), II, pp. 320–329. For the respect enjoyed by Dragomanov among Jewish revolu-

tionaries, see G. Gurevitch, "Zikhroynes," *YIVO Historishe Shriftn*, III, 1939, p. 229.

29. Dragomanov, *Sobranie...*, II, p. 327; and F. Kursky, "Di Zhenever 'Grupe Sotsialist-Yidn' un ir oyfruf 1880," *YIVO Historishe Shriftn*, III (1939), pp. 558, 561.

30. This was the judgment of E. Tcherikower in "Noch vegn der zhenever 'Grupe Sotsialistn-Yidn'," *YIVO Historishe Shriftn*, III (1939), p. 563.

31. Kurksy, "Di Zhenever...," p. 561.

32. M. Dragomanov, "Istorichekaia Polsha i velikorusskaia demokratiia, 1881–1882," *Sobranie...*, I, pp. 191–192, quoted in Bogucharskii, *Iz istorii...*, p. 223.

33. For the conversation with Ben-Ami, see the latter's "Moi snosheniia s M. Dragomanovym i rabota v Vol'nom Slove," *Evreiskaia Starina*, II (1915), p. 363. Ben-Ami claims that Dragomanov believed that a small Jewish sect committed ritual murder. Dragomanov's written remarks are found in his "Evreiskii vopros na Ukraine," *Sobranie...*, II, pp. 533, 539–540, quoted in Bogucharskii, *Iz istorii...*, pp. 222–223.

34. Dragomanov, "Evreiskii vopros...," quoted in Ben-Ami, "Moi snosheniia s Dragomanovym," *Evreiskaia Starina*, VIII (1916), p. 80.

35. Ibid., p. 81.

36. M. Dragomanov in *Vol'noe Slovo*, no. 38 (1882); cited in Ben-Ami, "Moi snosheniia...," *Evreiskaia starina*, II (1915), p. 356.

37. Ben-Ami, "Moi snosheniia...," *Evreiskaia starina*, I (1916), pp. 96–97.

38. Ibid., p. 97; M. Dragomanov, "Evreiskii vopros v slavianskom kruzhke v Londone," quoted in Bogucharskii, *Iz istorii...*, pp. 223–224; and Dragomanov, "Istoricheskaia Polsha...," pp. 234–235.

39. Tcherikower, "Yidn revolutsionern...," p. 172. The same opinion is expressed in Shmuel Ettinger, "The National Awakening of Russian Jews," *Jewish Quarterly*, 21 (Winter 1973), p. 14.

CHAPTER V: JEWISH RESPONSES TO THE POGROMS

1. *Razsvet*, 13 (March 26, 1881), pp. 491–492.

2. Ibid., 24 (June 11, 1881), p. 943.

3. *Nedel'naia khronika Voskhoda*, 1 (January 1, 1882), p. 3.

4. Chaim Chissin, *A Palestine Diary*, trans. Francis Miller (New York: Herzl Press, 1976), pp. 31–32.

5. For events in Odessa, see Ben Ami, "Odesskii pogrom...," pp. 25–40.

6. *Razsvet*, 4 (January 22, 1882), p. 138.

7. For the views of Jewish community leaders in the provinces, see Krasnyi-Admoni, *Materialy...*, pp. 203–204, 224–230, 299, 306, 311–316, 328–329, 425–429.

8. *Razsvet*, 17 (April 27, 1882), pp. 620–621.

9. Voytinsky, *Iz arkhiva...*, p. 228.

10. *Razsvet*, 9 (February 26, 1882), p. 335.

11. *Russkii Evrei*, 25 (July 23, 1882), p. 951.

12. *Razsvet*, 10 (March 5, 1882), p. 372.

13. Ibid., 11 (March 12, 1882), p. 407.

14. David Vital, *The Origins of Zionism* (London: Oxford University Press, 1975), p. 76.

15. *Razsvet*, 19 (May 8, 1881), pp. 730–731.

16. Ibid., 9 (February 26, 1882), p. 323.

17. Ibid., 26 (June 27, 1882), p. 979.

18. Ibid. p. 980.

19. Arthur Hertzberg, *The Zionist Idea* (New York: Atheneum, 1971), p. 169. For the diary notations, see M. Lilienblum, *Derekh Tshuva* (Warsaw: Achiassaf, 1899), pp. 22–49. Vital, *Origins...*, pp. 111–122, provides a fine explication of Lilienblum's views, as does Frankel, *Prophecy...*, in his excellent chapter on 1881–1882. See also the unpublished dissertation by Gersh. For a summation of Lilienblum's ideas in 1881 and later, see his *0 vozrozhdenie Evreiskago Naroda na sv. zeml' ego drevnikh otzov* (Odessa: Gornshstein, 1903).

20. These articles are found in *O vozrozhdenie...*, pp. 3–18.

21. Ibid., p. 14. Frankel, *Prophecy...*, p. 87, states that this article "tipped the balance in the *Razsvet* board toward Palestine and against America."

22. Lilienblum, *O vozrozhdenie...*, p. 17.

23. Hertzberg, *The Zionist Idea*, p. 170.

24. Ibid., pp. 170–171.

25. Ibid., p. 171.

26. *Razsvet*, 1 (January 1, 1882), p. 29.

27. Ibid., 27 (July 4, 1882), pp. 1051–1055.

28. Ibid., 52 (December 25, 1882), p. 2032. See also his articles, signed W, in *Razsvet*, 20, 21, 22, 27, 29 (1882).

29. Joel Geffen, "Whither: To Palestine or to America in the Pages of the Russian Hebrew Press *Ha-Melitz* and *Ha-Yom* (1880–1890), *American Jewish Historical Quarterly*, 59 (December 1969), p. 182. See also the letter from David Gordon, editor of *Ha-Magid*, published in Prussia, to the *Jewish Chronicle*, April 21, 1882, p. 6, supporting settlement in Palestine.

30. Geffen, "Whither...," p. 195.

31. Ibid., p. 197.

32. Ibid., p. 184.

33. On Smolenskin in the period 1881–1882, see Frankel, *Prophecy...*, pp. 61–64, 83–84, 87, 89, 90.

34. *Razsvet*, 1 (January 5, 1882), p. 3.

35. B. Netanyahu, *Road to Freedom* (New York: Scopus, 1944), p. 76. The book is a collection of Pinsker's essays, including *Auto-Emancipation*, from which the quote is taken. *Auto-Emancipation* was very quickly translated into Russian and appeared in *Razsvet* at the end of 1882.

36. Netanyahu, *Road to Freedom...*, pp. 77–78.

37. Ibid., p. 81.

38. Ibid., pp. 83–84.

39. Ibid., p. 91.

40. Ibid., p. 89.

41. Ibid., p. 95.

42. Ibid., p. 105.

43. Ibid., p. 48. This quote is found in the introduction by Netanyahu.

44. Ibid., p. 59.

45. The *Jewish Chronicle*, March 24, 1882, pp. 6–7.

46. The quote is from a letter by one of the members of Bilu in Palestine, Zeev Dubnov, to his brother, the historian, S. Dubnov, and it is found in S. Dubnov, "Pisma 'biluitsa' (1882–1884g.)," *Evreiskaia Starina*, VIII (1915), p. 106. Vital is particularly good on Bilu and on settlement in Palestine in the period 1881–1882, and so is Frankel. Additional information on Bilu can be found in Shulamit Laskov, "The Biluim: Reality and Legend," *Zionism*, II (Spring 1981), pp. 17–69, and by the same author, *Ha-biluim* (Jerusalem: Hasifria Hatsionit, 1979). The classic account of Bilu is found in A. Druyanov, ed., *Ketavim le-toldot Hibbat Zion ve-yishuv Erez Israel*, 3 vols. (Odessa: 1919; Tel Aviv: Ha Vaad Leyishuv Erets Yisroel, 1928, 1932).

47. Greenberg, *The Jews...*, II, p. 161.

48. Yehudah Leib Gordon, *Kitve Yehuda Leb Gordon: Shirah* (Tel Aviv: Hotsa'at Dvir, 1950), p. 31.

49. *Russkii Evrei*, 36 (Sept. 8, 1881), p. 1406.

50. *Razsvet*, 34 (August 21, 1881); 35 (August 28, 1881), pp. 1348–1350, 1384–1388, respectively.

51. Ibid., 40 (October 2, 1881), p. 1576.

52. Sidney Bailey, who emigrated during the pogrom years, recalled agents who created the impression that the Jews could build their own state in America in the same way that the Mormons had established themselves in Utah. See "Sidney Bailey's Memoir" in Uri D. Herscher, *Jewish Agricultural Utopias in America 1880–1910* (Detroit: Wayne State University Press, 1981), p. 148.

53. Mendes-Flohr and Reinharz, *The Jew in the Modern World*, p. 334.

54. *Razsvet*, 4 (January 22, 1882), p. 133.

55. For a personal recollection of Bokal, see "Sidney Bailey's Memoir," pp. 144–152.

56. Abraham Menes, "The Am Oylom Movement, " *YIVO Annual of Jewish Social Science* (1949), p. 16. For additional information on Am Olam, see also Frankel, *Prophecy...*, pp. 55–57, 66–67, 76, 94–96.

57. For 1881, see *Russkii Evrei*, 18, 24, 31, 33, 34. For 1882, see *Russkii Evrei*, 5, 6, 9, 21, 31, 33, 36, 39, 52.

58. *Russkii Evrei*, 31 (August 4, 1882), p. 1181.

59. On the need for Jewish self-defense, see the lead article by Landau in *Nedel'naia khronika Voskhoda*, 15 (April 9, 1882), p. 372.

60. Ibid., p. 371.

61. Ibid., pp. 369–371. See his remarks about Drenteln in *Nedel'naia khronika Voskhoda*, 35 (August 28, 1882), pp. 945–947, 963.

62. Ibid., 39 (September 25, 1882), pp. 1050–1051.

63. Ibid., 23 (June 5, 1882), p. 614.

64. Ibid., 35 (August 28, 1882), p. 948.

65. Ibid., p. 947.

66. Ibid., p. 949.

67. Ibid., p. 950.

68. This fear of endangering privileged positions may be behind the letter of Horace Günzburg to a prominent Jew in Manchester. The letter, which appeared in the *Jewish Chronicle*, July 1, 1881, p. 11, makes clear Günzburg's satisfaction

that no public meetings were convened in England to protest the Russian government's conduct during the pogroms.

69. Tsitron, *Shtadlanim*, p. 348.

70. *Russkii Evrei*, 20 (May 12, 1881), p. 765.

71. Vital, *The Origins of Zionism*, p. 72.

72. *Nedel'naia khronika Voskhoda*, 33 (August 4, 1882), p. 901.

73. Ibid., pp. 903–904.

74. Russkii Evrei, 32 (August 11, 1882), p. 1238.

75. Ibid.

76. Ibid., pp. 1239–1240.

77. Dubnow, *History...*, II, p. 307. A very detailed discussion of the Günzburg conferences is found in B. Dinur, "Tochniotov shel Ignatiev lepitron sheelat hayehudim veidot netzigay ha-kehilot bepetersburg bishnot tarma-B," *He-Avar*, X (1963), pp. 5–87.

78. Ibid.

79. *Razsvet*, 24 (June 13, 1882), pp. 898–903.

80. In the aftermath of the April conference, *Razsvet* devoted many articles to criticizing its participants for their unwillingness to lead and assist the emigration movement. See, for example, *Razsvet*, 19 (May 11, 1882), pp. 697–700; 25 (June 20, 1882), p. 942; and 26 (June 27, 1882), p. 979. Even before the conference, the paper had called for leadership and financial assistance from prominent and wealthy Jews, particularly the heads of the Jewish community in St. Petersburg. See *Razsvet*, 9 (February 26, 1882), p. 323.

81. *Nedel'naia khronika Voskhoda*, 39 (September 25, 1882), pp. 1050–1051.

82. For Gordin and the Spiritual-Biblical Brotherhood, see S. Ts, "Iakov Gordin," *Evreiskaia Entsiklopediia*, IV, pp. 687–688.

83. The letter was republished in *Russkii Evrei*, 27 (July 2, 1881), pp. 1046–1047.

84. For a critical Jewish response, see ibid., pp. 1042–1044.

85. A biography of Priluker and a discussion of New Israel's program is found in S. Ginsburg, *Mishumodim...*, pp. 90–118.

86. For a critical letter on New Israel from a member of the Jewish intelligentsia, see *Nedel'naia khronika Voskhoda*, 8 (February 19, 1882), pp. 184–185. The opposition to Priluker is briefly described in Frankel, *Prophecy...*, p. 57, and Ginsburg, *Mishumodim...*, pp. 97–98. The only Jewish writer of prominence who appeared receptive to Priluker and Gordin was the young Dubnov, who was just beginning his writing career. Dubnov soon lost interest in these radical ideas.

87. Ginsburg, *Mishumodim...*, p. 104.

CHAPTER VI: THE GOLDEN LAND

1. Cyrus Adler and Aaron Margalith, *With Firmness in the Right: American Diplomacy Affecting Jews, 1840–1945* (New York: The American Jewish Committee, 1946), p. 210.

2. Mark Wischnitzer, *To Dwell in Safety* (Philadelphia: Jewish Publication Society of America, 1948), p. 35.

3. Both statements can be found in the *New York Times*, February 2, 1882, p. 8.

4. U.S., *Congressional Record*, 47th Cong., First Sess., 1882, XIII, Part VII, Appendix, p. 653.

5. Wischnitzer, *To Dwell...*, p. 36.

6. Abraham Cahan, *Bleter fun mein leben*, 2 vols. (New York: Forvarts, 1926), II, p, 28.

7. B. Weinstein, *Ferzig yohr in der yidisher Arbeit Bavaygung* (New York: Veker, 1924), p. 12.

8. Zosa Szajkowski, "How the Mass Migration to America Began," *Jewish Social Studies*, IV (October 1942), p. 301.

9. E. Tcherikower, ed., *Geschichte fun der Yidisher Arbeiter-Bavaygung in di Fareinikte Shtaten* (New York: YIVO, 1943), I, p. 106. This is an absolutely superb source for East European Jewish immigration to the United States at the end of the nineteenth and the beginning of the twentieth centuries.

10. Ibid., p. 103. For rumors that the Alliance would send every Jew that arrived in Brody to America, see *Nedel'naia khronika Voskhoda*, 6 (February 5, 1882), p. 136.

11. Tcherikower, *Geschichte...*, p. 106.

12. Ibid. On October 21, 1881, *The Jewish Chronicle*, p. 4, published a letter from N. Leven of the Alliance disavowing the rumors.

13. Wischnitzer, *To Dwell...*, p. 44.

14. Leo Shpall, "The Diary of Dr. George M. Price," *Publications of the American Jewish Historical Society*, XL (December 1950), p. 175.

15. Brandes' account appears in Tcherikover, *Geschichte...*, pp. 391–396.

16. Alexander Harkavy, "Chapters From My Life," trans. Jonathan Sarna, *American Jewish Archives*, XXXII, no.1 (April 1981), pp. 37–39.

17. Shpall, "Diary...," p. 176.

18. Cahan, *Bleter...*, II, p. 28.

19. Shpall, "Diary..., "pp. 178–179.

20. Beginning in the 1890s, Jewish emigrants from Russia suffered many hardships in Germany as a consequence of stringently applied government regulation. See Zosa Szajkowski, "Sufferings of Jewish Emigrants to America in Transit through Germany," *Jewish Social Studies*, XXXIX (Winter-Spring, 1977), pp. 105–116.

21. Rubin's sea voyage and later experiences are described in Harris Rubin, "Worker on the Land," *American Jewish Archives*, XXXII, no. 1 (April 1981), pp. 7–34. For a recent discussion of the hardships experienced by emigrants on ship, see Pamela S. Nadell, "The Journey to America by Steam: The Jews of Eastern Europe in Transition," *American Jewish History*, LXXl (December 1981), pp. 269–284. According to Nadell, p. 269, "the emigrants traveling in steerage encountered unscrupulous steamship agents, unhealthy accommodations, wretched food, financial exploitation, and physical brutality."

22. Cahan, *Bleter...*, II, p. 33.

23. Shpall, "Diary...," p. 176.

24. Alexander Harkavy, "Chapters...," p. 39.

25. A good summary of American Jewish history is found in Arthur Goren, "Jews," *Harvard Encyclopedia of American Ethnic Groups*, ed. Stephen Thernstrom

(Cambridge, Mass.: Belknap, 1980), pp. 571–579. See also the relevant sections in Moshe Davis, *The Emergence of Conservative Judaism*, 2nd ed. (Philadelphia: Jewish Publication Society of America, 1965); Henry Feingold, *Zion in America* (New York: Hippocrene, 1974); Leon Jick, *The Americanization of the Synagogue* (Hanover, N.H.: University Press of New England, 1976); Bertram Korn, *American Jewry and the Civil War* (Philadelphia: Jewish Publication Society of America, 1961); and Jonathan Sarna, *Jacksonian Jew: The Two Worlds of Mordecai Noah* (New York: Holmes and Meier, 1980).

26. Emma Felsenthal, *Bernhard Felsenthal, Teacher in Israel* (New York: Oxford University Press, 1924), p. 226.

27. Paul R. Mendes-Flohr and Jehuda Reinharz, *The Jew in the Modern World*, p. 369.

28. Ibid., pp. 368–369.

29. On the Board, see Wischnitzer, *To Dwell...*, p. 31. For the *Jewish Messenger*'s generally hostile attitude toward Jewish immigration and the Russian Jews, see the following issues: June 25, 1869, p. 4; January 7, 1870, p. 4; and February 11, 1881, p. 4.

30. On support for Jewish immigration, see Wischnitzer, *To Dwell...*, p. 32.

31. Ibid.

32. Simon Kuznets, "Immigration of Russian Jews to the United States: Background and Structure," *Perspectives in American History*, IX (1975), p. 42. The long and detailed Kuznets article is far superior to earlier statistical studies on Jewish immigration.

33. Wischnitzer, *To Dwell...*, p. 43.

34. Zosa Szajkowski, "The Attitude of American Jews to East European Jewish Immigration (1881–1893)," *Publications of the American Jewish Historical Society*, XL (March 1951), pp. 222–223.

35. Ibid., p. 223.

36. Wischnitzer, *To Dwell...*, p. 41.

37. The *Jewish Messenger*, May 20, 1881, p. 4.

38. On calls for generosity in the treatment and handling of Russian Jews, see the *Jewish Messenger*, August 12, 1881, p. 4, and October 28, 1881, p. 4.

39. The *American Israelite*, November 11, 1881, p. 156. But some of his prominent Reform colleagues disagreed, advocating settlement in America. See the letter by Ludwig Philippson in the same issue, and the article by Rabbi Isaac Mayer Wise in the issue of August 5, 1881, p. 4.

40. Zosa Szajkowski, "The Attitude of American Jews...," p. 225.

41. Ibid., p. 265.

42. Ibid., p. 270.

43. Ibid., p. 225.

44. Ibid., p. 238.

45. Jacob Neusner, "The Impact of Immigration and Philanthropy upon the Boston Jewish Community (1880–1914)," *Publications of the American Jewish Historical Society*, XLVI (December 1956), p. 73.

46. Gilbert Osofsky, "The Hebrew Emigrant Aid Society of the United States," *Publications of the American Jewish Historical Society*, XLIX (December 1960), p. 181.

47. Zosa Szajkowski, "The European Attitude to East European-Jewish Im-

migration (1881–1893)," *Publications of the American Jewish Historical Society*, XL (December 1951), p. 138.

48. Ibid., p. 139.

49. Ibid., p. 140.

50. Ibid., pp. 148–153. Despite the attitudes of the committees, small numbers of Russian Jews did manage to settle in various European countries in the period 1881–1882. Their lot was not an easy one. They were often attacked in the anti-Semitic press, and they received meager assistance from the Jewish relief organizations, which had wanted them to move on to America. The most difficult struggle was to obtain some kind of employment. See Zosa Szajkowski, "How the Mass Migration to America Began," pp. 304–308. For a description of the harsh conditions experienced by Russian Jews in Paris, see *Nedel'naia khronika Voskhoda*, 12 (March 19, 1882), pp. 300–303.

51. Israel Friedlander, "The Present Crisis of American Jewry," *Past and Present: Collected Essays* (Cincinnati: Ark, 1919), p. 341.

52. The British were annoyed at the Americans because of the latter's emphatic insistence that only suitable emigrants be transported to America. The Americans wanted to have dependent women and children remain in Brody, at least temporarily. The Americans, of course, were responding to their own internal pressures. For the British view, see the *Jewish Chronicle*, June 30, 1882, pp. 3–4. On the dispute with the Mansion House Fund, and the finances of HEAS, see Zosa Szajkowski, "The Attitude of American Jews...," pp. 235–236, and 257–259.

53. See *Nedel'naia khronika Voskhoda*, 1 (January 1, 1882), pp. 19–20; for *Ha-Melits*, see Tcherikower, *Geshichte...*, p. 204.

54. *Russkii Evrei*, 12 (March 19, 1882), p. 471.

55. Tcherikower, *Geshichte...*, p. 213.

56. Ibid., pp. 213–214.

57. Leo Shpall, "The Memoir of Doctor George M. Price," *Publications of the American Jewish Historical Society*, XLVII (December 1957), p. 102.

58. Gilbert Osofsky, "The Hebrew Emigrant Aid Society...," p. 181.

59. Tcherikower, *Geshichte...*, p. 208.

60. Ibid.

61. Harkavy, "Chapters...," p. 40.

62. On the Ward's Island episode, see Shpall, "The Memoir of Doctor George M. Price," pp. 104–109, and Tcherikower, *Geshichte...*, pp. 207–209. For the British, what happened at Ward's Island was proof of American incompetence. See the *Jewish Chronicle*, November 10, 1882, p. 4.

63. Tcherikower, *Geshichte...*, p. 209.

64. Ibid.

65. Ibid., p. 208.

66. For Heilprin's role, see Osofsky, "The Hebrew Emigrant Aid Society...," p. 183; Gustav Pollak, *Michael Heilprin and His Sons* (New York: Dodd, Mead, 1912), pp. 190–220; and Cahan, *Bleter...*, II, pp. 131–138. Cahan called Heilprin the "most beloved" of personalities in the eyes of the immigrants.

67. Szajkowski, "The Attitude of American Jews...," p. 267.

68. Weinstein, *Ferzig yohr...*, pp. 30–36; and Tcherikower, *Geshichte...*, pp. 243–245.

69. Tcherikower, *Geshichte...*, p. 246.

70. Rubin, "Workers on the Land," p. 26.

71. Harkavy, "Chapters...," pp. 43–45.

72. The *American Israelite*, December 2, 1881, p. 181; January 20, 1882, p. 237; March 17, 1882, p. 301; and November 17, 1882, p. 170.

73. Leo Shpall, "Jewish Agricultural Colonies in the United States, *Agricultural History*, XIV (July 1950), pp. 126–129. For a recent discussion of American Jewish support for the agricultural colonies, see Uri D. Herscher, *Jewish Agricultural...*, pp. 22–26, 30, 49.

74. Gustav Pollak, *Michael Heilprin...*, p. 208.

75. Cahan, *Bleter...*, II, p. 115.

76. Ibid., p. 303.

77. Leo Shpall, "Jewish Agricultural Colonies...," p. 132. For a fine discussion of the colonies established in the United States, see Herscher, *Jewish Agricultural...*, pp. 31–84. See also his summary statement on the failure of Jewish agricultural colonization, pp. 108–121.

78. Tcherikower, *Geshichte...*, p. 253. A detailed discussion of Jews returning to their place of origin is found in Jonathan D. Sarna, "The Myth of No Return: Jewish Return Migration to Eastern Europe, 1881–1914," *American Jewish History*, LXXI (December 1981), pp. 256–268. Sarna places the rate of return in the 1881–1900 period in the range of 15 to 20 percent, and claims, p. 265, that "inability to find work was a prime cause of return migration."

79. Tcherikower, *Geshichte...*, p. 245.

80. Wischnitzer, *To dwell...*, p. 31.

81. The cartoon and the controversy generated by it appear in Tcherikower, *Geshichte...*, pp. 390, 396–399.

82. Cahan, *Bleter...*, II, p. 415.

Glossary

Aliyah: (Hebrew) "Going up," referring to immigration into Palestine. Some migrations are know by their numbers, hence, the First Aliyah (1882–1903).

am olamkes: (Yiddish) Members of the Am Olam organization which aspired to agricultural settlement in the United States.

biluim: (Hebrew) Members of Bilu, a group seeking to establish communal farms in Palestine.

bosiaki: (Russian) The "barefoot brigade," itinerant workers who moved into the Ukraine in the period prior to the pogroms and participated in the attacks on the Jews.

chalutzim: (Hebrew) Pioneers, Jews who settled in agricultural communities in Palestine.

chometz: (Hebrew) Food that cannot be eaten during Passover.

desiatina: (Russian) 2.7 acres.

Druzhina: (Russian) The Holy League, a secret organization attempting to protect the Tsar and disrupt the revolutionary movement.

duma: (Russian) Town council.

feldsher: (Russian) Doctor's assistant.

guberniia: (Russian) A province.

haluka: (Hebrew) Charity collected in Jewish communities for the pious poor Jews of Palestine.

Hasidism: A pietistic religious movement originating among the Jews of Poland in the eighteenth century. Its adherents are known as Hasidim.

Haskalah: (Hebrew) The Jewish enlightenment movement which began in Berlin in the eighteenth century and had enormous influence on Jews all over Europe.

heder: (Hebrew) The first school for a Jewish child in Eastern Europe.

kahal: (Hebrew) The self-governing body of Jewish communities in the Russian Empire.

Kahal: The mythical international organization invented by Russian and European anti-Semites.

kashruth: (Hebrew) Jewish dietary laws.

kolkhoz: (Russian) Soviet collective farm.

kulak: (Russian) Wealthy peasant.

mashgiach: (Hebrew) A person trained to ensure that producers and distributors of kosher food have complied with kashruth.

maskilim: (Hebrew) Followers of the Haskalah.

meshchanstvo: (Russian) The lower middle class.

narod: (Russian) The people.

narodnovoltsy: (Russian) Members of the revolutionary organization Narodnaia Volia.

oblast: (Russian) Region, district.

obrusenie: (Russian) Russification.

obshchina: (Russian) Commune.

ORT: (Russian) Abbreviation of three Russian words meaning Society for the Spread of Manual Work [among Jews]. It was established in 1880 in Russia by wealthy Jews and is now an international organization providing vocational training for Jews.

Pale of Settlement: The area in Tsarist Russia in which Jews were permitted to live.

parnossa: (Hebrew) Livelihood.

pogromshchiki: (Russian) People carrying out the pogroms.

pomeshchiki: (Russian) Landlords.

prikaz: (Russian) An order.

pud: (Russian) A Russian weight equal to about 36 pounds.

rekrutshchina: (Russian) The system of conscripting Jewish boys during the reign of Nicholas I.

sblizhenie: (Russian) Rapprochement, term used by some Jewish writers to describe the future relationship between Jews and the Russian people.

sephardim: (Hebrew) Jews of Spanish and Portuguese origin.

shtadlan: (Hebrew) A representative of a Jewish community designated to defend its interests before the authorities.

shtadlanut: (Hebrew) The system of Jewish advocacy and intercession by specially chosen people.

slianie: (Russian) Confluence or merger, term used by some Jewish writers to describe a more pervasive assimilation than was the case with sblizhenie.

Talmud: (Hebrew) Collections of Jewish law and lore compiled in Babylonia and Palestine.

tref: (Hebrew) Food that is not kosher.

tsadik: (Hebrew) A pious, saintly man, a Hasidic leader.

ukaz: (Russian) Decree, edict.

versta: (Russian) 3,500 feet.

yeshiva: (Hebrew) Traditional institution of higher Jewish learning where the Talmud was studied.

Yiddishkeit: (Yiddish) Love of Yiddish culture; a profound personal sense of Jewishness.

Yishuv: (Hebrew) The modern Jewish community in Palestine.

Zemsky Sobor: (Russian) Landed Assembly, an institution composed of different classes which met with Grand Princes and Tsars in the medieval and early periods of Russian history.

zemstvo: (Russian) Elective rural council in pre-revolutionary Russia.

zhid: (Russian) A pejorative term for Jews, equivalent to the English yid.

Bibliographical Essay

The sources utilized for this book fall into two categories: primary sources, consisting of newspapers, memoirs, and government documents, and secondary sources, both books and articles. Of particular value were the three Russian Jewish weeklies: *Razsvet*, *Russkii Evrei*, and *Nedel'naia khronika Voskhoda*. All three had correspondents in the cities and towns of the Pale of Settlement. They also published large numbers of letters. As a result, these three periodicals provide an insight into the period that would be difficult to obtain from other sources. The nature of the general onslaught against the Jews, the responses of various segments of the Jewish community, and the efforts of prominent and of ordinary Jews to defend themselves and the rest of the Jewish people are laid out in their pages. The Russian Jewish papers, together with the sources discussed below, contributed most decisively to my understanding of various aspects of the subject.

GENERAL WORKS

The most helpful general studies on Russian Jewish history are Simon Dubnow [Dubnov], *History of the Jews in Russia and Poland*, trans. I. Friedlaender, 2 vols. (New York: Ktav, 1975); Louis Greenberg, *The Jews in Russia*, 2 vols. (New Haven: Yale University Press, 1944); I. Sosis, *Di Geshicte von di yidishe gezelshaftleche shtremungen in russland in XIX y.hy.* (Minsk: Meluche, 1929); Salo Baron, *The Russian Jew under Tsars and Soviets* (New York: Macmillan, 1964); and Iu. Gessen, *Istoriia evreiskago naroda v rossii*, 2 vols. (Leningrad: 1927). Dubnov also published in the years 1915–1916 a long series of articles entitled "Iz istorii vos'midesiatikh godov" in the journal *Evreiskaia Starina* of Petrograd. Anyone looking at Russian Jewish history in this period ought to begin with Dubnow. Mina Goldberg's inaugural dissertation, "Die Jahre 1881–1882 in der Geschichte der russischen Juden," is of substantial interest. It was published by Friedrich-Wilhelms-Universität zu Berlin, 1933.

Other valuable general sources are the sixteen-volume *Evreiskaia Entsiklopediia* published in St. Petersburg from 1906 to 1913, and the more recently published *Encyclopedia Judaica*, 16 vols. (Jerusalem: Keter Publishing House, 1971–1972). Not an encyclopedia but encylopedic in scope is Jonathan Frankel's *Prophecy and Politics; Socialism, Nationalism and the Russian Jews, 1862–1917* (London: Cambridge University Press, 1981). It is the best study on the subject and has rapidly become the definitive account. I. Orshanskii, *Evrei v rossii* (St. Petersburg: Bakst, 1877), is a good contemporary account of the political, economic, and social status of Russian Jewry. An indispensable source for Russian language literature on the Jews in Russia before 1889 is *Sistematicheskii ukaztel' literatury o evreiakh na russkom iazyke* (St. Petersburg: A.E. Landau, 1892).

RUSSIAN JEWRY BEFORE THE POGROMS

For the Jewish community in the reign of Nicholas I there is now available an excellent monograph by Michael Stanislawski, *Tsar Nicholas I and the Jews* (Philadelphia: Jewish Publication Society of America, 1983). It fills a gap not only in the English language literature but in that of other languages as well. The begining of the Haskalah in the Russian Empire is examined in Jacob Raisin, *The Haskalah Movement in Russia* (Philadelphia: Jewish Publication Society of America, 1913); I. Zinberg, "Levinzon i ego vremia," *Evreiskaia Starina*, III (1911), pp. 504–541; and Steve J. Zipperstein, "Jewish Enlightenment in Odessa," *Jewish Social Studies*, XLIV (Winter 1982), pp. 19–36.

The policies of the government of Alexander II in relation to Russian Jewry are discussed in volume I of Greenberg's *The Jews in Russia*. I. Orshanskii, *Russkoe zakondatel'stvo o evreiakh* (St. Petersburg: Landau, 1877); and L. Levanda, *Polny khronologicheskii sbornik zakonov i polozhenii kasaiushchikhsiia evreiev* (St. Petersburg: Trubnikov, 1874) are the most detailed accounts of Russian legislation affecting the Jews. The uproar over anti-Jewish remarks in the journal *Illiustratsiia* is well covered in John D. Klier, "The Illiustratsiia Affair of 1858; Polemics on the Jewish Question in the Russian Press," *Nationalities Papers*, V, no. 2, pp. 117–135.

The activities of the Jewish intelligentsia in the 1860s and 1870s are examined in the fine monograph by Alexander Orbach, *New Voices of Russian Jewry: A Study of the Russian Jewish Press of Odessa in the Era of the Great Reforms, 1860–1871* (Leiden: Brill, 1980). I. Sosis published the following articles in *Evreiskaia Starina* on the Jewish intelligentsia in the 1860s, 1870s, and very early 1880s: "Obshchestvennaia nastroenia epokhi velikh reform," VII (1914), pp. 21–41, 182–197, 341–369; "Natsional'ny vopros v literature 60-kh godov," VIII (1915), pp. 38–56; "Period obruseniia," VIII (1915), pp. 129–146; "Na rubezh dvukh epokh," VIII (1915), pp. 324–337; and "Period Krizisa," IX (1916), pp. 46–60, 194–209. Markus Kagan's "K istorii natsionalnogo samosoznanii," *Perezhitoe*, III (1912), pp. 136–157, discusses the rise of Jewish national consciousness in response to growing anti-Semitism at the end of the 1870s.

Moshe Leib Lilienblum's writing appears in his collected works, *Kol kitve Moshe Leib Lilienblum* (Krakow and Odessa: Y. Tseitlin, 1910–1913). Irving Gersh's "Moshe Leib Lilienblum: An Intellectual Biography" (Ph.D. diss., Brandeis University, 1967) is a good secondary source. Lev Levanda has not received the attention he deserves; therefore it is necessary to seek his numerous publications in their original form. His novel, *Goriachee Vremia*, was serialized in the journal *Evreiskaia Biblioteka* (St. Petersburg) in 1872. His reaction to the pogroms is found in a series of articles written primarily for *Razsvet* in 1881 and 1882. Orbach also has some good sections on Levanda in the sixties and seventies. Smolenskin's publications are found in his collected works, *Kol sifre Perez Smolenskin* (Wilna: M. Katzenelenbogen, 1901). Linetski's popular novel, *Dos Poylishe Yingel*, appears in a fine translation by Moshe Spiegel, *The Polish Lad* (Philadelphia: Jewish Publication Society of America, 1975).

Easily the best source on Jews in the Russian revolutionary movement in the 1860s and 1870s is E. Tcherikower, "Yidn revolutsionern in Rusland in di 60-er un 70-er yohrn," *YIVO Historishe Shriftn*, III (1939), pp. 60–172. This is an absolutely superb piece of scholarship, and it is a pity that it is not available to a more general audience. Jonathan Frankel's *Prophecy . . .*, is also excellent on this period. The article by N. I. Sidorov, "Statisticheskie svedeniya o propagandistakh 70kh godov v obrabotke III Otdeleniia," *Katorga i ssylka*, I (1928), pp. 27–56, provides interesting statistical data on Jewish participation in the Russian revolutionary movement in the 1870s.

The economic and social situation of Russian Jewry on the eve of the pogroms is treated in a number of works. *Sbornik materialov ob ekonomicheskom polozhenii evreiev v Rossii*, 2 vols. (St. Petersburg: Izdanie evreiskago kolonizatsionnago obshchestva, 1904), is a detailed study of Jewish life in Russia, based on the 1897 Russian census, the most reliable up to that time. The *Sbornik* makes educated guesses for the 1860s, 1870s, and 1880s. An American summary of the data presented in the *Sbornik* appeared in 1907 in I. M. Rubinow, *The Economic Condition of the Jews in Russia* (Washington, D.C.: U.S. Labor Bureau). In the 1880s the Tsarist government formed the Pahlen Commission to examine the status of Russian Jewry. Its report, *Obshchaia Zapiska vysshei kommisii dlia peresmotria deistvuiushchikh o evreiakh v imperii zakonov* (1883–1888), presents much interesting material on Jewish life prior to the outbreak of the pogroms, especially on Jewish poverty.

The Jewish community in St. Petersburg is dealt with in two books by Shaul Ginsburg: *Amolike Petersburg* (New York: Tashid, 1944); and *Mishumodim in Tsarishn Russland* (New York: Cyco, 1946). As in the case of Tcherikower, Ginsburg's work is not known by many students of Russian or even Russian Jewish history. This is unfortunate because he was a fine historian. Tcherikower, "Yidn revolutsionern . . . ," is good on the Jewish plutocracy and so is S. L. Tsitron, *Shtadlanim* (Warsaw: Ahisfr, n.d.). A very detailed discussion of the Society for the Diffusion of Enlightenment Among the Jews is found in E. Tcherikower, *Istoriia Obshchestva dlia rasprostraneniia prosveshcheniia mezhdu evreiami v Rossii* (St. Petersburg: 1913).

THE POGROMS

The best source on the pogroms is the Russian Jewish press. The *Jewish Chronicle*, published in London, provides much valuable material. An indispensable Russian governmental source is the long report on the pogroms that was written by Prince P. I. Kutaisov, who toured the affected area on assignment for the government and whose report was passed on to the highest authorities. It was edited by G. Ia. Krasnyi-Admoni and published in the 1920s under the title, *Materialy dlia istorii antievreiskikh pogromov v Rossii*, vol. 2 (Petrograd: Gosudarstvennoe izdatel'stvo, 1923). The first part of the book contains messages and reports of government officials in the areas experiencing pogroms. The bulk of the book contains Kutaisov's report. The report of the Pahlen Commission also gives useful material.

Two articles written by Jews who lived through the pogroms shed interesting light on them: [P. Sonin], "Vospominaniia o iuzhnorusskikh pogromakh 1881 godu," *Evreiskaia Starina*, II (1909), pp. 207–218; and Ben-Ami [M. Rabinovich], "Odesskii pogrom 1881 goda i pervaia samooborona," *Evreiskii Mir*, 5 (1909), pp. 18–49. Another article, written shortly after the events by one who witnessed them is [S. Dubnow], "Anti-evreiskoe dvizhenie v Rossii v 1881 i 1882 g.," *Evreiskaia Starina*, I (1909), pp. 88–109, 265–276. Dubnow originally wrote this article for the Pahlen Commission.

Foreign diplomats were stationed in many parts of the Russian Empire and provided their governments with reports and analyses of the pogroms. The reports of Austrian officials appear in N. M. Gelber, "Di Rusishe Pogromen in di 80er yohren in sheyn fun estraykisher diplomatisher korespondents," *Historishe Shriftn*, II (1937), pp. 466–496. British accounts of the pogroms are in *British Documents on Foreign Affairs: Reports and Papers from the Foreign Office Confidential Print*, ed. Domenic Lieven, Part I, Series A: *Russia, 1859–1914*, 2, *Russia, 1881–1905* (Frederick, Md.: University Publications of America, 1982).

Two very good secondary sources on the pogroms are *Die Judenpogrome in Russland*, ed. A. Linden [Leo Motzkin] (Köln; Judischer Verlag,1910); and I. Michael Aronson, "Geographical and Socioeconomic Factors in the 1882 Anti-Jewish Pogroms in Russia," *Russian Review*, 39 (January 1980), pp. 18–31. For the Druzhina, see Stephen Lukashevich, "The Holy Brotherhood: 1881–1883," *American Slavic and East European Review*, XVIII (December 1959), pp. 491–509; as well as the articles by V. M. Smel'skii under the title "Sviashchennaia Druzhina" in *Golos Minuvshago na chuzhoi storone*, 1, 2, 3, 4, 5–6 (1916), pp. 222–243, 135–162, 155–176, 95–110, 86–105, respectively; and V. D. Novitskii, *Iz Vospominanii Zhandarma* (Leningrad: Pribor, 1929). Anti-Jewish sentiment in the reign of Alexander II is discussed in Ginsburg's *Mishumodim...*, particularly the section on Iakov Brafman; in A. E. Kaufman, "Evrei v russko-turetskoi voine 1877 goda," *Evreiskaia Starina*, VIII (1915), pp. 57–72, 176–182; and in Hans Rogger, "Government, Jews, peasants and land in post-emancipation Russia," *Cahiers du monde russe et sovietique*, 17 (January-March and April-September 1976), pp. 5–25, 171–211, respectively. Dostoyevsky's attitude toward the Jews is stated most emphatically in his *Diary of a Writer*, which can be found in his collected works *Polnoe sobranie sochinenii v tridtsati tomakh*, specifically vol. 25, *Dnevnik pisatelia za 1877 god Ianvar-Avgust* (Leningrad: Izdatel'stvo Nauka, 1983). A recent work which focuses on Dostoyevsky's anti-Semitism is David Goldstein, *Dostoyevsky and the Jews* (Austin: University of Texas Press, 1981).

RUSSIAN AND FOREIGN RESPONSES TO THE POGROMS

The government's attitude toward the pogroms is examined in a number of works. The views of Alexander III on the pogroms and the Jews are discussed in R. M. Kantor, "Aleksandr III o evreiakh pogromakh 1881–83 g.g.," *Evreiskaia Letopis*, I (1923), pp. 151–158. E. A. Peretts, a government official, kept a diary, later published, which has informative material: *Dnevnik E. A. Perettsa 1880–1883 g.g.* (Moscow and Leningrad: Gosudarstvennoe Izdatel'stvo, 1927). The memoirs of another high-ranking official, Prince V. P. Meshcherskii, *Moi vospominaniia* (St. Petersburg: 1877–1898), are also useful. Peter Zaionchkovsky, an eminent Soviet historian, has written an extremely helpful book, *The Russian Autocracy in Crisis 1878–1882*, trans. Gary Hamburg (Gulf Breeze, Fla.: Academic International Press, 1979). Kutaisov's report is also revealing in this regard.

The work of Ignatiev, the Ministry of the Interior, and the *guberniia* commissions are analyzed in Iu. Gessen, "Graf N. P. Ignatiev i 'Vremennyia pravila' o evreiakh 3 Maia 1882 goda," *Pravo*, 30 and 31 (1908), pp. 1630–1637, 1678–1687, respectively; I. Michael Aronson, "Russian Bureaucratic Attitudes towards Jews 1881–1894" (Ph.D. diss., Northwestern University, 1973) and the same author's "The Attitudes of Russian Officials in the 1880s towards Jewish Assimilation and Emigration," *Slavic Review*, 34, no. 2 (March 1975), pp. 1–18. Another fine piece of work is Hans Rogger, "Russian Ministers and the Jewish Question 1881–1917," *California Slavic Studies*, VIII (1975), pp. 15–76. One of the Jewish members of a *guberniia* commission has written an account of his activity that reveals the difficulties faced by those who sought to defend the Jews: M. Mandelshtam, "Ignatievskaia komissia v Kieve 1881 g.," *Perezhitoe*, IV (1913), pp. 44–64.

The views of prominent personalities of the period are covered in Robert F. Byrnes, *Pobedonostov: His Life and Thought* (Bloomington: Indiana University Press, 1968); *Pisma K. P. Pobedonostova k Aleksandru III*, 2 vols. (Moscow: 1925); Martin Katz, *Mikhail N. Katkov: A Political Biography 1881–1887* (The Hague: Mouton, 1966); and Stephen Lukashevich, *Ivan Aksakov 1823–1886: A Study in Russian Thought and Politics* (Cambridge, Mass.: Harvard University Press, 1965).

The way in which people in other parts of the world became aware of the pogroms is shown in E. Tcherikower, "Naya materialn vegen di pogromen in Rusland onheyb di 80er yohren," *Historishe Shriftn*, II (1937), pp. 444–445. Foreign reaction to the pogroms was covered in the London *Jewish Chronicle* and in the Russian Jewish press, which had correspondents reporting from Paris, London, Berlin, Vienna, and New York; Zosa Szajkowski has dealt with this in "The European Attitude to East European Jewish Immigration (1881–1883)," *Publications of the American Jewish Historical Society*, XLI (December 1951), pp. 127–162.

The attitude of the Russian press and the Russian intelligentsia to the pogroms is covered in great detail by all three of the major Russian Jewish weeklies, *Razsvet, Russkii Evrei*, and *Nedel'naia khronika Voskhoda*. Each one contains a special section devoted to surveying the views of the Russian press. G. B. Sliozberg, one of the greatest Jewish attorneys in pre–1917 Russia, wrote of Russian society during the pogrom years in *Dela minuvshikh dnei; zapiski russkago evreia*, vol. 1 (Paris: Izdanie komiteta po chestvovaniiu 70-ti letnogo iubileia, 1933). The journal *Otechestvennye zapiski* exemplifies the ambivalent attitudes of Russian liberals. Turgenev's views of the pogroms are found in his *Pisma, tom trinadtsatyi, kniga pervaia, 1880–1882* (Leningrad: Izdatel'stvo Nauka, 1968). The position taken on the pogroms by prominent merchants and industrialists is shown in I. G. Oksman, "Otlik moskovskikh promyshlennikov na anti-evreiskie besporiadki,"

Krasnyi Arkhiv, XIV, 1 (1926), pp. 258–260. *Nedel'naia kronika Voskhoda*, 20 (May 15, 1882), also has material on this subject.

For the Narodnik movement the crucial sources are the newspapers and bulletins of Narodnaia Volia which appear in Vasily Iakovlev Bogucharskii, *Literatura Partii Narodnoi Voli* (Moscow: 1907). Of extraordinary value for this subject and for the specific question of Jews in the Russian revolutionary movement is *YIVO Historishe Shriftn* III (1939). The entire volume of some eight hundred pages contains numerous articles on the Jewish role in the Russian revolutionary movement before 1897. A fine source for essential material on Akselrod is V. S. Voytinsky et al., *Iz arkhiva P. B. Akselroda* (Berlin: Russkii revoliutsionnyi arkhiv, 1924). For a good general discussion of the Narodnik movement, with some interesting information on its attitudes toward the Jews, see V. Ia. Bogucharskii, *Iz istorii politicheskoi borby* (Moscow: Russkaia Mysl, 1912). Articles of interest in this connection include: Abraham Ascher, "Pavel Axelrod: A Conflict between Jewish Loyalty and Revolutionary Dedication," *Russian Review*, 24, No. 3 (1965), pp. 249–265; the several articles by Ben-Ami entitled "Moi snosheniia s Dragomanovym," in *Evreiskaia Starina*, for 1915–1916; Shmuel Ettinger, "The National Awakening of Russian Jews," *Jewish Quarterly*, vol. 21 (Winter 1973), pp. 9–14; Erich Goldhagen, "The Ethnic Consciousness of Early Russian Jewish Socialists," *Judaism*, 23 (1974), pp. 479–496; Mark Kiel, "The Jewish Narodnik," *Judaism*, XIX (1970), pp. 295–310; G. P. Ia. Krasnyi-Admoni, "Literatura podpolia i pogromy," *Vestnik Literatury*, no. 3 (16) (1920), pp. 10–16; M. Mishkinsky, "Al Hadeot Ha-kdumot shel ha-sotsialistim hamahapkhanim shelanu neged ha-yehudim," *He-Avar*, XXI (1975), pp. 20–34; the same author's "Tenuat ha-poalim ha-yehudit beRusyah ve-ha-tenu'ah ha-sotsialistit ha-polanit," *Asufot*, 1, no. 14 (1970), pp. 81–132; and S. Valk, "G. G. Romanenko," *Katorga i ssylka*, 48 (1928), pp. 36–59. For Dragomanov and the Jews, the best sources are his collected works, *Sobranie politicheskikh sochinenii M. P. Dragomanova*, 2 vols. (Paris: Osvobozhdenie, 1905); and the articles by Ben-Ami.

JEWISH RESPONSES TO THE POGROMS

The best source on this topic is the Russian Jewish press. The views of all sorts of Jews are expressed in its columns and letters, and the great debates of the period are the subjects of editorials and articles. The *Jewish Chronicle* is also helpful. Frankel's *Prophecy...*, is excellent on the debates of the 1881–1882 period. A fine source on the pro-Palestine movement is David Vital, *The Origins of Zionism* (London: Oxford University Press, 1975). B. Netanyahu, *Road to Freedom* (New York: Scopus, 1944) contains Pinsker's *Auto-Emancipation* along with other material by Pinsker. Arthur Hertzberg, *The Zionist Idea* (New York: Atheneum, 1971) has some of the writings of early East European Zionists. The debate over America and Palestine is summarized in Joel Geffen, "Whither: To Palestine or to America in the Pages of the Russian Hebrew Press *Ha-Melitz* and *Ha-Yom* (1880–1890)," *American Jewish Historical Quarterly*, LIX (December 1969), pp. 179–200. Y. L. Gordon's poems are found in *Kitve Yehuda Leb Gordon: Shirah* (Tel Aviv: Dvir, 1950). For the reaction to the pogroms of young educated Jews, see Chaim Chissin, *A Palestine Diary*, trans. Francis Miller (New York: Herzl

Press, 1976). Kutaisov in Krasnyi-Admoni, *Materialy...*, reveals the attitudes of Jewish provincial leaders.

For Bilu there are a number of interesting articles and books. S. Dubnow, "Pisma 'biluitsa' (1882–1884 g.)," *Evreiskaia Starina*, VIII (1915), pp. 100–111; Shulamit Laskov, "The Biluim: Reality and Legend," *Zionism*, 2 (Spring 1981), pp. 17–69; a book by the same author, *Ha-Biluim* (Jerusalem: Hasifria Hatsionit, 1979); and the classic account of Bilu, A. Druyanov, ed., *Ketavim le-Toldodt Hibbat Zion ve-yishuv Erez Israel*, 3 vols. (Odessa: 1919, Tel Aviv: Ha Vaad Leyishuv Erets Yisroel, 1928, 1932). The conferences convened by Günzburg are discussed in B. Dinur, "Tochniotov shel Ignatiev lepitron sheelat hayehudim veidot net-zigay ha-kehilot bepetersburg bishnot tarma-B," *He-Avar*, X (1963), pp. 5–82.

Am Olam is discussed in Abraham Menes, "The Am Oylom Movement," *YIVO Annual of Jewish Social Science* (1949), pp. 9–33. Iakov Gordin and the Spiritual-Biblical Brotherhood are covered in volume 4 of the *Evreiskaia Entsiklopediia*. The most extensive discussion of Iakov Priluker is in Ginsburg, *Mishumodim*. David Roskies' *Against the Apocalypse: Responses to Catastrophe in Modern Jewish Culture* (Cambridge: Harvard University Press, 1984), is an important work but appeared too late to be included in this study.

ENCOUNTERING AMERICA

The best general work is E. Tcherikower, ed., *Geshichte fun der Yidisher Arbeiter-Bavaygung in di Fareinikte Shtatn*, vol. 1 (New York: YIVO, 1943). The East European roots of the immigration and the process of adapting to American life are covered superbly in this book. Mark Wischnitzer, *To Dwell in Safety* (Philadelphia: Jewish Publication Society of America, 1948) is a good source. Irving Howe, *World of Our Fathers* (New York: Harcourt Brace Jovanovich, 1976) is a magnificently written account of the immigrant experience in New York City. An excellent statistical survey of Jewish immigration is Simon Kuznets, "Immigration of Russian Jews to the United States: Background and Structure," *Perspectives in American History*, IX (1975), pp. 35–124. An extremely helpful work is Jeffrey S. Gurock's recently published *American Jewish History: A Bibliographic Guide* (New York: Anti-Defamation League, 1983).

Some especially fine memoirs of immigrants who arrived in 1881–1882 are: Abraham Cahan, *Bleter fun mein leben*, 2 vols. (New York: Forvarts, 1926); Leo Shpall, "The Diary of Dr. George M. Price," *Publications of the American Jewish Historical Society*, XL (December 1950) and XLVll (December 1957), pp. 101–110, and 173–181, respectively; the articles by Harris Rubin and Alexander Harkavy in *American Jewish Archives*, XXXIII, no. 1 (April 1981), pp 7–34, 35–52; and Bernard Weinstein, *Ferzig yohr in der yidisher Arbeit Bavaygung* (New York: Veker, 1924). The Cahan books are the best known and are considered classics. The Russian Jewish newspapers are also good sources since they contain many letters from settlers in the United States.

The attitudes of American Jews toward the immigrants are expressed in Jewish periodicals such as the *Jewish Messenger* and the *American Israelite*. These attitudes and American Jewish efforts to assist the immigrants are discussed in a number of articles, of which the following are most helpful: Jacob Neusner, "The Impact of Immigration and Philanthropy upon the Boston Jewish Community (1880–

1914)," *Publications of the American Jewish Historical Society*, XLVl (December 1956), pp. 71–85; Gilbert Osofsky, "The Hebrew Emigrant Aid Society of the United States," *Publications of the American Jewish Historical Society*, L (December 1960), pp. 173–188; Jonathan Sarna, "The Myth of No Return: Jewish Return Migration to Eastern Europe, 1881–1914," *America Jewish History* (December 1981), pp. 256–268; and Zosa Szajkowski, "The Attitude of American Jews to East European Jewish Immigration," *Publications of the American Jewish Historical Society*, XLI (March 1951), pp. 221–280. For relations between native Jews and the immigrants in the 1880s, 1890s and first years of the twentieth century, the interested reader should consult Gurock's bibliography. Native Jewish attitudes appear to have changed in subsequent years.

The Jewish agricultural experiments in the United States are treated in two very fine essays: Leo Shpall, "Jewish Agricultural Colonies in the United States," *Agricultural History*, XIV (July, 1950), pp. 120–146; and Uri Herscher, *Jewish Agricultural Utopias in America, 1880–1910* (Detroit: Wayne State University Press, 1981). Michael Heilprin's activity is discussed in Gustav Pollak, *Michael Heilprin and His Sons* (New York: Dodd, Mead, 1912).

Index

About the Author

STEPHEN M. BERK is a Professor of History at Union College, Sche-
nectady, New York. His articles have been published in *Soviet Jewish
Affairs, Canadian-American Slavic Studies, Russian History,* and *The Oral
History Review.*